Russia and the American Revolution

Nikolai N. Bolkhovitinov

Russia
and the
American Revolution

translated and edited by
C. Jay Smith

THE DIPLOMATIC PRESS
TALLAHASSEE, FLORIDA

Library of Congress Cataloging in Publication Data

Bolkhovitinov, Nikolaı Nikolaevich, 1930-
    Russia and the American Revolution.

    1. United States—Foreign relations—Russia.
    2. Russia—Foreign relations—United States. 3. United
States—History—Revolution, 1775-1783—Foreign public
opinion, Russian. I. Title
E249.B6413   973.3'2'7   75-42220
ISBN 0-910512-20-5

© 1976   The Diplomatic Press, Inc.

A list of other Diplomatic Press publications
appears at the back of this book.

Composition by Action Graphics, Tallahassee
Printed and bound by Rose Printing Co., Inc.
Manufactured in the United States of America

THE DIPLOMATIC PRESS, INC.
1001 Lasswade Drive
Tallahassee, Florida 32303

Foreword

Russo-American relations are older than the United States. Russian and American scientists had been in touch with each other since the middle of the eighteenth century; official contacts between the American Philosophical Society in Philadelphia and the Academy of Sciences in St. Petersburg had been established in the early 1770's. American merchants made their way to Russia by 1763.

When the American Revolution erupted, the English government solicited Russian help. It was after Catherine the Great refused to provide George III with Russian troops that Hessian soldiers were recruited. Russia proclaimed her armed neutrality in the war and cautiously counseled Britain to make peace with the colonists and to recognize their independence.

The present book details the early diplomatic, cultural, and economic relations between Russia and America on the basis of unpublished archival material. It focusses on Russian policy toward the struggling nation and on the impact of the American revolution on Russian thinking. At the same time it offers a new perspective for our perception of events in America by relating how they looked through Russian eyes.

The author, Dr. Nikolai Nikolaevich Bolkhovitinov, a distinguished Soviet historian, has written many books on the United States and on international relations, including *Doktrina Monro* (The Monroe Doctrine, 1959), *Stanovlenie russko-amerikanskikh otnoshenii 1775-1815* (Origins of Russo-American Relations 1775-1815, 1966), and *Russko-amerikanskie otnosheniia 1815-1832* (Russo-American relations 1815-1832, 1975). He is one of the compilers and editors of the multi-volume series *Vneshniaia politika Rossii XIX- nachala XX veka* (Foreign policy of Russia of the 19th and the beginning of the 20th century, 1960-   )and a member of the editorial boards of the journal *Novaia i noveishaia istoriia* (Modern and contemporary history) and of the annual *Amerikanskii ezhegodnik* (American yearbook). Since 1958 Dr. Bolkhovitinov has worked at the Institute of History (renamed in 1968 the Institute of General History) of the Academy of Sciences of the U.S.S.R. At the same time he has lectured and directed theses in the history of the United States at Moscow State University (1967-1974), the University of Simferopol (1974-1975) and other educational institutions.

Bolkhovitinov's above-mentioned work on the origins of Russo-American relations is to be published by the Harvard University Press this year. Written as his doctoral dissertation, it was researched in the late 1950's and early 1960's. The present work incorporates some of the material published in that book and in other works of the author as a stepping stone for new thoughts and investigations. Russia and the American Revolution zooms in on a briefer span of history than the earlier volume. It analyzes Russian policy in detail and reproduces in the appendix the unpublished correspondence of Russian diplomats about the American War of Independence. It is the product of additional research by Bolkhovitinov in American as well as in Soviet archives and takes into account the various studies published since 1966 in the Soviet Union, the United States, and Western Europe on the attitude of Russia toward the American Revolution and the founding of the United States.

The translation of the present book was made from the original manuscript provided by the Novosti Press Agency Publishing House, Moscow, through the Information Department of the Embassy of the U.S.S.R., and updated through personal correspondence with the author. At Dr. Bolkhovitinov's suggestion chapters on John Ledyard's journey to Siberia and on John Paul Jones in Russia were deleted to minimize the repetition of facts related in his book on the origins of Russo-American relations. The illustrations were also obtained from the Novosti Press Agency Publishing House.

Dr. C. Jay Smith, who has rendered the work into English, is professor of history at the Florida State University in Tallahassee. Among his own books are The Russian Struggle for Power 1914-1917 and Finland and the Russian Revolution 1917-

1922. He was thus in a position to clarify the text for the American reader by a number of explanatory notes, mostly of a biographical nature.

George Alexander Lensen

Tallahassee, January 1976.

Contents

PART ONE
Russian Diplomacy and the American Revolution

PART TWO
Russian Society and the American Revolution

Introduction

Two centuries ago, in the flames of a revolutionary war for independence, a new state was born—the United States of America. The Americans proclaimed their independence officially on July 4, 1776, but in a certain sense this was already only a formality, or, more exactly, the logical culmination of a process. Since April 1775, they had been upholding their freedom and independence with arms in hand, struggling with the troops of the British King, George III.

Precisely in North America, in the words of Karl Marx, was proclaimed the first Declaration of the Rights of Man, and "the first impulse to the European revolution of the 18th century was given."[1] Vladimir Ilyich Lenin also gave a high evaluation to the struggle of the American people against England, naming it "one of those great, truly liberating, truly revolutionary wars, of which there were so few amidst the overwhelming mass of wars of conquest."[2]

An enormous, indeed immeasurable, range of documentary publications and a still greater number of various historical works, hundreds and thousands of monographs and research articles have been devoted to the American revolution of the 18th century, not to mention countless popular publications, the biographies of the "Founding Fathers," the textbooks, the anthologies, etc.[3]

The international aspect of the American War for Independence and the policy of the principal European Powers, and in the first place, the position of France, have been subjected to detailed investigation. In this connection, it is enough to name the well-known works of Samuel F. Bemis and also the monograph of Richard B. Morris on the conclusion of the Treaty of Paris of 1783, based on the study of the archival materials of almost all the principal European capitals from Madrid to Stockholm, and also on extensive American documentation. The only thing that did not seem to be at the disposal of R. B. Morris was the documents of the Russian archives, which, of course, could not fail to be reflected in the contents of those pages of the book where there is discussion of the policy of the Petersburg Court.[4]

The works of Academician Ye. V. Tarle (in particular his unpublished manuscript about the foreign policy of Catherine II), of Academician A. L. Narochnitsky, and of Corresponding Member of the Academy of Sciences of the U.S.S.R. A. V. Yefimov, have great significance for the study of the history of international relations in the foreign policy of the Russia of the 18th and early 19th centuries. In the pages of *The History of Diplomacy* and in *Sketches on the History of the U.S.A.,* A. V. Yefimov reviewed, from a Marxist position, a number of the most important problems of the foreign policy of the young American Republic, and also demonstrated the significance of Russia's position in the years, difficult ones for the U.S.A., of the struggle for national independence.[5] However, a detailed investigation of Russia's position in the period of the American War for Independence has been greatly hampered as a result of the absence of an appropriate documentary base. To a wide circle of specialists, the basic Russian diplomatic correspondence of the end of the 1770's and the beginning of the 1780's has remained little known. The publication of the political correspondence of Catherine II was carried out only to the end of 1777.[6] The papers of the French, English, Austrian, and Prussian Ministers in St. Petersburg appeared still earlier in scattered publications, and a valuable collection of Russian documents on the history of the proclamation of armed neutrality[7] was transformed recently already into a unique bibliographic rarity, to find which, even in the central Soviet libraries, turned out to be surprisingly difficult.

As a result, even professional historians, not to mention the general public, knew little about the concrete actions of the Tsarist Government and its attitude towards the rebelling colonists. It was well known, of course, that in the fall of 1775, Catherine II refused to grant the request of the English king concerning the despatch of a corps of 20,000 Russian soldiers to America, and on February 27/March 9, 1780, issued a declaration of armed neutrality. From the other side, recently already documentary materials have been published, and also some monographs, on the mission of the American Francis Dana, who, over the course of two years (1781-1783), unsuccessfully sought in St. Petersburg official recognition of the United States.[8]

To find a satisfactory explanation of the position of the Tsarist Government in this question turned out to be not so simple, and in general almost nothing reliable was known about the attitude of Russian society toward the American Revolution, the participation of emigrants from Russia in the War for Independence, and the commercial contacts of both countries, except for some works in the field of literary history about A. N. Radishchev, N. N. Novikov, and F. V. Karzhanin. (Research of Academician M. P. Alekseyev, Ye. M. Dvoychenko-Markova, G. P. Makogonenko, A. I. Startsev, and others.)[9]

Precisely this situation served as the reason for our carrying out at the end of the 1950's and the beginning of the 1960's a systematic inspection of the central Soviet archives for the purpose of bringing to light the documents relating to Russia's position in the period of the American War for Independence, and also a study of the newspapers, journals, and books of the 18th century in which American subjects were touched. On the basis of these materials, separate articles were written, and also appropriate chapters of a doctoral dissertation which was published in 1966 in the form of a monograph.[10] It soon became apparent, however, that this work serves more as a point of departure and stimulus for new investigations than as some sort of final or culminative stage in the study of Russia's position during the American revolution of the 18th century.

A series of special investigations has appeared in the course of the last ten years in the Soviet Union, in the U.S.A., and in the countries of Western Europe, in which many important problems connected with the attitude of Russia toward the War for Independence in North America and the formation of the

United States were reviewed. Among their number one may name the works of Yu. Ya. Gerchuk, M. N. Nikolskaya, B. I. Rabinovich, A. I. Startsev (U.S.S.R), and also R. B. Morris, D. Griffiths, N. S. Saul (U.S.A.), D. Boden (F.R.G.), P. Dukes (Great Britain), A. Rasch (Denmark), and others. Although the professional level, methodology, and scientific significance of these works is far from uniform (about which we must still make mention in the appropriate subdivisions), as a whole they extend and deepen substantially understanding of many important aspects of Russo-American relations of the 18th century.

All these circumstances, and also supplementary work in the Soviet and American archives, have forced us to return to a review of the whole complex of problems connected with the position of Russia in the period of the American Revolution, and to prepare a special monographic investigation of this theme. Of course, we could not avoid some repetition of facts and materials already well known and in the first place, of the text of the 1966 monograph mentioned above. However, basically the present book is an original investigation, and a summary of the previous works of the author. An attempt is made in it to offer a complete and many-sided presentation, both about the position of Tsarist diplomacy in the period of the American War for Independence, and also about the attitude of Russian society towards events in America. The mercantile, scientific, and cultural ties in the 1760's, 1770's, and 1780's, the participation of Russian emigrants in the events in North America, and also the arrival of the Americans in Russia, are, moreover, studied in detail.

Varied published sources have been widely used in the present work—official documents; diplomatic correspondence; records of the Continental Congress; essays; correspondence, the diaries and memoirs of political leaders, students, literary figures; the works of travellers and of contemporaries who studied events; the press; statistics—as well as numerous works of Soviet, American, and West European authors. But the primary base for the investigation was formed by the very rich and in many instances unknown or insufficiently studied archival materials. In the front rank thereof are the documents of the Archive of the Foreign Policy of Russia, of the Central State Archive of Ancient Acts, of the Central State Archive of the Navy of the U.S.S.R., of the manuscripts of the divisions of the Institute of Russian Literature (Pushkin House), of the Leningrad Division of the Institute of the History of the U.S.S.R., of the Archive of the Academy of Sciences of the U.S.S.R., and many others. Materials were also drawn from the National Archives of the United States in Washington, the Massachusetts Historical Society, the Pennsylvania Historical Society, the American Philosophical Society, and a number of other archives where the author did research on the academic exchange in 1968 and in 1975. The administrations and staffs of all these organizations invariably furnished the author gracious cooperation and valued assistance.

Nikolai Nikolaevich Bolkhovitinov

Moscow, January 1976.

PART ONE

Russian Diplomacy
and the
American Revolution

1

Rejection of Alliance with England
1775-1779

On April 19, 1775, shots rang out in battles at Lexington and Concord which announced the beginning of the armed struggle of the North American colonies of England for independence. Attempts of British soldiers to seize an arms depot and to arrest the popular leaders of the colonists, Samuel Adams and John Hancock, ended in failure. Having lost 273 men killed and wounded, the well trained and well armed soldiers were forced to pull back to Boston. The uprising against the yoke of the mother country took on a mass character, and quickly spread to the other British colonies in North America. A true outburst of revolutionary enthusiasm took place in New York. A crowd of patriots seized the city arsenal and divided the arms among the populace. The chief of the city militia reported that all his soldiers were "Sons of Liberty," and the British commander moved his troops aboard a warship.[1]

On May 10, 1775, in an atmosphere of revolutionary enthusiasm, there convened in Philadelphia the Continental Congress, which adopted a resolution concerning the organization of an army of 20,000, at the head of which was put the outstanding political and military leader George Washington. Although proponents of reconciliation still predominated in the make-up of the Congress (in July, for the last time, a so-called "olive branch" petition was sent to George III), real events continued to develop rapidly in a revolutionary direction. Moreover, the English King completely ignored the peace petition, and on August 23, 1775, declared the colonies in a state of rebellion.[2] As a result, the revolutionary faction in the colonies won a final victory. Contributing much to this was the publica-

1

tion in January, 1776 of the famous pamphlet of Thomas Paine, "Common Sense," of which a huge number of copies for that time, more than 100,000, was sold out. While unmasking the legend of the "divine origin" of royal power, Paine wrote about the founder of the English dynasty, William the Conqueror, as a "French Bastard," who landed in England "with an armed Banditti" and who ruled "against the consent of the natives," and reached the conclusion: "Nothing can settle our affairs so expeditiously as an open and determined declaration for independance."[3]

A half-year later, on July 4, 1776, the Continental Congress unanimously adopted a Declaration of Independence written by Thomas Jefferson, the text of which read: "We hold these truths to be self evident: that all men are created equal; that they are endowed by their Creator with unalienable rights; that among these are Life, Liberty, and the pursuit of Happiness." At the basis of the Declaration lay the idea of popular sovereignty, and the establishment of a government is directly connected with the guarantee of inalienable rights and the consent of the governed. "That whenever any form of government becomes destructive of these ends," it is pointed out in this historic document, "it is the right of the people to alter or to abolish it, and to institute new government," which would be the most likely to effect their safety and happiness. More than this, "when a long train of abuses and usurpations" evinces the design to reduce the people "under absolute despotism, it is their right, it is their duty to throw off such government, and to provide new guards for their future security."[4]

The beginning of an armed struggle in North America throughout its length and breadth confronted England with the problems of allies. The position of Russia took on special significance for Great Britain. The English Government counted on receiving precisely from Russia the help of which it now stood in such need. And the British ministers more than once had the occasion to regret the fact that in the past, they had been too unyielding in negotiations about the conclusion of a treaty of alliance. We recall in this connection that from the time of the coming into existence of Nikita Ivanovich Panin's "Northern System," Anglo-Russian relations developed in a friendly direction, which is explained, in particular, by mutual opposition to the influence of France.* It was pointed out in detailed

*TRANSLATOR'S NOTE: Nikita Ivanovich Panin was one of the outstanding Russian statesmen of the 18th century, and the role he played in both domestic and foreign affairs goes far towards explaining the attitudes which the author of this book shows that he took toward the War of the American Revolution. Born in Danzig in 1718, Panin spent his childhood in Pernau, where his father was the Russian commandant. In 1740, he became an officer in the Guards regiments in St. Petersburg, and in the next year played a role in the palace revolution which seated Empress Elizabeth on the Russian Throne. Entering the diplomatic service, he was made Minister to Denmark in 1747, but in the next year, exchanged that post for that of Minister to Sweden, which he held until 1760. Charged with implementing in Stockholm the traditional Russian endeavor to keep the Swedish monarchy weak, so as to ward off a Swedish war of revenge, Panin developed there a liking for constitutional, as opposed to autocratic, monarchy, which he retained after returning home.

Panin was out of favor in St. Petersburg after 1756 because he opposed Russia's support of Austria and France against Prussia in the Seven Years War, and was surprised when he was recalled home in 1760 to become the tutor of Grand Duke Paul Petrovich, officially regarded as the son of the future Emperor Peter III and the future Empress Catherine II. In 1762, he participated in the palace revolution which replaced Peter III with Catherine II only because he thought he was arranging for the accession of his pupil, Paul Petrovich, to the throne. However, Catherine II and her favorites, the Orlov brothers, while secretly disliking Panin, found it expedient to allow him to play a major role in the new regime. He continued to be the tutor of Grand Duke Paul Petrovich, now Heir to the Throne, until the latter married.

Panin tried unsuccessfully during 1762-1763 to persuade Catherine II to limit the autocratic powers of the Russian Sovereign, through a reform of the Senate and the establishment of a Permanent Imperial Council of six members. However, the Empress turned over the direction of the College of Foreign Affairs to him between 1763 and 1781. His "Northern System" reflected his earlier distaste for Empress Elizabeth's alliance with the Houses of Hapsburg and Bourbon, and his admiration for King Frederick II of Prussia. However, the interests of Russia, Prussia, Great Britain, Sweden, Denmark, and Poland were too diverse for the "Northern System" to have much chance of success. Both Sweden and Poland struggled against Russian influence in their domestic affairs during 1763-1773, and Frederick II of Prussia took advantage of this situation. Sweden escaped Russian control after King Gustaf III established a strong monarchy in 1772. Russia's intervention in Poland, to prevent a similar development there, led to war with Turkey in 1768, and that war forced Panin, much against his will, to go along with the desire of Prussia for a partial partition of Poland during 1772-1773, one in which Austria joined in order to preserve the balance of power in Eastern Europe. Moreover, as the author of this book points out, although Great Britain helped Russia in her war of 1768-1774 with Turkey, to the extent of facilitating the transfer of the Baltic Fleet to the Mediterranean, the London Government deprecated extensive Russian gains at Turkey's expense.

instructions to the Russian Minister in London, Ivan Grigoryevich Chernyshev* of July 24/August 4, 1768: "We are relying
on the Northern System, and we are considering how there
may be a greater and closer union of the Northern Powers on
the one direct point of our common interest, in order to bring
about thereby a strong balance in the European Courts against
the Houses of Bourbon and Austria, and tranquillity in the
North, and to be completely free of their influences, which have
so often produced calamitous consequences therein."[5]

Already in 1762, the English Ambassador, James Hobart, the
second Earl of Buckinghamshire, received instructions to strive
for the conclusion of a treaty of alliance and a commercial
treaty with Russia.[6] An important trade treaty with Great Britain
was signed in St. Petersburg on June 20/July 1, 1766.[7] The negotiations concerning the conclusion of a treaty of alliance did
not yield practical results. English diplomacy was not inclined
to furnish definite support to Russia in her relations with

---

*TRANSLATOR'S NOTE: I. G. Chernyshev was the younger brother of Field Mar-
shal Count Zakhar Grigoryevich Chernyshev (1722-1784), who acquired military fame
during the Seven Years War, and was appointed by Emperor Peter III in 1762 to lead
a campaign against Austria on behalf of Prussia which was never fought. Under Catherine II, Z. G. Chernyshev was Vice-President and then President of the College of War,
Governor-General of Belorussia, and Commandant of Moscow.

By the time of the War of the American Revolution, Panin was completely out of
favor with Catherine II, and during 1774-1778, the Empress effected a reorientation
of Russian foreign policy involving alignment with Austria rather than with Prussia,
which, as the author points out, had a certain impact on Russia's role in the War of the
American Revolution. However, Panin remained officially in charge of Russian foreign
policy during 1774-1781, partly because of his closeness to the Heir to the Throne,
partly because his brother was charged with the suppression of the peasant uprising of
1773-1774 led by Pugachyov. There are some indications that at the time of the start
of the War of the American Revolution, Panin hoped for a new palace revolution which
would lead to the installation of Grand Duke Paul Petrovich on the Throne, and the
implementation of a constitutional project drawn up by his close friend, Denis Ivanovich Fonvizin. As the author of this book points out, Panin finally lost out in 1781 in a
struggle with the new imperial favorite, Grigory Aleksandrovich Potyomkin. He died in
1783.

Panin was as interested in the ideas of the French Enlightenment as Catherine II
claimed to be; Catherine herself described him as an "Encyclopaedist." Foreign diplomats were impressed by his learning and sophistication. In private, he led the life of a
typical 18th century sybaritic Voltairean gentleman.

NIKITA IVANOVICH PANIN
Chairman, College of Foreign Affairs, 1762-1781
*He blamed the British for upsetting his Northern
System with their American war.*

MAKERS
OF
RUSSIAN
FOREIGN
POLICY,
1775-1783

At right: Ivan Sergeyevich
Baryatinsky, Minister to
France, 1773-1785.
*Benjamin Franklin re-
assured him about the
American threat to East-
ern Siberia.*

Below: Arkady Ivano-
vich Morkov, Peace Ne-
gotiator in the Hague
and Paris, 1781-1783.
*He barely missed signing
the Anglo-American
peace treaty of 1783.*

At Left: Ioann-Matias
Simolin, Minister to
Great Britain, 1779-1785.
*He deplored the intran-
sigeance of Lord North's
Government.*

Sweden, Poland, and Turkey, stubbornly refusing, in particular, to include a war of Russia with Turkey in the *causus foederis* (literally, "the condition of the alliance"—the circumstances under which she would have to enter the war on the side of her ally), which was precisely what interested the Russian Government the most at that time.[8] Later, in the period of the Russo-Turkish War of 1768-1774, though she also adopted on the whole a benevolent position towards Russia, England was in no hurry, nevertheless, to assume the obligations of an ally. On the other hand, she was not tardy in intervening in the conflict, and in implementing her mediation, which was in turn decisively rejected by Russia.[9]

The war in America exerted a vital influence on the subsequent development of Anglo-Russian relations, laying bare the hitherto concealed contradictions, and changing to a certain degree even the very nature of those relations. On September 1, 1775, the English King, George III, sent a personal envoy to Catherine II. Playing on the monarchical sentiments of the Empress, the King "sent greetings" in expressions high-flown in form, and in essence, requested Russian soldiers for participation in the suppression of the uprising of his subjects in North America.[10] Detailed instructions were furnished to the British Minister in St. Petersburg to seek the despatch of a corps of 20,000, and the project of an appropriate treaty was forwarded.[11]

Rumors about the unusual request of George III and the possible despatch of Russian troops overseas aroused serious concern, both in America, and also in Western Europe. Already on September 21, 1775, the French Minister of Foreign Affairs, Charles Gravier, Comte de Vergennes,* sent his Minister in

*TRANSLATOR'S NOTE: It was somewhat ironic that both Vergennes and Panin, each in a different way to be sure, should have played pro-American roles during the War of the Revolution, since much of the long diplomatic career of Vergennes was devoted to thwarting the designs of Russia in Eastern Europe. Born at Dijon in 1717 into a family of the *noblesse de la robe,* he entered the diplomatic service in 1740. After various assignments in western Europe, he went to Constantinople as Minister Plenipotentiary in 1754. His first task was to prevent a Turkish attack on France's allies of the Seven Year's War, Austria and Russia. However, after the advent of Panin's "Northern System" in 1763, Vergennes worked vigorously to bring about a Turkish attack on

St. Petersburg, the Marquis de Juigné, special instructions in which he expressed alarm on the subject of the possible despatch of Russian soldiers to America, and asked him to verify the accuracy of these rumors at all costs.[12] According to a communication of the Russian Minister in Paris, Prince Ivan Sergeyevich Baryatinsky,* in the fall of 1775, they were already naming in the press a concrete number of Russian soldiers (30,-000), in "reciprocity" for which, England "is giving three million pounds sterling." Referring to various interpretations of "this deal," Baryatinsky reported in particular "that if the colonies should have the desire to be reconciled with England, then the introduction of foreign troops will arouse in them great refractoriness, and may lead to their declaring themselves truly independent of England." As for Russia, "it is almost unbelievable that Her Imperial Majesty would be pleased to consent to such a deal, however close the alliance that prevails between the two Courts, since such an action is not in accord with the humanitarian, peace-loving, and disinterested sentiments of Her Majesty." If England was striving "to suppress the freedom of the colonies and to subject them completely to her authority," then Catherine II, on the contrary, "is showing compassion untiringly in the matter of furnishing her people relief and some freedom through new laws."[13]

*TRANSLATOR'S NOTE: The well-connected Prince Baryatinsky was the scion of a powerful family of the Russian nobility, and served as Minister in Paris between 1773 and 1785.

Russia, as a means of distracting the latter from Polish affairs. He was recalled to France in 1768 because he failed to produce results soon enough, but in 1771, he was sent as Ambassador to Stockholm, where he played a major role in the anti-Russian coup of King Gustaf III in 1772. Because he was so disliked by the Russians and Prussians, he was transferred to Copenhagen in 1772, and two years later, brought back to Paris to be the Foreign Minister of the new King, Louis XVI. Despite the support he rendered the Americans, Vergennes was a bitter opponent of the various reform schemes associated with the names of Turgot, Necker, and Calonne, but he died in 1787, too soon to witness the beginning of the great French Revolution. As Foreign Minister, though mainly concerned with the diplomacy of the War of the American Revolution, Vergennes kept an uneasy eye on the affairs of Eastern Europe. Though reconciled to the idea of the eventual partition of Poland and Turkey by 1774-1787, he hoped to gain compensating advantages for France in western Europe.

Although there may be some room for argument, of course, on the subject of the "humanitarianism" and "disinterestedness" of Catherine II, the principal conclusion, to this effect, "that it is obviously not for Russia to furnish aid to England against the colonies," arouses no doubts, the more in that in St. Petersburg, they were not badly informed about the real state of affairs in North America. Already in the 1760's, and in the first half of the 1770's, Russian diplomats abroad were informing the Tsarist Government, in detail and quite objectively, about the development of a conflict between the American colonists and the mother country. Characteristic in this regard, in particular, was a report of the Russian Minister in London, Aleksey Semyonovich Musin-Pushkin,* of October 31/November 11, 1774, in which the firm determination of the American colonists to uphold their rights against the encroachments of the English authorities was emphasized. "Letters received here yesterday from America," reported Musin-Pushkin to the Chairman [*Pervoprisutstvuyushchy*] of the College of Foreign Affairs, Nikita Ivanovich Panin, "emphasize in a most convincing way how firm, and so almost unanimous, is the intention of the local inhabitants not to obey any orders such as are inclined, however little, towards the confirmation of the right of legislating for them here. . . . It has already been decided by the general congress in Philadelphia not to export any American goods here, and not to receive there any from here."[14]

The Russian Minister in London not only correctly evaluated the situation which was unfolding at that time, but also was able to see clearly the consequences of the conflict with the colonies, both for the internal life of England, and also for her international position. Musin-Pushkin wrote in that same report to St. Petersburg: "Such a situation justly alarms the administra-

---

*TRANSLATOR'S NOTE: Musin-Pushkin represented Russia in both London and Stockholm in the time of Catherine II, and was awarded the title of Count by that Empress in 1779. He should not be confused with his more famous relative, Aleksey Ivanovich Musin-Pushkin, who was Procurator of the Holy Synod, President of the Academy of Arts, a historian and archaeologist, and the indefatigable collector of ancient Russian chronicles.

tion here, and the more in that all the advantages which trade and factories here receive, both from raw materials brought here from America, and from goods manufactured here and exported there, are well known to it. The local annual exports herefrom attain, in general, a value of no less than three million pounds sterling, while New York Province sends in six hundred thousand pounds sterling annually, and Philadelphia Province, often seven hundred thousand. Any shutting off of such exports, if it does not undermine all manufactures here completely, at least injures them very perceptibly. An aroused France, and Spain, will not fail to intervene in the dispute between England and her colonists. Two frigates under the flag of the former have already appeared near Boston, loaded, as is heard, with various military supplies, while the latter has already despatched five warships from Ferrol, probably to America."[15]

Subsequent events, as is well known, confirmed the correctness of these assumptions: the conflict with the colonies in America not only affected the economy of Great Britain "very perceptibly," but also led her into a war with France and Spain, which were striving to use the "disagreement" in their own interests.

That which seemed so obvious to a foreign diplomat clearly did not find lodgment in the heads of George III and of the members of the conservative Government of Lord North. The English ministers did not desire to pay attention to commercial "consideration," and proceeded to a "frightful proclamation of the Americans as rebels."[16]

The short-sighted policy of the ruling circles of Great Britain did not leave the colonists any recourse except an armed struggle. "An internecine war with them seems the more unavoidable," Russian Minister Musin-Pushkin justly wrote in February, 1775, "in that they are pushed thereto by the extremity either of obeying all laws here, contrary to custom, or of fighting against that which is, so to speak, burdensome, and also restrictive of their natural and legal rights."[17] Reporting that "great reserves of all military weapons, with a sufficient quantity of powder" were found in various localities of America, Musin-

Pushkin continued further: "The people there, leaving their ordinary occupations, are engaging in military exercises voluntarily. The enthusiastic spirit in them encompasses to an equal degree all ranks and callings; it is beginning to manifest itself in Virginia Province more strongly even than it has also operated up to now in New England itself."[18]

Although the royal troops carried out a "hostile attack" on the provincial American militia, they suffered a severe defeat already in the first engagement. "The inhabitants who had hastened thither from various places with arms, threw back the royal troops, and pursued them as far as the warship itself, under the guns of which they could guarantee their safety from attack, with losses, however, of around 150 men. All this took place, Most Gracious Sovereign, on April 8/19, probably without any formal plan of internecine war. The Americans, considering this event the precise beginning thereof, besieged Boston with an impressive number of their militia, with the intention of taking possession of it."[19]

Some time later, the same A. S. Musin-Pushkin reported that according to news received from New York, "the inhabitants there, taking up arms, took possession of the fortress of the capital and the garrison, and the leaders of this uprising established a new administration, subject only to the general American congress."[20]

Catherine II herself took an extremely skeptical attitude towards the "abilities" and "virtues" of George III, and in a letter to her friend Madame Bjelke in the summer of 1775, caustically remarked that the loss of the "worthless sister"* caused her greater grief "than the defeat of his troops in America." And further along she continued: "His best subjects overburden (literally, "bore") him very much, and that often even...."[21] Catherine II deliberately did not make a treaty,

---

*TRANSLATOR'S NOTE: Catherine II had in mind Caroline Matilda, Consort of the Danish King Christian VII, who died on May 10, 1775. The Danish Queen was the sister of George III. After 1768, she and her mentally ill husband came under the spell of the court physician, Count Johan Frederick Struensee, who by 1771-1772 had become a virtual dictator. After his overthrow, Caroline Matilda was imprisoned, after it was discovered that she had been Struensee's mistress.

while laying down a highly significant qualification: she obviously did not want to recognize directly the legality and justice of the uprising of George III's subjects. On the whole, however, the Empress took into account realistically enough the perspectives of the war in America, when she ended the letter with the words: "With all my heart I desire that my English friends come to an understanding with their colonies, but my forebodings have come true so much that I fear that already in my lifetime, we will have occasion to witness the falling away of America from Europe."[22] It is therefore not surprising that the English King's expectations of Russia's support were not justified, and that in a letter of September 13/October 4, 1775, Catherine replied to her most august correspondent politely, but with a quite definite refusal. "The extent of the assistance, and the place designated for it, not only alter the idea of my proposals," wrote the Russian Tsaritsa, "but even exceed the means of which I may dispose for furnishing service to Your Majesty. I am scarcely just beginning to enjoy peace, and it is well known to Your Majesty that my Empire stands in need of a rest." Noting "the embarrassments which would arise in case of the employment of so significant a corps in another hemisphere," Catherine II alluded also to the unfavorable consequences "of such a concentration of Our forces solely for the suppression of an uprising not supported by a single one of the foreign Powers."[23]

All attempts of the English Minister, Robert Gunning, to bring about a favorable decision through Panin and Aleksey Grigoryevich Orlov,* or simply to tone down the refusal, produced

---

*TRANSLATOR'S NOTE: Orlov was the younger brother of Grigory Grigoryevich Orlov, leader of the palace revolution of 1762, and thereafter the reigning favorite at the Court until 1775. G. G. Orlov was the father of Catherine II's illegitimate children. Though both Orlov brothers were loaded with rewards and honors, neither had much ability. A. G. Orlov was only the nominal leader of the Russian naval expedition to the Mediterranean which defeated the Turks at Chesmé in 1770. G. G. Orlov failed in efforts to make peace with the Turks in 1772. A. G. Orlov did repress an uprising of the Don Cossacks in 1765 and G. G. Orlov, an uprising in Moscow, in 1774. Both brothers were out of favor by the time of the American Revolution. G. G. Orlov died in 1783, and A. G. Orlov was forced to go into exile during the reign of Emperor Paul.

no results. The Minister ascribed the failure to the intrigues of the all-powerful Grigory Aleksandrovich Potyomkin and the Chernyshev brothers,[24]* but this was not the main thing, of course. In making the decision, Catherine II could not fail to take into account, in the first place, the internal and international situation of Russia: the war with Turkey (1768-1774) had been concluded only relatively recently, and the awe-inspiring events of the peasant war under the leadership of Yemelyan Ivanovich Pugachyov (1773-1775)** were too fresh in memory to think of the defense of the interests of the English King in America. As the French Minister of Foreign Affairs, Comte de Vergennes, wrote in the fall of 1775, the Russian Empress, not being assured of the quietude of her own subjects, would scarcely agree to being deprived of a part of her army, and all of the navy, for the sake of *"la vaine gloire"* of the subjugation of the rebelling Americans.*** The Russian landlords, in the opinion of Vergennes, were extremely interested in the preservation of their property, and would scarcely agree to look on quietly at the destruction of their serfs "for the settling of internal discords in America."[25]

Not having received Russia's support, the British cabinet adopted the recruitment of soldiers among the ruling princes

---

*See TRANSLATOR'S NOTE above on Chernyshevs.

**TRANSLATOR'S NOTE: Pugachyov was born among the Don Cossacks and served in the Russian Army during the Seven Years War and the Turkish War of 1768-1774. Deserting in 1771, he was hounded by the authorities for two years and roamed about among the Cossack and Old Believer communities in the valleys of the Terek, Volga, and Ural Rivers. He started his uprising against the Government among those communities in the summer of 1773, claiming to be the deceased husband of Catherine II, Emperor Peter III. By December 1773, he headed a force of 30,000 men with 86 guns. His decision to besiege Orenburg, which fell in March, 1774 gave the Government a chance to concentrate overwhelming forces against him. After a number of severe defeats, he was handed over to the authorities by his own supporters in September, 1774, and executed in Moscow in January, 1775.

***TRANSLATOR'S NOTE: The exact words of Vergennes in this letter were: "Les Seigneurs ont pris patience tant qu'il s'agisesoit du soutien de l'interest de l'Etat bien ou mal etendu; mais verroient ils avec le meme sang froid leurs cerfs décimés pour une enterprise aussi étrangère à la securité et au bien etre de la Russie, et par consequent aussi romanesque que de prendre sur elle d'apaiser les troubles intériours de l'Amérique."

of Germany.[26] In the end, hired soldiers did not bring any special successes to the English Crown: the uprising in North America spread more and more, and the hope of pacification practically ceased to exist. "They are talking here more than ever about the affairs of England with her colonists, and they think that England is in extremely bad circumstances," reported the Russian Minister in Paris, Baryatinsky, to Vice-Chancellor Ivan Andreyevich Osterman[*] on May 25/June 6, 1776. "The evacuation of the city of Boston produced, so they say, a great sensation among the royalists, and satisfaction on the part of the Americans. Among the public here, they are trying to verify whether they have the most accurate news that the English troops were expelled therefrom by force, but the Ministry here does not give out anything about this, and the English royalists who are here refute these rumors, and offer the assurance that General Howe left that place according to orders, in line with a plan offered to the Ministry by his brother. They are also saying here publicly that allegedly he, General Howe, at the time of the evacuation of Boston, weathered a storm of such magnitude that all his ships were so scattered that they do not know where a great part of them are.... The Duke of Richmond who, as Your Excellency knows, is a part of the Opposition to the present English ministry, said in confidence to some of his friends here that he thinks that the colonies will never agree to any peace proposals. On all occasions, the Court here continues to offer assurances to England as to the continuation of friendship and peace. A rumor recently came to me from a quite reliable source, it seems, that allegedly there is already an American

---

[*]Osterman was the son of the famous Heinrich Johann, or Andrey Ivanovich Osterman, a German who entered Russian service in 1704, and was a major figure in the formulation of Russian foreign policy from 1707 until his disgrace at the hands of Empress Elizabeth in 1741. I. A. Osterman, born in 1725, found it expedient to go abroad in 1741, but was allowed to enter the Russian diplomatic service in 1757. After service in the Paris and Stockholm Embassies, Osterman joined the College of Foreign Affairs in St. Petersburg in 1774. Although given the title of Vice-Chancellor, he was overshadowed, first by Panin, and then, after 1781, by Bezborodko, in the making of Russian foreign policy. He was briefly, 1796-1798, State Chancellor and President of the College of Foreign affairs under Emperor Paul, and died in 1804.

emissary here with whom the Ministry here is having conversations. If this is really true, then this matter is moving forward very secretively, since they still do not leak out at all who such emissaries might be, and with which of the ministers they are having conversations. Commerce between the Americans and France is now in quite a state of activity. They say that, of the American ships in almost all the French ports, no small number came in under their own flags . . . ."[27]

The adoption by the Continental Congress of a Declaration of Independence became known in Europe in August, 1776. "The publication of this document and the promulgation of a formal declaration of war against Great Britain, offer evidence of all the courage of the leadership there," reported the Counsellor of the Russian Embassy, V. G. Lizakevich, from London.[28]

Although the outcome of the struggle still seemed not completely clear to the European diplomats, it was obvious that in any case the influence of England was diminished significantly and serious changes had taken place in the general system of international relations. "The disputes which have taken place between England and her American colonies and the resulting war itself," wrote Panin in a secret report to Catherine II in October, 1776, "foretell apparently impressive and early changes in the present position of the European Powers, and consequently, in the general system. Whether the colonists succeed in establishing the independence now claimed by them or whether England finally succeeds through exhaustive efforts in subjecting them to her authority, which without internal exhaustion of those colonists in the end may not be presupposed in a reasonable way, it behooves us in both these cases, however, to consider it as probable that the Court of London will lose very much of its present reknown. . . ."[29]

In accordance with the degree of the development of military operations in America and the aggravation of the contradictions of the European Powers, Paris, the capital of England's principal rival in Europe, took on ever greater significance as the center of the diplomatic struggle. It was there that Benjamin Franklin came in December, 1776, and started secret conversations with the French Government. Making reference to his arrival in a detailed report in code of December 4/15, 1776, Russian Minister Baryatinsky emphasized the importance of Franklin's mission, and the enormous impression produced by him in France. "The public is so taken with him," wrote Baryatinsky, "that they no longer talk about anything else except the reasons for his arrival here...." In reporting further about "the sensation which he produced" in the French capital, and about the supposed purposes of his mission, Baryatinsky remarked that, according to "the general opinion" of the diplomatic corps, "the arrival of the Franklins here" is producing, of course, "an important evenement"[30] (from the French *événe-ment*—event).

In the spring of 1777, Baryatinsky devoted a special report to the Marquis de Lafayette, who along with other French officers went to Bordeaux, "engaged a ship," armed it, "paying five thousand livres for all this," and went to America "with the intention of entering the service of the struggling colonies." The Russian Minister reported further that Lafayette revealed "his intention to Franklin and [Silas] Deane, and asked their advice thereon." Both Americans "praised his enterprise, but did not give him any advice, but on the contrary, said to him that they have need only of engineer and artillery officers, but that other officers were not necessary to them; however, such a dry answer could not deflect him." In leaving France, Lafayette put his domestic affairs "in good order, and took with him ready cash, more than a hundred and fifty thousand livres and a large quantity of muskets and ammunition." According to the words of Baryatinsky, this event produced "a great sensation among the public and at the Court. All are extremely impressed that such a young man, being in the very best circumstances here, took such a strange part, but along with this, they draw the conclusion that he is perhaps also clever in thinking out his whole conduct in this enterprise, and in the keeping of a secret. The King is very upset by this action," wrote the Tsarist diplomat, and he referred later to the opinion of the French Government "that if England takes them captive and deals with them with all severity, the Court here may not make any solicitations on their behalf."[31]

News of the capitulation of the English troops under the command of General Burgoyne at Saratoga on October 17, 1777, delivered a serious blow to the international prestige of England. Musin-Pushkin, the Russian Minister in London, viewed very skeptically the new military preparations of England, thinking correctly that their result would be only a further tightening up of the forces of the rebelling colonists. "Good sense itself showed," remarked the Russian Minister in London in December, 1777, "that from the beginning of the intentions here against America, the Americans were strengthened not otherwise than precisely to the degree of the prernature preparations threatening them here."[32]

After long delays, Vergennes, the Minister of Foreign Affairs of France, signed two important treaties concerning an alliance and concerning trade with the American Minister, Benjamin Franklin, on February 6, 1778.[33] Commenting on unofficial reports of the conclusion of a treaty and its terms, Russian Minister Baryatinsky wrote to St. Petersburg on February 26/March 9, 1778: "France made a mistake in waiting a long time to do this, since she could have had more advantageous terms with the Americans if she had made up her mind on this in the month of July last; then the Americans would have protected themselves with ties to France, and they would perforce have owed their independence to her assistance. Now, however, the Americans feel that they are winning freedom with their own resources, and they conclude, moreover, that France decided to move towards them only when she was accurately advised about the adventure of General Burgoyne. As to the factor of time, they think that the treaty mentioned must be announced in the month of next April; moreover, they say too that already the plan of war with England has been made here. The Spaniards will operate in the Mediterranean Sea, and France, on the Ocean."[34]

It is impossible not to notice in this connection that in the course of the whole period of the War of the American Revolution, Paris remained one of the most important centers, if not the main center, of information about international politics, and in particular, about events connected with the war in America, both for the Tsarist Government, and also for Russian society. The richest information is contained above all, in the reports of the Russian Minister in Paris, Baryatinsky. Moreover, representatives of the high aristocracy, and also important leaders of Russian culture, often travelled from Russia to France. Among their number, one may mention Princess Yekaterina Romanovna Dashkova,* Count Andrey Petrovich Shuvalov,** Count Ivan Grigoryevich Chernyshev,*** Denis Ivanovich Fonvizin,**** and others. It is impossible not to say something about the last of these especially. An outstanding leader of Russian culture, an illustrious writer of the 18th century, Fonvizin served after the end of 1769 in the College of Foreign Affairs, and was the secretary, close assistant, and friend of Panin.[35]

During 1777-1778, Fonvizin travelled to Europe as a private person, and was in Montpellier and Paris for a long time. During his stay in France, Fonvizin corresponded regularly with his sister, and with Pyotr Ivanovich Panin, brother of the head

*TRANSLATOR'S NOTE: On Princess Dashkova, see Translator's Note, Chapter Six.

**TRANSLATOR'S NOTE: Count Shuvalov (1744-1789) was the son of one of the Shuvalov brothers who were all powerful during the reign of Empress Elizabeth. He himself was high in the favor of the Court during the time of Catherine II. Appointed to her Legislative Commission in 1767, he was from 1768 to 1783 head of a commission charged with translating into Russian and publishing the works of the *philosophes* of the French Enlightenment. He performed other useful public service in the development of Russian historical studies, the development of Russian banking, and the development of city planning for St. Petersburg and Moscow. A fervent admirer of Lomonosov and Voltaire, he was a minor literary figure and patronized the fine arts.

***See Translator's Note above on Chernyshevs.

****TRANSLATOR'S NOTE: Fonvizin was born in 1744 and died in 1792. Though he is not regarded as a major Russian literary figure, his satires and plays had significance because they criticized autocracy and serfdom. Though Fonvizin's name betrayed the Baltic German origin of his family, it had been settled in Russia for two centuries before his birth. Born in Moscow, he was educated at the University founded there in 1755. Though he embarked early on his literary career, he worked as a translator in a minor government department from 1763 to 1769 before serving as Panin's chief assistant in the College of Foreign Affairs from 1769 to 1784. In addition to his travels in France during 1777-1778, he was abroad in Germany and Italy during 1784-1785. Towards the end of his life, he ran into increasing difficulty with the censorship.

of the Foreign Affairs Office. The letters of Fonvizin—a remarkable example of the elegant prose of the 18th century—are interesting for us as valuable historical documents which recorded important events of the international life of that time. In his letters, Fonvizin more than once invited attention to the relations of England and France, which were becoming strained in connection with the war in America. "The Englishmen are not able to endure it here," wrote Fonvizin on December 31, 1777/January 11, 1778. "Although they treat them very politely to their faces, nevertheless they abuse them behind their backs, and laugh at them . . .Their American affairs are being reduced to extremity itself, and they are in such despair as to think it necessary to withdraw from America, and to declare war on France: since from time immemorial, every time England has been reduced to great unhappiness, she has always had the resources for, and the custom of, declaring war on France."[36]

Some time later, in March, 1778, Fonvizin reported in a letter to Pyotr Ivanovich Panin that "the state of affairs here is so bad that war is, of course, unavoidable." France was concluding "a treaty with the Americans, as with an independent Power. . . . In a word, although war has not been formally declared, they nevertheless expect its declaration from hour to hour. Franklin, the American Chargé at the Court here, is, they say, being accredited in a few days as the Minister Plenipotentiary from the United American States."[37] In general, Fonvizin mentioned Franklin frequently, and in particular, he reported in August, 1778, about his encounter with him. "To a gathering which took place in the present year under the name of the *rendezvous des gens de lettres* (*i.e.,* encounter of literary people)," wrote Fonvizin, "they sent me an invitation, and also the same to the glorious Franklin, who is living here as Minister from the American United Provinces. He, the glorious English physicist Magellan,* and I were received excellently well, even

---

*This third honored guest at the literary gathering in Paris in the summer of 1778 had a career which illustrates, as did those of Franklin and Fonvizin, the cosmopolitanism of the eighteenth century, at least in the worlds of literature, learning and science. Born in Portugal in 1723, he was originally named João Jacinto de Magalhães, but was

to the extent that on the next day, they printed something in the newspapers about our visit."[38] Commenting on the encounter of Fonvizin with Franklin in Paris, P. V. Vyazemsky wrote: "The representative of the young enlightenment of Russia was an interlocutor with the representative of young America."[39]

It is necessary to say that Benjamin Franklin skillfully took advantage of his outstanding position as a savant and literary figure known to all the world for the establishment of unofficial contacts with the diplomatic representatives of the European countries. He had such contacts with the Russian Minister in Paris, Baryatinsky. More than this, in October, 1779, the Tsarist Government itself formally breached the principle of the non-recognition of the diplomatic representatives of the rebelling Americans.

The reason was that in the fall of 1779, a report came to St. Petersburg from the Governor-General of Irkutsk, Klichka, of the appearance in the region of "Cape Chukotsk" [*i.e.,* Kamchatka] of "unidentified" foreign ships. This news disturbed the Tsarist Government so strongly that it decided to instruct its Minister in Paris, Baryatinsky, to establish contact with the "Chargé from the American colonies," Benjamin Franklin, on the question mentioned. In informing Baryatinsky "about the ships which came to those shores," the Chairman of the College of Foreign Affairs, Panin, wrote that Catherine II, "suppos-

---

later known outside Portugal as Jean Hyacinthe Magellan. He was a descendant of the great Portuguese navigator who had discovered the maritime passage from the Atlantic to the Pacific two hundred years earlier, and was at first a monk who obtained a reputation in the fields of chemistry and mineralogy. In 1764, he abandoned monasticism, the Catholic faith, and Portugal and moved to England. After a decade of serving as tutor to wealthy young men during their grand tours of Europe, he was elected a Fellow of the Royal Society in 1774; subsequently he became an honorary member of the Academies of Science in Paris, Madrid, and St. Petersburg. His last years (he died in 1790) were devoted to perfecting the making of scientific instruments. Magellan was the friend of the outlandish Hungaro-Polish count, Mauritius August Benyowski, with whose exploits the author of this book deals in this chapter. The Anglo-Portuguese physicist lent Benyowski the money for the latter's expedition to Madagascar in 1784, but it was never returned, since Benyowski was shot by the French Government as a pirate. Later, Magellan arranged for the publication of an English edition of Benyowski's memoirs.

ing them to be American, and from Canada, was pleased to instruct me to let Your Excellency know about this, and moreover, the Most High was pleased to issue an order that, while making reference to the voyage of the latter to the above mentioned shores to the Chargé from the American colonies, Franklin, who is in your place of residence, you ask him in your name whether he will undertake to investigate whether these ships were really American ones, and from what place; and that if and when he ascertains that they were actually from America, you inquire whether it will not be possible already for him, in such a case, to obtain and deliver to you an account of their journey and a chart, so that upon consultation of them, it may be seen whether it would be convenient or possible to establish direct navigation between districts here and America itself by a direct and shortened route. In conclusion, I say to you for your information that Her Majesty was pleased also to issue an order that in case of the arrival in those places again of some sort of unidentified foreign ships, that coats of arms be made and sent to the Chukotsk people for hanging from trees along the shore of their abode, so as to show thereby to people approaching with ships that these places belong to the Empire of Her Majesty."[40]

The document cited has significant interest for the investigator of Russo-American relations. Above all, we must keep in mind that this was the first official order, and one emanating directly from Catherine II and Panin, to a Russian representative abroad to make reference "to the Chargé from the American colonies, Franklin." It is evident from Panin's letter, moreover, that already at this time, the Russian Government was displaying interest "in the establishment of direct navigation between districts here and America itself by a direct and shortened route." Finally, the document cited is one more sign of the constant fears of Tsarist Russia with respect to the security of its possessions in the North Pacific, and the effort to protect them from foreign rivals.

The question arises as to why the news of the appearance of "unidentified" foreign ships at distant "Cape Chukotsk" could disturb the Tsarist Government so strongly in the 1770's that it considered it possible to forget about diplomatic niceties, and to turn directly to the representative of the "rebellious" American colonies, Benjamin Franklin. The reasons for the concerned attitude of the Tsarist Government become more understandable if one recalls the notorious "uprising" organized in 1777 in Bolsheretsk by Mauritius August Benyowski, who promised to return to the shores of Kamchatka later in foreign ships.[41]

Benyowski himself (1746-1786) was a person with an unusual and complicated biography. Sprung from the Polish aristocracy, he was born in Hungary, took part in the uprising of the Polish confederationists against Russia, and subsequently, in a conspiracy of supporters of the Heir to the Russian throne, Paul I, and in the end, was sent by the Government of Catherine II to remote Bolsheretsk. Bound up with his destiny in a fantastic manner were events in Poland and in Kamchatka, bold journeyings and adventures, links with Benjamin Franklin, twofold visits to the United States, and finally, the history of the island of Madgascar, where for some time, Benyowski was "emperor."[42]

Events which followed the "uprising" of Benyowski in Bolsheretsk, and the memory of his threat to return to Kamchatka with foreign support, brought about the excitement and the suspiciousness, acute enough already, of the Tsarist authorities. More than this, the American angle of Benyowski's activity, his ties with Kasimierz Pulaski and Benjamin Franklin, and also the trip to the United States in 1779, could also bring about directly the emergence of suspicion concerning the "American" origin of the "unidentified" foreign ships which were at the shores of "Cape Chukotsk." Although there are no direct documentary confirmations of this supposition (except for simple chronological correspondence), it is impossible not to take into account its probability.

In carrying out the order given him, Russian Minister Baryatinsky reported to Panin from Paris in December, 1779: "By virtue of Your Excellency's instructions of October 11 relative to the report coming from the Governor of Irkutsk, Mr.

Klichka, about the two ships which appeared at the islands of the Chukotsk coasts, thought to be from Canada, I made inquiries in a private conversation with Franklin, as to whether he has any reports as to what sort of ships these might be, and whether he does not have a chart of the position of those seas, and the route taken from Canada to Kamchatka? Franklin replied that up to now, so far as he knows, this route has not yet been discovered, and consequently, he has no charts. He knows only that an ancient Spanish writer, whose name he does not remember, alleges that ships went out from a strait named Hudson, which lies above Canada in the land called Labrador, and proceeded to Japan; but it seems to him that this route, if it has been discovered, will be extremely difficult, not to say impossible; as to the ships mentioned which have put in an appearance, he thinks that they are either Japanese, or those of the Englishman Cook, who left England three years ago to travel around the world."[43]

The supposition of Franklin to the effect that the ships sailing to the Russian possessions in the North Pacific were actually the third expedition (1776-1780) of the illustrious English navigator, James Cook, turned out to be quite well-founded. Cook's ships (*Resolution* and *Discovery*) first appeared on the shores of the Russian possessions in the far north of the Pacific Ocean already in 1778. James Cook did not succeed in finding the Northwest Passage, and on the Asiatic coast, the prospect of close acquaintance with the militant tribes of the Chukchi, who greeted the English ships in a very hostile manner, did not attract him. Turning to the south, the Cook expedition reached the island of Unalaska in October, 1778, (one of the largest of the Aleutian Islands, with a good natural harbor). Sent ashore, the American John Ledyard observed that the island had already been explored recently by Russian navigators, and that Russian traders were on it. Precisely here took place Ledyard's first acquaintance with Russians. Gerasim Izmailov, who was on the island of Unalaska, in company with a large group of Russians and local inhabitants in twenty canoes, came to James Cook's ship. A splendid seaman and a distinguished cartographer, Izmailov was quickly able to find a common language with the English sailors, and did Cook's expedition enormous service. According to the testimony of Cook himself, the Russian sailor was well informed about the geographic discoveries made in this region, and pointed out at once mistakes in the charts which had been issued to him [Cook].[44]

One must keep in mind that, in travelling in the northern part of the Pacific Ocean, Captain Cook, like Vancouver later, already knew about the many very important geographic discoveries made in this region by Russian navigators. As is well known, Cook used the works of Miller and Stählin. Vancouver also valued highly the Russian discoveries, making use in particular of the charts received by him from Russian entrepreneurs.[45]

English ships appeared again on the shores of the Russian possessions in the spring of 1779, after the death already of Captain Cook in the Hawaiian Islands. When two foreign warships entered Petropavlovsk Harbor on April 18/29, real panic arose in Kamchatka: all were convinced that the foreign ships had appeared with hostile intentions. It soon became clear, however that the ships which were arriving had no relationship to Benyowski, and were travelling for scientific purposes. After mutual recognition, a joyous welcome was given to the expedition. The English received "great help" in provisioning, of which they were in dire need, and could send to the homeland the report of Cook's death. To the English ships were sent "22 fat cattle" and also 250 *puds* of rye bread.[46] Upon leaving hospitable Petropavlovsk Harbor, the expedition proceeded "along the coasts of Asia" to the north, and again attempted to find the Northwest Passage to the Atlantic. However, on this occasion, owing to the ice, the English navigators were forced to give up their intent, and on July 19, 1779, they turned back. At the beginning of the fall of 1779, the expedition returned to Kamchatka.

It thus may not be doubted that the "unidentified" foreign ships which sailed to the Chukotsk shores, news of which they received in St. Petersburg in the fall of 1779 from the Governor of Irkutsk, Klichka, were actually the ships of Cook's expedition. At the same time, it seems, Klichka himself had already informed his superiors about their arrival in Petropavlovsk Harbor earlier, in connection with which, the order followed from St. Petersburg in August, 1779, to charge to the treasury the provisions and cattle expended, and since the voyage to Kamchatka "made it already well known to foreigners, to put it in a state of defense."[47]

This last order "caused not a little trouble to the anxious Klichka," who sent about special couriers "in all directions."[48] The bustle of the Irkutsk Governor caused concern to his Petersburg superiors also, who in the fall of 1779 had to wrack their brains about the origins of the "unidentified" foreign ships. Along with this, this bustle had one obviously positive result: they made the decision in St. Petersburg concerning a direct approach to the "Chargé from the American colonies,"Benjamin Franklin.

On the whole, despite the obvious hostility of monarchical circles to the rebellious republicans, American diplomacy enjoyed marked success in playing on the contradictions of the European Powers. The young republic, V. I. Lenin noted, skillfully took advantage, in its interests, of "the differences between the French, the Spaniards, and the English"; the American peoples fought "alongside the troops of the French and Spanish oppressors against the English oppressors."[49]

The position of England became ever more difficult. The extension of the conflict, the entry into the war of France and Spain, elevated still more the significance of the position of the mighty Northern Power. The gaze of the London Court was fixed on St. Petersburg. England was still counting on obtaining the support of Russia, if not against America, then at least against the European Powers. One of the most capable English diplomats was sent to the Russian capital, the young James Harris (subsequently Lord Malmesbury),[50*] who at the begin-

*TRANSLATOR'S NOTE: James Harris, first Earl of Malmesbury (1746-1820) was indeed one of the ablest British diplomats of the period 1768-1797. After attending

ning of 1778 renewed the negotiations about the conclusion of an alliance. In transmitting the project of a treaty of alliance in April, 1778, Harris wrote about the necessity of undermining the "ambitious plan of the House of Bourbon." Laying strong emphasis on its "candor" and "artlessness," the English Government did not forget at all to stipulate, "exclusively for commercial reasons," that war with Turkey not be included in the *casus foederis*. Simultaneously, it magnanimously agreed not to extend the operation of the treaty to the war which was taking place in America.[51]

The reply of the Russian Government, delivered in a note of Panin to Harris of May 6/17, 1778, offered little consolation to the London Court. Panin wrote that "although Her Imperial Majesty understands all the significance of the adherence" of Great Britain to the Northern System, she "is forced with deep regret to recognize that she considers the existing situation as completely unsuitable for the conclusion of an alliance between the two Courts."[52]

The subsequent approaches of the English Government, which proposed already the conclusion of a defensive alliance "without any qualifications whatsoever," were not crowned with

---

Winchester College and spending time with his father, a Lord of the Treasury, in London, he became a friend of Charles James Fox and William Eden at Oxford during 1763-1765. After a year of travel and study on the continent, he was sent to the Madrid Embassy by Lord Shelburne, and managed to ward off a Spanish attack on the Falkland Islands in 1770. He served as Minister Plenipotentiary in Berlin during 1772-1776. His mission to St. Petersburg lasted from1777 to 1783. As Ambassador there he had to spend 20,000 pounds out of his private fortune. He complained of the Russian climate and of the duplicity of Catherine II. As a Member of Parliament during 1770-1774 and 1780-1788, he backed Fox and the Whigs, and hence the policy of eventual reconciliation with the United States. Despite his Whig politics, William Pitt the Younger made much use of his diplomatic talents. As Minister, and then Ambassador, to the Netherlands during 1784-1788, he meddled in Dutch politics on behalf of the Stadtholder, in connection with an Anglo-Prussian effort to ward off a Dutch revolution like the one in France in 1789. Later, during the War of the First Coalition, he tried, but failed, to cause Prussia to act more effectively against the First French Republic. He also failed in efforts to negotiate a peace treaty with that Republic during 1796-1797. He was created Baron Malmesbury in 1788 and Earl of Malmesbury in 1800. His talents as a diplomat were highly praised by Talleyrand, the great master of the diplomatic art.

success.[53] In explaining the position of Russia, Panin emphasized in December, 1779 "that the conclusion of a defensive
alliance by its very nature cannot coincide in time with a war
in progress, especially such a one as the existing war, serving
as a cause of the outbreak of which were circumstances which
were always excluded from the treaties of alliance between
Russia and England, as not having a relationship to the possessions of those countries in Europe."[54] Still earlier, in July,
1779, it was pointed out to the new Russian Minister in England, Ioann-Matias Simolin,* in the most categorical way, on
the subject of the negotiations concerning a treaty of alliance,
that "the very question cannot arise" in the existing "critical
and delicate situation" of the London Court.[55]

Thus, from the very beginning of the war of the English colonies in North America for independence, the Russian Government, firmly and unshakeably, pursued a policy of stringent
neutrality, decisively rejecting all attempts of England to tie it
down to the obligations of an ally.

The position taken by the Russian Government received a
high rating in the United States. "We are not a little pleased
to find from good authority," wrote George Washington to
Lafayette in the spring of 1779, "that the solicitations, and
offers of the Court of Great Britain to the Empress of Russia,
have been rejected with disdain."[56] On another occasion, noting the definite refusal of Catherine II to conclude any sort of
treaty of mutual assistance with England, Washington emphasized that the Russian Government motivated its position "in
terms breathing a generous regard to the rights of mankind."[57]

It is necessary to say that while dicoursing on "the welfare of
mankind," the Government of Catherine II proceeded, of
course, above all from the state interests of Russia itself, and
from a sober evaluation of the general international situation.

---

*TRANSLATOR'S NOTE: Ioann-Matias Simolin (1720-1790) claimed descent from
the Polish King Stefan Batory, and was made a Baron by the King of Poland in 1776.
Actually he was the son of a Lutheran pastor of the Finnish town of Abo (Turku). He
served as Russian Minister in Copenhagen, Stockholm, London, and Paris.

A detailed analysis of the general international situation, and of the system of the foreign policy of Russia in connection with the war of England in Europe and America, was given in a secret report of the College of Foreign Affairs to Catherine II in the summer of 1779. The report expressed the joint opinion of the Chairman of the College of Foreign Affairs, Panin, of the Vice-Chancellor, Osterman, and of the other members of a secret committee of the College of Foreign Affairs, the Bakunin brothers;* it was worked out in a session of July 31/August 11, 1779.[58] This document has prime significance for an understanding of the general policy of Russia in connection with the war which England was waging. "Her American colonies," it is pointed out in the report, "having been turned, through the *fault* [emphasis of the author] of the British Government itself into an independent and self-governing area, are not struggling against her, save within their own dwellings and lands, defending their new status solely to the degree of her attacks."

From the above quotation, it is completely evident that the Russian Government not only considered the separation of the colonies from the mother country an accomplished fact, but also saw the reason therefor in the "personal fault" of the English cabinet. More than this, it was pointed out in the report directly that the separation of the colonies from England not only did not contradict the interests of Russia, but was advantageous to her, since Russian goods could with success replace the wares which had been sent earlier to the English market from America, and, moreover, mutually advantageous direct trade relations would be developed with America itself. "... The loss by England of her colonies on a firm basis," the report concluded, "is not only not injurious, but rather may still

*TRANSLATOR'S NOTE: The Bakunin brothers were sons of Vasily Mikhailovich Bakunin, an official of the College of Foreign Affairs in the time of Peter I, and one who specialized in dealings with the Kalmyks. The two brothers both had the same name, Pyotr Vasilyevich, and were distinguished as "Senior" and "Junior". P. V. "Senior" lived from 1724 to 1782, and P. V. "Junior", from 1734 to 1786. P. V. "Junior" was a rival of Bezborodko. The two brothers were great-great-uncles of the famous revolutionary, Mikhail Aleksandrovich Bakunin.

be useful for Russia in the area of her commercial interests, since in time a new direct branch of commerce with Russia will be opened up from America, and may be exploited for the obtaining of mutual necessities at first hand."

We must keep in view that all this was expressed, not as the opinion of an individual statesman, however influential, but as the result of the collective work of the persons who managed the foreign policy of the country; the very character of the document—a secret report to the Empress—gave its contents special significance.

The authors of the report held to a very skeptical opinion about the English Government of the time. "Truly the internal condition of the English Court and ministry is not such as to be able to arouse confidence therein at home and abroad." They expressed special dissatisfaction with respect to the activity of England on the sea. "Though surrounded by a quantity of the most powerful enemies, she does not, nevertheless, desist from the seizure of neutral ships, and to become more and more angry over the most innocent cargoes, and to exasperate other peoples."

On the whole, the authors of the report concluded from this that in connection with the definition of Russia's position, "our own (i.e., Russian) interests and the very basis of all our policy" —the Northern System—must be taken into consideration. In this connection they recommended, while holding fast to the policy of stringent neutrality, that the Northern System be simultaneously built up, and particularly, that "contact be established with, and counsel be taken with" Denmark and Prussia "in good time and frankly" about "joint measures." Thereby, in their opinion, a path would be prepared for Russia towards entry into the role of a powerful mediator for the reconciliation of the contending parties. The subsequent activities of the Russian Government corresponded, in broad outline, with the views presented in the secret report.

The text of the report analyzed and also other documents brought forward in the present chapter show quite definitely that the Russian Government was not guided at that time in its attitude towards the War of the American Revolution by the principles of legitimism and did not look upon the Americans as "rebels" and "insurrectionists" against a lawful monarch. It is clear that even Catherine II limited herself to jeers at the expense of George III, and considered the separation of the North American colonies from England as practically unavoidable. As for Panin and his closest associates, they looked upon the cause of the uprising in North America as the "personal fault" of the British cabinet, and thought that the separation of the colonies from the mother country not only did not contradict the interests of Russia, but was even advantageous to her.

THE SEMIRAMIS OF THE NORTH AND THE SQUIRE OF MOUNT VERNON

CATHERINE II
Empress, Tsaritsa, and
Autocrat of All the Russias,
1762-1796

She kept his portrait out of Russia.
. . . He praised her Declaration of
Armed Neutrality. . . . She asked
him for an American Indian dictionary.

GEORGE WASHINGTON
Father of His Country

2

The Armed Neutrality
1780

The most important formal international action undertaken by Russia in connection with the war which Great Britain waged with the United States and the European Powers was the proclamation of armed neutrality in 1780.

The idea that the original impulse which in the final analysis led to the issuance of a declaration of armed neutrality was the operations of the American privateer *General Mifflin,* under the command of Daniel McNeill, has been expressed again comparatively recently in American literature.[1] In May, 1778, the American privateer, armed with twenty guns and a crew of 150 men, sailed to North Cape, where it captured eight British ships, and then five more in the English Channel. Thereby a threat arose to British trade with Russia via Archangel, which was carried on mainly in English ships. Taking advantage of this occasion, British Minister James Harris tried to obtain the support of the Tsarist Government, and at first glance, the deployment subsequently in 1779 of a Russian squadron may seem directed against the rebelling colonists. David M. Griffiths, mentioned above, is inclined to evaluate the action of Russia in precisely this way.

Actually, however, not only is no sort of "anti-American" tendency to be discerned in the actions undertaken by Russia, but such an outlook was from the very beginning rejected by the Tsarist Government itself. The thoughts of Panin on the subject of "the pleasure" of Catherine II concerning "the opening next summer of the trade and navigation of foreign peoples to the city of Archangel," confirmed on December 22, 1778/ January 2, 1779, have special interest in this connection. "This restriction must, however, be based on rules common to all

31

recognized Powers, that is, that the sea is open, and that every nation is free to carry on its navigation on open waters," wrote Panin, and he proposed further "to issue precise instructions" to the commander of the squadron deployed, "so that during his cruise he did not clash at all with English, French, and American privateers which were encountered, but advised them to withdraw to other waters . . . because all navigation of this region proceeded solely to the harbors and shores" of the Russian Empire.[2] The most important thing is that although the operations "of a single American privateer" served as the reason for the "restriction" mentioned, Panin emphasized especially the necessity of the observance of a strict neutrality, and of an impartial attitude towards all belligerent parties, including America. "I also consider a procedure vis-à-vis the American privateers which is the same as that vis-à-vis the English and French ones to be suitable for the reason that our own merchant ships in all other seas not be subjected to their vengeance and seizure, like those of the nations which are themselves suffering from their hostile attacks. It is well known that the Americans have in European waters no small number of armed ships, all of which would begin to harry our merchant fleet."

The "most humble judgments" of Panin were given "monarchical approbation" and on January 26/February 6, 1779, an appropriate order to the Admiralty College followed, in which it was emphasized that the Russian ships were being deployed "for the protection and general defense of trade to ports here, without distinction of nationality." Catherine II instructed the squadron to show the "respect" which "it is appropriate to maintain without interruption towards the various belligerent Powers, in accordance with the stringent neutrality being maintained by Us."[3]

On February 28/March 11, 1779, a note was sent to the Governments of England and France in the form of a declaration, in which notice was given of Russia's intention to send out "a squadron of her ships of the line and frigates, which will be ordered to defend trade and navigation in the approved fashion, driving away from this coastal zone any privateer which appears there, wihout exception, and without regard to its national registry."[4]

Although the Russian Government emphasized its impartiality and neutrality in the formal sense, in practice the actions of Russia took on, not an anti-American, but an anti-English, slant, inasmuch as Great Britain, with her strong naval fleet, strove to dictate her terms to the ships of all the rest of the countries.

Musin-Pushkin, the Russian Minister in London, was already reporting frequently about the insolent actions of the "English privateers," which were boarding "all ships encountered by them, without any regard for the various flags."[5] "Unfriendly representations" went to the London Court systematically on this subject from the representatives of the neutral countries. In particular, Simolin, the successor of Musin-Pushkin as Russian Minister in London, was instructed in a rescript of Catherine II of November 8/19, 1779 to make "the strongest representations" on the subject of the seizure of two ships of the Riga merchants, Karl Behrens and Company.[6]

Finally, at the beginning of 1780, in connection with the seizure by Spain of the merchant ship *Svyatoy Nikolay* (*Saint Nicholas*), the Government of Russia considered it necessary, "before outrages to the Russian merchant flag are transformed into a dangerous habit," to give notice to London, Paris, and Madrid of the decision "to use, on our part, all means and all forces available to us for complete protection and its enforcement, with the firm intention, however, of reconciling them, in a solemn and inviolable way, with the rules of the most stringent impartiality and neutrality in the course of the present war."[7] They were talking of the despatch of a new squadron to the North Sea in the summer "for the ejection from waters thereof all privateers, and the guarantee of the free navigation to Our ports of all friendly peoples in general," and about the outfitting in Kronshtadt of a supplementary fleet composed of 15 ships and 4 frigates.[8]

In order that the foreign states, and above all, the belligerent Powers, "through a misunderstanding or because of unwarranted assumptions," should not fall into "erroneous conclusions," and should not take advantage of the measures undertaken by Russia with "her own resources," the famous Declaration of Armed Neutrality was issued simultaneously on February 27/March 9, 1780, based, as was pointed out in the rescript, "on the simple, honorable, and undisputed principles of natural law," on the one hand, and "on the wording of the terms of Our commercial treaty with Great Britain," on the other hand.

It was pointed out in the Declaration: (1) that neutral ships may freely visit the ports of belligerent Powers; (2) that the goods of belligerent Powers on neutral ships are permitted to pass without hindrance, with the exception of war contraband; (3) that only objects enumerated in Articles 10 and 11 of Russia's treaty of 1766 with England are considered war contraband (i.e., arms, military supplies, etc.); (4) under the definition of a blockaded port falls only a port into which entry is actually hampered by naval forces; (5) these principles will serve as the rule in the definition of the legality of prizes.[9]

The proclamation of an armed neutrality had enormous international significance: now firm principles were established in the international law which governed the maritime trade of neutral Powers in wartime. By this act, as Friedrich Engels remarked, Catherine II "first formulated in her name and in the name of her allies the principle of 'armed neutrality' (1780) — a demand for the limitation of the rights to which England laid claim for her warships in the open sea."[10]

In the course of 1780-1783, practically all the neutral countries of Europe adhered to the declaration, which was officially registered by appropriate agreements. France and Spain also recognized the principles put forward by Russia. A literature difficult to cover—books and documentary publications of German, French, English, Danish, American, and other foreign authors (not to speak even of the Russian ones!), among which may be encountered statesmen, historical scholars, jurists, professional diplomats, etc.—has been devoted to the history of the armed neutrality, the origin of the principles of Russia's declaration, and their significance.

But nevertheless, the problems connected with the history and significance of the armed neutrality have still always remained not completely clear. The most contradictory views are expressed, in particular on the question of the author of the famous formal act of 1780. Among the main pretenders they name: Panin; Catherine II; Count Andreas Peter Graven von Bernstorff, the Danish Minister of Foreign Affairs; Frederick II, King of Prussia; Vergennes, the Minister of Foreign Affairs of France; and others. At one time von Döhm and Count Goertz[11] created a version to the effect that the proclamation of armed neutrality was no more than an accidental act, the result of a Court intrigue, and of the rivalry of Count Panin and Prince Potyomkin. As for Catherine II, in their opinion she understood so little the real significance of the declaration, drawn up on the initiative of Panin, that she thought that it was being proclaimed in the interests of England.[12]

However, already in the older Russian works (Leshkov, Danevsky, and others), it was being justly observed that the proclamation of armed neutrality was the natural result of preceding events, and that the general interests of Russia herself, which corresponded at that time to the general principles of the famous declaration of 1780, were the reason for its proclamation.[13]

The maritime trade of Russia in the second half of the 18th century was mainly in the hands of the English merchant class, and carried on in British ships. The natural striving of Russia was to free herself from excessive dependence on England, in order to encourage the development of her own, and neutral, navigation. In 1775, 414 ships (of them, 17 Russian ones and 236 English ones) were used in foreign trade, and in 1787, already 2,015 ships (including 141 Russian ones and 767 English ones).[14]

One must also consider that the principles of the declaration of 1780 were not something completely new: many of them were already being encountered earlier in treaty texts (it is characteristic that in the declaration itself there is a reference to the trade treaty of 1766 with England), diplomatic correspondence, works of scholar-jurists, etc. It is well known, for example, that the reply of Danish Foreign Minister Count Bernstorff of September 29, 1778, to the Russian Government on the question of the defense of maritime navigation in accordance with a defined system of principles, was based on materials presented to the Ministry of Foreign Affairs of Denmark by the well known jurist, Max Hübner.[15]

Finally, we must note especially that the Russian declaration of 1780 asserted as the essence of the matter that same principle which, in 1776, on the proposal of John Adams, the Continental Congress of the United States approved ("free ships, free goods"), i.e., the right of free trade of neutral countries in wartime in any goods with the exception of direct military contraband.[16] Later this principle was reflected in the text of the trade treaty of 1778 between France and the United States mentioned above. In this connection, it was demonstrated objectively that the Russian Government, in promulgating a declaration of armed neutrality, was asserting (it goes without saying, by virtue of its own interests) one of the principles in the name of which the rebelling colonists in America were fighting. It was therefore no accident that many years later the President of the United States, James Madison, wrote about armed neutrality as about "the American doctrine," and emphasized that its proclamation by the Russian Government in 1780 constituted "an epoch in the history of maritime law," and noted that the United States was "especially interested" in supporting it.[17]

The reasons for the wide acceptance of the declaration of 1780 and its significance in the history of international relations come down to the fact that the principles of armed neutrality were prepared by preceding events, by the development of the theory of maritime law, and by the practice of merchant navigation. Remarks to the effect that the Russian Government allegedly did not understand the significance of the formal action undertaken by it, and that Catherine II even thought that she was doing a favor to England by her declaration, do not deserve any sort of serious consideration. Actually, the British Government itself, as we have seen, did not give up during all these years the idea of possible support on the part of Russia. Already on November 5, 1779, the "sincerely devoted brother" of Catherine II, the English King George III, asked about a demonstration of Russian naval forces which would be capable, in his words, "of reestablishing and strengthening the peace of Europe, of dissipating the league organized against me (*i.e.*, George III), and confirming the system of the balance, which this league is trying to destroy."[18] Catherine II carried out such a demonstration by sending a squadron to the North Sea and promulgating the declaration of armed neutrality, but this demonstration was not on behalf of, but against, Great Britain.

In reports to London, British Ambassador James Harris exerted not a little effort in order to slander the declaration of armed neutrality in every way, and also to play down its significance. Reference is often made in the literature to the fact that Catherine herself remarked in a conversation with Harris on December 7/18, 1780: "What sort of harm is this armed neutrality, or rather, armed nullity, doing to you?"[19] But not without reason did Fyodor Fyodorovich Martens write that "the sharp-witted English diplomat did not fail to observe that by calling her grandiose plan a trifle or a nullity, Catherine II, while reassuring him, was also poking fun at him."[20]

Despite the abundance of persons mentioned in the literature to whom are ascribed great services, sometimes exceptional ones, in the preparation of the proclamation of armed neutrality, and despite the minuteness of the investigations which have been conducted, the actual role of the individual persons involved (for example, Franz Ulrich Theodor Aepinus)* remains not completely clear up to the present time. Little is known also as to the role of Pyotr Vasilyevich Bakunin in the

---

*TRANSLATOR'S NOTE: On Aepinus, see Translator's Note, Chapter Six.

direct preparation of the project of the declaration, although on this point, there are testimonies of contemporaries, including Semyon Romanovich Vorontsov and Catherine II herself.[21] For a long time, the activity of the Russian Minister in the Hague, Dmitry Alekseyevich Golitsyn,* also remained outside the field of vision of the scholars.[22] Nevertheless, to him belonged, if not a decisive role, than all the same a quite vital role, both in the preparation of the proclamation of armed neutrality, and also, especially, in the establishment of the first Russo-American diplomatic contacts.[23]

To the interesting and unique figure of Golitsyn there belongs a place not at all ordinary in the history of Russian diplomacy. A person of wide reach, with a many-sided education, the author of works on the theory of electricity, on mineralogy, geography, political economy, and philosophy, Prince Golitsyn occupied during 1762-1768 the post of Minister in Paris, and then was transferred to the Hague. He was an honorary member of several academies and scientific societies (including the Academies of Science in St. Petersburg, Berlin, Stockholm, and elsewhere), was a friend of Voltaire, Diderot, and Mercier de la Rivière, and was especially close to the Physiocrats. Precisely to him belongs the merit of the posthumous publication in 1773 of the famous book of the philosophe-materialist Claude-Adrien Helvétius, *On Man (De l'homme)*, and also the working out of a project, radical for that time—if also very restricted in principle—of the abolition of serfdom in Russia, one which foresaw the liberation of the peasants through purchase and without land.[24]

*TRANSLATOR'S NOTE: As the author indicates, Prince Dmitry Alekseyevich Golitsyn, who belonged to one of the most famous of the Russian noble families, was an enthusiastic disciple of the leading figures of the French Enlightenment, but he spent most of his adult life abroad, and published his writings in the French language. Born in 1734, he was attached to the Russian Embassy in Paris from 1754 until his appointment as Minister to the Hague in 1768. He died in the Dutch capital in 1803. His publications included *Lettre sur quelques objects d'Électricité (1778)*, *Défense de Buffon (1793)*, and *De l'esprit des economistes ou les economistes justifies d'avoir posé par leurs principes les bases de la revolution francaise (1796)*. He also published articles in the *Works* of the St. Petersburg Free Economic Society, of which he was a member.

Being in the Hague, Golitsyn systematically maintained contacts with American agents, at first with Charles W. F. Dumas, and then with John Adams; he exchanged correspondence with Benjamin Franklin, and even received a reprimand from St. Petersburg for forwarding a portrait of George Washington, which Catherine ordered sent back.[25] In May, 1782, he was also given strict orders to refrain from official recognition of John Adams as the American Minister.[26]

In contrast to many of his colleagues — dull and self-satisfied Tsarist officials — Golitsyn not only held independent views on a number of important questions, but systematically gave advice in St. Petersburg to Panin, Osterman, and Catherine II herself (not to speak even of his relative Field Marshal Aleksandr Mikhailovich Golitsyn), which is not often encountered in the diplomatic practice of that time.

Holding special interest for the history of the proclamation of the February declaration of 1780 is, in particular, a letter of Golitsyn to Panin of February 7/18, in which the Minister justified the project of a treaty of alliance of Russia and Holland, with the participation of Denmark and Sweden, "solely for the purpose of the defense of the trade of the contracting Powers and the support of neutrality and of free navigation."[27] He reported about this project as if it were a plan of Holland, and called it "just, wise, and correct." "As for the advantages from this treaty," wrote Golitsyn, "Your Excellency understands them better than I. The English and the Germans, while seizing all the ships of the Republic, are making its trade difficult to such a degree that the Dutch will be forced to withdraw therefrom, as a consequence of which, the sale of our goods suffers, since in practice, ever since the beginning of the war of America with England, only Russia alone has had the occasion to send hemp, canvas, and lumber to the belligerent Powers. However, it is precisely these goods which the English are taking away from the Dutch most zealously. I must also advise Your Excellency that it is known to me from a reliable source that the Court of Versailles will not object to the forming of an alliance between the Republic and our Court, and even between all the Northern Courts, and that at the present time, it desires peace, if only such would be concluded on well-advised terms, the principal one of which is freedom of trade and navigation for all European nations."

Developing his ideas in detail in a letter to Panin in March, 1780,[28] Golitsyn remarked: "In my opinion, the most important advantage which may derive from this would be that of moving forward in the role of mediators between the belligerent Powers: they cannot turn down this mediation; the Empress will force them to peace and dictate their terms, as she did at the Congress of Teschen. The basic purpose which it is necessary to keep in view in concluding the present alliance consists precisely of this."

It is difficult for us to reach a final judgment as to the degree of the influence of Golitsyn on the proclamation of armed neutrality by the Russian Government. In any case, his advice could not fail to hasten the unfolding of events. We invite attention also to a curious chronological coincidence: Golitsyn's letter of February 7/18, 1780, as the stamp thereon testifies, was received in St. Petersburg on February 26/March 8, 1780, and already on the following day, February 27/March 9, the famous declaration of armed neutrality was signed. The Russian Government moved forward as the initiator of the creation of a league of neutral Powers for the defense of mercantile navigation. We are far from drawing any sort of categorical conclusions from the simple chronological coincidence. Golitsyn's letter was, so to speak, the last drop which filled to overflowing a cup already filled to the brim. There is no doubt too that the activity of Golitsyn in the Hague deserves the special attention of historians.

The actions of Russia had no small significance for the improvement of the international position of the United States, the sapping of the naval might of England, and her diplomatic isolation. Benjamin Franklin gave a high rating to the armed neutrality, writing the American agent in Holland, Charles W. F. Dumas, in June, 1780: "I approve much of the Principles of the Confederacy of the Neutral Powers, and am not only for respecting the Ships as the House of a Friend, tho' containing the Goods of an Enemy, but I even wish for the sake of humanity that the Law of Nations may be further improv'd, by determining, that, even in time of War, all those kinds of People, who are employ'd in procuring subsistence for the Species, or in exchanging the Necessaries or Conveniences of Life, which are for the common Benefit of Mankind, such as Husbandmen on their lands, fishermen in their Barques, and traders in unarm'd Vessels, shall be permitted to prosecute their several innocent and useful Employments without interruption or Molestation, and nothing taken from them, even when wanted by an Enemy, but on paying a fair Price for the same."[29]

In characterizing an international situation favorable for the United States which unfolded after the proclamation of armed neutrality, George Washington remarked that the declaration of Russia, in which all the other states of Europe joined, was humiliating "to the Naval pride and power of Great Britain."[30]

Giving an exceptionally high rating to Russia's declaration was John Adams, who viewed it as an act scarcely less hostile to England than a declaration of war. In particular, in a letter of April 26, 1780, to the President of the Continental Congress of the United States, and relying on the materials of the English newspapers and the debates in Parliament, John Adams reported the enormous dissatisfaction in England with the proclamation of armed neutrality by Russia. Along with this he thought that the rectification of international law for which the Russian Government was working, would be advantageous for all countries, and especially for the United States.[31]

During September-October,1780, the declaration of armed neutrality became the object of a special discussion of the Continental Congress of the United States. At the session of September 26, 1780, Robert Livingstone introduced a resolution to recognize that the rules contained in the Russian declaration were "useful, wise, and just." Like other members of the Congress too, he thought that Russia's declaration claimed "the earliest attention of a rising republick."[32]

In accordance with the recommendations of a committee created for the review of this question on October 5, 1780, the Continental Congress passed a special resolution fully approving of the declaration of Catherine II as based on "the principles of justice, equity, and moderation." The resolution provided for the preparation of appropriate instructions for the warships of the United States,[33] and also empowered the American representatives abroad to join in the principles proclaimed by Russia.[34]

Mention is sometimes made also in the literature of a letter of the President of the Continental Congress, Samuel Huntington, which was allegedly sent to the Russian Government, and which even contained a passage where something was said about "the great and dear ally" of the United States.[35] Meanwhile, in the text of the letter, there was talk of the desire of Congress that its "feelings and measures" be brought as soon as possible to the attention "of His Most Christian Majesty (Sa Majesté Très-Chrétienne)," i.e., the French King Louis XVI.[36] Naturally, therefore, the words about "the great and dear ally" of the United States referred to France, and not to Russia. At the same time, the fact itself of the approval in October, 1780 by the Continental Congress of the declaration of armed neutrality, and of the despatch of appropriate instructions to the commanders of American warships actually took place, and the Russian Government became well informed about it, both through the French Minister in St. Petersburg, Charles-Oliver de Saint-George, Marquis de Vérac,* and also directly from the American representatives in Europe, Charles W. F. Dumas and John Adams. In forwarding the decision of the

*TRANSLATOR'S NOTE: Born in 1743, Vérac entered the French diplomatic service as Minister to Cassel in 1772 after a military career. After service in Copenhagen as well, he was sent as Minister to St. Petersburg in 1779 to negotiate the neutrality of Russia in France's war with Great Britain. He left Russia in 1784, and served subsequently in the Netherlands and Switzerland. He resigned and became an émigré in 1791, after the French King's flight to Varennes. Returning to France in 1801, he was restored to his military rank after the Restoration in 1814, and died in 1828.

Continental Congress to the Russian Minister in the Hague, Golitsyn, John Adams wrote on March 8, 1781 that he was happy "to be the instrument of the formal commitment of the United States of America to fidelity towards the transformation of international maritime law, which does such honor to the present age."[37]

On the whole, the issuance of the declaration of armed neutrality in 1780, and the formation subsequently of a league of neutral countries headed by Russia, had first-rank significance in the history of the international relations of this period. The declaration of armed neutrality, directed in essence against the maritime despotism of Great Britain, was advantageous for all other states, and especially for the United States. It was no accident therefore that the leaders of the young republic welcomed it, and that the Continental Congress officially approved the principles proclaimed by Russia. Subsequently, over the course of many decades, the defense of the rights of neutral navigation became a lasting basis of Russo-American rapprochement.

3

The Mediation Proposal
1780-1781

Along with the proclamation of armed neutrality, a most important action of Russian diplomacy in 1780-1781 was the advancement of a proposal concerning mediation between England and her enemies. In the secret report of the College of Foreign Affairs to Catherine II of July 31/August 11, 1779, which is cited above, it was noted that the acquirement "of the enviable role of mediatrix in the present war encompassing all parts of the world" would be in the interests of Russia. With her ambitious plans, Catherine II was not hesitant to become the "arbiter of affairs" at the time of the conclusion of a peace which "will embrace all parts of the inhabited world."[1]*

In this connection, one of the main purposes of the proclamation of armed neutrality was the effort to fortify the international authority of Russia and to attribute great significance to her peace initiative. Referring to this question, Panin remarked in a report to Catherine II in March, 1780 that the union of the neutral Powers "gives still greater importance to our impartial efforts to reestablish peace in Europe."[2] Golitsyn, the Russian Minister in the Hague, in presenting a plan for an alliance of neutral Powers for the defense of mercantile navi-

*TRANSLATOR'S NOTE: By 1780, Catherine's desire for general peace clearly reflected her absorption with her "Greek Project" which involved the expulsion of the Turks from southeastern Europe, the cession of the western Balkans to Austria, the establishment of a principality for Potyomkin in modern Rumania, and the reestablishment of the Byzantine Empire in Constantinople, with a Russian prince as its ruler. Her first two grandsons, born in 1778 and 1779, respectively, were given Greek names, Alexander and Constantine. The older one eventually became the Russian Emperor Alexander I (1801-1825), but the younger one, Grand Duke Constantine Pavlovich, never came close to the throne of a revived Byzantine Empire, and had to be satisfied with the role of Russian Viceroy in Poland between 1815 and 1830.

gation, remarked in his turn that his basic goal was "to put an end to the war between England and the House of Bourbon, by offering her the mediation of the Empress and the [Dutch] Republic."[3]

Although the general history of the negotiations which were crowned by the signing of peace treaties in 1783 between England, on the one hand, and the United States, France, and Spain, on the other, is well known, their initial period, and above all, the role of Russia in the early stages of the complex diplomatic struggle which preceded the opening of concrete negotiations, has remained not completely clear until recently. Thus, the well-known authority on the diplomatic history of the War of the Revolution, Professor Samuel F. Bemis, remarked that the mediation was in essence directed against the independence of the United States, and would have led to a significant part of its territory remaining in the hands of Great Britain.[4] Meanwhile, attentive acquaintance with the contents of the peace proposals of the Russian Government, and to the circumstances in the course of which they were advanced, makes it possible to evaluate their objective significance quite otherwise.

In a preliminary and unofficial way, the peace proposals of Russia were advanced by Panin in a conversation with the new French Minister in St. Petersburg, the Marquis de Vérac, at the end of the summer of 1780. The head of the Russian Office of Foreign Affairs was convinced already at this time that the English could never subdue again their rebelling colonies. However, in order to secure the independence of America, without thereby wounding the pride of Great Britain, one had, in his opinion, to conclude an armistice initially, after which the French King would be able to query each of the colonies separately with regard to whether it desired to preserve its independence. More than this, Panin stated frankly in this connection that he viewed American independence as advantageous "for all countries, and especially for Russia." In accordance with his plan, America would receive "complete freedom to decide her own fate, and . . . during the armistice, she would be able to trade freely with all countries." Adding up the totality of everything about which Panin frequently spoke, the French Minister reported that therefrom "there is reason to suppose that Russia is moving secretly towards leaving independence to the Americans."[5]

At first glance it may appear that Panin's proposals were completely unreal, and moreover, not too favorable to the rebelling Americans. In diplomatic circles it was supposed that in case of the implementation of this plan, both Carolinas "were more likely than not to remain true to the British Crown."[6] Already in June, 1780, Catherine II informed the Austrian Emperor Joseph II[*] of her desire "that peace be concluded and that a part of the colonies receive independence."[7] Finally, in December, 1780, in a private conversation with the British Minister, James Harris, the Empress expressed herself on this subject especially firmly: "Make peace—begin conversations with your colonies . . . , try to disunite them."[8]

Speaking generally, there is nothing surprising in the fact that the Tsaritsa, during a private audience, cynically recommended to the English Minister an attempt to divide the rebelling colonies (the actions of the monarch were in close correspondence with her moral norms). In the given instance, however, there is something else important: Catherine II (not to speak even of Panin) understood that it was already impossible to conquer the rebelling Americans by force of arms, and counselled the English to make peace as soon as possible. (Moreover, even in the representation of the Tsaritsa, a part of the colonies would have to receive independence.)

In connection with the analysis of the proposals of the Russian Government, it is also extremely important to take account of

---

[*]Joseph II was Holy Roman Emperor from 1765 to 1790, but ruled the Austrian hereditary domains jointly with his mother, the Empress Maria Theresa, until 1780. A far more sincere enlightened despot than Catherine II, he stirred up rebellions in those domains through his reforming efforts of the 1780's. Thereby he was prevented from furnishing effective support to Catherine during her second war with the Turks between 1787 and 1792.

the concrete circumstances, and the time of their advancement. We recall that already for several years, a hard and exhausting war had been going on without an apparent prospect of success. A significant part of the territory of the United States, including New York, was occupied by British troops. In May, 1780, the English inflicted a heavy defeat on the army of the United States at Charleston, as a result of which, a route was opened for an offensive into South Carolina and Georgia. On August 16, the troops of General Cornwallis won yet another victory in the South at Camden, South Carolina.[9]

Already in November, 1778, the ally of France, Spain, proposed a peace settlement on the basis of *uti possidetis* (literally, "as you possess"—according to the territories occupied at that time by the belligerent parties), analogous to the way in which the United Provinces of Holland obtained their independence after the armistice of 1609.[10] The French Minister of Foreign Affairs, Comte de Vergennes, expressed interest at the end of 1778 in such a type of armistice, on the condition that England agree to withdraw her troops from North America.[11]

Compared to the Spanish proposals, Panin's project had significant advantages. If, in accordance with the principle of *uti possidetis,* New York remained in the hands of the English King, then Panin proposed to hand over the decision of the question of independence to the review of the American states themselves (each separately). The principle of the self-determination of the states would naturally lead the overwhelming majority (if not all) of the former English colonies in North America to independence. The young American researcher David Griffiths recently came to precisely such a conclusion.[12]

The significance of the Russian proposals becomes completely clear if the attitude of the Comte de Vergennes towards them is taken into account. According to the words of the French Minister, Panin advanced in conversation with Vérac "several ideas" brought forth to resolve the main difficulty—

the question of America's independence—this true "Gordian knot of the present war *(le noeud Gordien de la présent guerre)*."[13]

If this knot were cut, then already there would be no doubt that peace would be the direct consequence. The Powers interested in the reestablishment of peace would scarcely be able to refuse to seek an explanation from the "United Provinces of America" of their intentions, and to receive from each of them separately an "authenticated declaration" of the desire to remain in a state of independence. In the opinion of Vergennes, this would in no respect destroy the honor of France and the obligations undertaken by her. The Americans would remain "arbiters and masters" of their situation. "If any one of the United Provinces preferred to return under the rule of England, the King's obligations would not be affected to any degree," since the guarantee of the French Government did not extend to them in this case. In sum, this would be acceptable to France, and at the same time, honorable for Great Britain. And the United States itself was not in principle against the conclusion of an armistice and the intervention of the neutral Powers, on the condition that this led later to the recognition of its independence.[14]

In instructions looked over by us, Vergennes sympathized also to an exceptionally high degree with the league of neutral countries headed by Russia. In the words of the French Minister, the "real" goal of the existing war consisted of all nations enjoying freedom of navigation. Expressing agreement with Russia's moving forward into the role of "mediator and arbiter", Vergennes reckoned that in this event, at the time of the conclusion of the peace treaty a reflection of the principle of the declaration of Catherine II on armed neutrality would enter therein.[15]

Already on October 24/November 4, 1780, the Marquis de Vérac informed Panin of the benevolent attitude of the French Government towards the Russian peace proposals, and on the following day, he transmitted the full text of the despatch of Vergennes of October 12, 1780.[16] This despatch was destined for the eyes of the Empress only, and the Minister emphasized especially its deeply confidential character. Panin himself also carried on his negotiations with Vérac in strict secrecy, and this perhaps explains in part the barrenness of searches for some sort of official protocols or memoranda of conversations with the French Minister in the files of the College of Foreign Affairs. Nothing was known about them either by James Harris, or by his friend, Grigory Aleksandrovich Potyomkin. "I could not receive any sort of supplemental information about the proposal laid before the Empress concerning mediation," the English Minister reported with regret to Lord Stormont, the Secretary of State for the Northern Department at the British Foreign Office, from St. Petersburg in October, 1780. "Prince Potemkin declares his ignorance of this measure, and that nothing of the kind appears amongst the papers sent to him . . . I find it every day more difficult to do business here," James Harris complained in this letter. "Prince Potemkin is either not able or afraid to assist me, and my enemies have in their possession every other avenue of the Court. Your Lordship, however, may be assured I will struggle to the last."[17]

The British diplomat did not doubt that already recently "the most perfect understanding" existed between Panin and Vérac.[18] Soon his fears received official confirmation from the mouth of the head of the Office of Foreign Affairs. According to the testimony of Harris, Panin, in a conversation with him, rated very highly "the prudence, the moderation, the good conduct" of the enemies of Great Britain, and along with this, laid blame on the English indirectly. He expanded in detail on the power, resources, and high morale of the enemies of Great Britain, and, referring to the obvious inequality of forces in the conflict which was in progress, expressed himself definitely in favor of the speediest conclusion of peace. Calculating that "nothing could result to us from" the continuation of the struggle "but distress and ruin, he (*i.e.*, Panin)," wrote Harris, "strongly advised our making peace . . . on terms which might meet the ideas of *all* the belligerent powers." In the words of Harris, the Russian Minister argued "the Bourbon cause with as much warmth, but with less eloquence, than the Minister of Versailles would have done," and the English "never must expect anything but evil" from Panin.[19]

On October 27/November 7, 1780, official instructions were sent to the Russian Ministers in London, Paris, and Madrid, in which the interest of the Tsarist Government was expressed in "the reestablishment of general peace in Europe," and the desire was expressed "to see an end soon to the sufferings of the people, and particularly, the shedding of innocent blood, in whatever way it is to be achieved."[20] When in December, 1780, Simolin, the Russian Minister in London, made an official representation to the English Government about mediation (the well known *"insinuation verbale"*), Lord Stormont preferred to draw in Austria as well as a mediator", and thus possibly to paralyze the undesirable consequences of the Russian initiative."[21] In order to confront the Tsarist Government with a fait accompli, and to deprive it of freedom of choice, the proposal about drawing Austria into the mediation was made "directly" to the Vienna cabinet through the British Ambassador, Sir Robert M. Keith. Taking into account the character of Russo-Austrian relations (the preparation of the conclusion of a treaty of alliance), and the ever growing interest of Russia in her support in Eastern politics, it was in practice impossible to decline cooperation with Austria. Being forced to consent to joint Russo-Austrian mediation, Panin proposed nevertheless to pursue his original peace plan. The detailed memorandum about mediation which was presented to Catherine II and approved by the Russian Empress on January 22/February 2, 1781, has special interest in this connection.[22]

In this document, at the very beginning, attention is invited to the difference in principle between the positions of the belligerent Powers on the question of the independence of the rebelling colonies. If England considers "inconsistent with her honor acceptance of the independence of the American settlements," France, "by binding herself to the rebels by a formal agreement, rests her honor on the contrary event. Extreme necessity alone, and virtual exhaustion, would be capable of extracting from each of them ideas contrary to these, but the position of the belligerent Powers seems far removed from this phase."

In these circumstances, both mediators must adopt a completely impartial position and offer their plan of pacification, foreseeing in the first instance the conclusion of "an armistice of two or three years in Europe and other parts of the world." (In the memorandum it is specially stipulated that "the American settlements must be included" in this armistice.) In case of the extreme stubbornness of Great Britain over the recognition of an American Plenipotentiary, the armistice could be concluded "by means of mediators, that is, with the full consent of both sides, in a formal act announced through their ministers here."

The Russian Government noted especially that "means must not be taken away from the American settlements of negotiating with the English Crown and concluding treaties with it in common, or individually, by provinces." Moreover, the possibility was foreseen that "France will show pliability in exiting with honor from her obligation, and from the war itself, being satisfied, for example, with a guarantee of the pacts made between England and the American colonies, and various trade advantages granted to her."

As for the locale of the peace negotiations, the Russian Government, "both for the convenience of His Majesty the Emperor [Joseph II], and because of the convenience of the location of that city," agreed to elect for Vienna, "in accordance with which, the Imperial Russian Minister, Prince Dmitry Mikhailovich Golitsyn* must be designated and empowered to deal with the belligerent Powers jointly with the Imperial Ministry, to make appropriate proposals on the subject of mediation, and to maintain direct relations with our Ministers at other Courts."

---

*TRANSLATOR'S NOTE: Prince D. M. Golitsyn should not be confused with his relative, Prince Dmitry Alekseyevich Golitsyn, the Minister at the Hague at this time.

In close correspondence with the contents of the memorandum analyzed, a Tsarist rescript and full powers were sent to Dmitry Mikhailovich Golitsyn on February 4/15, 1781, to act "as mediator," as well as to cooperate in the conclusion "of treaties, conventions, or other acts which will be considered necessary for the complete and final settlement of all disputes, and for the full and complete pacification of the present confusion."[23] Along with the rescript of February 4/15, 1781, a whole array of supplementary materials (including the above-mentioned memorandum on mediation), calculated to give Golitsyn the fullest possible picture of the mission entrusted to him, was sent to Vienna.[24]

Simultaneously, the Russian diplomatic representatives in London, Paris, and Madrid were instructed to cooperate "in the general suggestions and explanations for the achievement of the desired" peaceful settlement. "Because of our heartfelt desire to return peace and quietude to mankind," it was pointed out in the rescript to Simolin, the Russian Minister in London, on February 4/15, 1781, "we are gladly using all means available to us in the present important negotiation." To explain the choice of the Austrian capital as a place for the conduct of the forthcoming peace congress, the Tsarist Government pointed out that Vienna "is centrally located for all the Powers," and there "already are several ministers there," which made unnecessary "new and useless expenditures."[25] "In all discussions with the belligerent Powers and with other Powers," it was recommended to the Russian diplomats that they "enter as little as possible into a dissection of American affairs, so as not to show partiality to one side, and, no less, in order to avoid all mistakes there."[26]

Along with the joint Russo-Austrian mediation in Vienna, the Tsarist Government entrusted to its Ministers in London and the Hague "the important commission of the mutual reconciliation of England and Holland." Simolin, the Minister in London, and Dmitry Alekseyevich Golitsyn, the Minister in the Hague, were ordered to offer both Governments their friendly services and "formal mediation." "The nature and form of our good services and mediation," Catherine II wrote, "must naturally depend on the personal will" of the British cabinet and of "the Estates General, after a preliminary contact about this with them."[27]

Although the Russian Minister in London "exerted all efforts in order to convince the British ministry to agree with the intentions of the Empress," and to enter into a separate reconciliation with Holland, they gave him to understand that England did not consider it possible to accept these proposals, while referring to the joint Russo-Austrian mediation, and the forthcoming negotiations in Vienna. "It seems that they flatter themselves here with the hope," wrote Simolin, "that the mighty influence of the Empress in union with the influence of the Emperor [Joseph II] must guarantee the desired success—a universal pacification, for which they think it possible to continue to exert themselves."[28]

For the Russian Government, it was no secret that the real reason for the attack of England on Holland was the adherence of the latter to the system of armed neutrality. For this reason, England did not desire the conclusion of peace with Holland, fearing that in the contrary event, the Republic would use the fruits of the "new system" advanced by Russia "in favor of the trade and the navigation of the neutral nations."[29]

On May 21, 1781, Prince Dmitry Mikhailovich Golitsyn, the Russian Minister in Vienna, and the Austrian Chancellor, Prince Wenzel Anton von Kaunitz-Rietberg, sent to the Governments of France, Spain, and England their concerted proposals, "designed to serve as a basis for negotiations concerning the reestablishment of general peace." This document (by the way, already less favorable for the United States than the initial Russian proposals) foresaw: (1) that at the congress in Vienna, all proposals advanced by the belligerent parties without exception would be reviewed. Simultaneously, parallel negotiations must be carried on between Great Britain and the "American colonies" about the reestablishment of peace in America, "but without any sort of intervention of other belligerent parties, and of the two Imperial Courts, unless their inter-

vention on this score should be officially requested and offered."
(2) Peace with the "American colonies" could be signed only
simultaneously with the conclusion of a peace treaty between
the other belligerent countries, and both agreements made
subject to the "solemn guarantees" of the mediators, and also
"any other neutral Power whose guarantee the belligerent
parties may consider necessary." (3) In order to make the
peace negotiations independent of unexpected eventualities
connected with military operations, the conclusion of a general
armistice for the term of one year was proposed, during which
the status quo was to be maintained. (4) In approving "this
plan of negotiations," the belligerent Powers would have to
request the mediators to open a session, and to supply their
representatives without delay with full powers and the instructions necessary for the success of the negotiation."[30]

It is easy to see that at the base of these articles lay the well-
known proposals of Panin, into which, however, the Government of Austria had introduced a number of vital changes. We
note in particular that in the Russian proposals, there was
talk of the "American settlements," and not of the "American
colonies." The duration of the armistice was foreseen as two
or three years, and not as one year, etc. The Austrian version
of the Russian proposals thus turned out to be more unfavorable for the United States, but Dmitry Mikhailovich Golitsyn
and his high command in St. Petersburg did not want to quarrel
with their new ally on the subject of these "trifles."

"I did not hesitate, Most Powerful Sovereign Lady," Golitsyn
reported to St. Petersburg, "to consent to the proposal of Prince
Kaunitz, the more in that, in the month of April last, he informed me of the formal acceptance of the dual mediation of
both Imperial Courts which followed from the French and
Spanish Courts, and also then gave appropriate notice to the
Court of Your Most High Imperial Majesty as to that acceptance."[31]

During conversations with the French Ambassador in Vienna,

Louis-Auguste le Tonnelier, Baron de Breteuil,* the Austrian Chancellor touched on the question of American representation and proposed that each state send to the congress its own representative. Although at first the Ambassador took a negative attitude towards this idea, his chief in Paris, recalling the proposals made at one time by Panin, considered it possible to fall in behind the Austrian Chancellor. Vergennes understood that such a course of action would be more acceptable to Great Britain, and thought that despite the differences, even those states which were occupied anew by the English were bound by the obligation to achieve their independence.[32]

The idea of plural representation of the rebels possibly still attracted Vergennes also because his relations with the American plenipotentiaries appointed by the Continental Congress for the conclusion of a peace treaty and a trade treaty with Great Britain, already at the end of 1779, were turning out to be totally bad. The egotistical and suspicious John Adams was in many respects on opposite sides to Benjamin Franklin, who, as is well known, possessed a rare skill in maneuvering, and striking diplomatic tact, which made it possible for him to win the confidence of the French cabinet, and an enormous success in the Parisian salons. Even the very form of presenting John Adams as "the colleague of Mr. Franklin" always re-

*TRANSLATOR'S NOTE: Born in 1733, Baron de Breteuil was of considerable importance in both French diplomacy and French domestic politics in the eighteenth century. He began his diplomatic career at Cologne in 1758, and two years later became the Minister in Russia. Catherine II liked him, but later, in Stockholm, he helped prepare the coup d'état of 1772 which she very much disliked. He went to Vienna first in 1770, but was soon transferred to other posts before returning there a second time in 1778. Upon returning to France in 1783, he became a Minister of State. Though a favorite of Louis XVI, he was ousted from office by Calonne. Having opposed the convocation of the Estates-General in 1789, he was made head of the Government after the second dismissal of Necker in that year. The Fall of the Bastille forced the King to dismiss a Government which was anathema to the new National Assembly, but Breteuil fled abroad with a secret commission from the King to work for the intervention of foreign Powers in French affairs. Needless to say, he remained abroad until the establishment of the Consulate made it possible for him to return to France in 1802. He died in 1807.

minded the lawyer from Massachusetts of the popularity of his illustrious fellow countryman at the Court, in the *haut monde*, among scholars and literary people, and to no slight degree, among the French ladies. Not without surprise did Adams reflect that French women (in contrast to American ones) nourished "an inexplicable inclination to fall in love with old men."[33]

Franklin did not succeed in changing the "strait-laced" Adams into a more easy-going Adams, and in the summer of 1781, Vergennes was forced to call in the American plenipotentiary from the Hague in order to discuss with him the perspectives of a peace congress in Vienna. Having scarcely succeeded in becoming acquainted with the Austro-Russian proposals, Adams hastened to send to Philadelphia a letter about their obvious inacceptability for the United States. "I can never agree to the mediation of any powers, however respectable, until they have acknowledged our sovereignty, so far at least as to admit a minister plenipotentiary from the United States as the representative of a free and independent power."[34]

While not objecting to separate negotiations with England, Adams at that time was definitely against an armistice on the basis of the status quo, which was foreseen in the third article of the Austro-Russian proposals. Such an armistice would lead, after its conclusion, only to "another long and bloody war." The necessary terms would therefore be: (1) preservation in full measure of the existing treaties of alliance throughout all the duration of the armistice, and right up to the final recognition by England of American independence, and (2) the withdrawal prior to the armistice "of British land and naval armaments" from all parts of the United States.[35]

After further thought, the American Plenipotentiary cooled off and calmed down. Some of the proposals of the mediators began to seem to him already fully satisfactory. Thus, for example, the proposal about a separate treaty between the United States and England seemed to him "to be a benevolent invention to avoid several difficulties" — to save the "national pride" of Great Britain and to avoid preliminary recognition of American independence (inasmuch as the Imperial Courts might consider such recognition inconsistent with their role of mediators, and even of neutral countries). "I cannot see that the United States would make any concession, or submit to any indignity, or do anything inconsistent with her character if their Minister should appear at Vienna, or elsewhere with the ministers of other powers, and conduct any negotiation with a British minister, without having the independence of the United States or his own title and character acknowledged or ascertained by any other power except France until the pacification should be concluded." In agreeing to go to Vienna and take part in the peace congress, Adams withdrew all earlier objections, with the exception of those which related to the status quo and the armistice.[36]

Adams came to the most important conclusion, however, exactly ten days after Comte de Vergennes acquainted him with the content of the Austro-Russian proposals. The conversation was about the idea of sending to Vienna representatives of all thirteen American states for the subsequent peace negotiations with Great Britain. The experienced lawyer and specialist in constitutional law reminded Vergennes that the Articles of Confederation had been ratified and sent "to all the courts and nations of the world." The European newspapers could broadcast this constitution, and now it was well known to all. "By this constitution all power and authority of negociating with foreign powers is expressly delegated" to the Confederation Congress. "If the two imperial courts should address their articles to the States separately, no governor or president of any one of those Commonwealths could even communicate it to the legislature." And therefore there was no other way for the transmission of anything to the American people than through the Congress of the United States. In taking account of all these circumstances, Adams pointed out that the very "idea of summoning ministers from the thirteen States may not be countenanced at all."[37]

According to the well-turned expression of Professor Richard B. Morris, John Adams "had put a spoke in the wheel, and the mediation soon came to a stop."[38] The modest lawyer from Massachusetts, without special doubts, crossed out the cunning and complex plan of peace negotiations advanced initially in St. Petersburg by Panin, given preliminary approval in Paris by the Comte de Vergennes, and finally, revised in Vienna by Prince Kaunitz. It became clear that negotiations were possible only with the representatives of one sovereign state—the United States of America.[39]

The main cause of the failure of the Russo-Austrian project of mediation lay, however, not in the position of John Adams, the more in that he always expressed agreement to participating in a peace congress in Vienna, but to the stubborn lack of desire of England "to consent to the idependence of America." According to the testimony of Russian Minister Simolin, "this point has such enormous significance for the most important interests of England and her prestige," that the British cabinet "will never give way in this question and there will not be any progress in the peace negotiations so long as France will insist on this condition."[40]

Referring to the reply of the British cabinet to the joint Austro-Russian proposals, Simolin wrote N. S. Khotinsky in Paris in June, 1781 that therein "is contained a rejection of negotiations insofar as they relate to the American colonies, with which they firmly intend to do business only as with subjects, and therefore everything that relates to them in the first, second, and third preliminary articles is considered inacceptable and contradictory to the integrity of the King, to the basic interests of his nation, and to the rights of his Crown. It looks as if the King, the ministry, and the nation have decided they would sooner go down with arms in hand than to consent to dishonor . . . If the two Courts, moving forward in the capacity of mediators, do not find any means for the reconciliation of the parties, then the time of the beginning of negotiations about general peace will be put off still more."[41]

Even on November 15, 1781 (*i.e.,* already after the surrender of the troops of General Cornwallis at Yorktown, but before anything about this event became known in London), Lord Stormont, in a conversation with Simolin, categorically rejected the possibility of the recognition of the independence of the United States or the concession of Gibraltar to Spain.

In the words of the conservative Lord, "the British nation is fighting for its vital interests and its political existence," and it would not sign "a shameful peace even if the French seize the Tower [of London]." As for the "absurd demand of Spain concerning the offer of a full guarantee of the concession of Gibraltar," Stormont thought that with such an excuse, he would be able "to demand in advance the concession of Madrid." As Russian Minister Simolin wrote, "the only arbiter" in this serious confrontation of interests could become arms alone.[42]

As we have seen, the general situation in 1781 was little favorable to the success of proposals concerning mediation. "In politics as in other things," Frederick II [of Prussia] remarked on this subject, "to everything its time.... No one eats cherries in February if they do not ripen in June."[43] Of course, at the disposal of the mediators, and in particular of Russia, were some means of making the British cabinet more conciliatory. The most decisive of the Russian diplomats, in the first place, Dmitry Alekseyevich Golitsyn, proposed already at the beginning of 1781 that direct military pressure be exerted on England.

"Let the Sovereign Empress send out 20 of Her ships," wrote the Russian Minister in the Hague to Panin on January 29/ February 9, 1781. "Let the [Dutch] Republic add 30 of hers, and Sweden and Denmark, 20 more. Let this united squadron be disposed along the coast of Holland in such a way that the Dutch ports remain in its rear, and thus it is enabled neither to take any risks, nor to fear any one. Let them, besides, close the Baltic Sea completely for the English, and valiantly resist the parry, so that, by depriving them thus of any sort of supplies and equipment, they will be able to knock some sense into them. In order, finally, to incline them in this direction, it would be possible to threaten to move against them with all these forces."

"If these plans should be carried out, then, in my opinion, mediation will be proposed to the Empress unfailingly. In this case, peace will be concluded on just and well-advised terms, and consequently, advantages acquired for the rest of the states of Europe."

"(1)Moreover, freedom of navigation and trade will be guaranteed for all the European nations. (2)England would be forced to accept a new maritime code for neutral states, as the Sovereign Empress has so wisely found. (3)It would be possible to recognize the independence of the Americans, inasmuch as England has been stubborn on this point, although it cannot be hoped in any way to subjugate them at any time, even if they confront them with their own forces. Consequently, we must in the future remove this stumbling block. (4)It would be possible through the subsequent terms of this peace to re-establish the balance between England and France. I think it is not in the interests of Europe that the latter become the predominant Power, but it is in the interests of each of us that a balance of forces exist between these two Powers."[44]

Golitsyn's recommendations were too radical for them to be capable of winning approval in St. Petersburg to the full extent. It is true that in the secret report of Panin, Osterman, and the Bakunin brothers to Catherine II in April, 1781, for the "inclining" of the London Court "to a greater spirit of conciliation," the deployment beyond the Sound "for a set period of a Russian, Danish, and Swedish squadron, and their cruising in such proximity to each other that they represent a powerful and ready naval militia" was recommended. Simultaneously, however, the members of the Foreign College emphasized that "the inviolable rule" was the preservation "in all stringency" of neutrality with respect to all belligerent Powers, "since under the shadow thereof, our own Russian navigation will be established and grow from year to year."[45]

The secret report surveyed by us was one of the last important documents prepared by the College of Foreign Affairs under the leadership of Nikita Ivanovich Panin. In May, 1781, Panin was sent on vacation, and then definitely removed from the leadership of foreign affairs. Grigory Aleksandrovich Potyomkin linked the removal of Panin with the actions of British Minister James Harris, and in particular, with a conversation of the British Minister with Catherine II in March, 1781.[46] Although Potyomkin, according to all appearances, somewhat overrated the "services" of his English friend, objectively the departure of Panin turned out to be very opportune for British diplomacy. "The Prussian, French, and Dutch Ministers," wrote Harris, "consider themselves left without a head."[47]

The correspondence about mediation was carried on simultaneously with negotiations concerning the conclusion of a treaty of alliance with Austria.[48] Thereafter, to the degree that the interest of the Tsarist Government grew in Eastern affairs, in the alliance with Austria, and in the annexation of the Crimea, its interest in mediation in European and American affairs diminished. In this same regard, actually all the threads of mediation were concentrated in Vienna, and then in Paris, where Russian influence turned out to be quite limited.

Along with this, the very fact of the advancement by Panin of a concrete plan of mediation, and the subsequent frequent démarches of the Russian Government in favor of the conclusion of peace could not fail to be of use to the opening of direct negotiations, and to a final peace settlement.

4

Francis Dana's Mission
1781-1783

The rejection by Catherine II of the proposals of Great Britain on the conclusion of a treaty of alliance, the proclamation of the Declaration of Armed Neutrality, and finally, Panin's proposal as to a peace settlement, changed essentially the initial idea about Russia's attitude towards the War of the American Revolution, and even led to the spreading in America of hopes too optimistic and not well founded. In taking account of the significance of Russia's position, and evaluating highly the proclamation by Catherine II of armed neutrality, the Continental Congress adopted in the middle of December, 1780, a resolution about the necessity of the despatch to St. Petersburg of an American diplomatic representative. A commission was created for the drawing up of full powers and instructions to the new Minister, one composed of John Duane, John Witherspoon, and James Madison, and as candidates for the vacant post, Francis Dana, Arthur Lee, and Colonel Alexander Hamilton were put forward.[1]

Francis Dana, "late delegate in Congress from the State of Massachusetts Bay, and a member of the council of said state," turned out to be the choice for the post of Minister on December 19, 1780.[2] On that same day, the President of the Continental Congress, Samuel Huntington, signed the appropriate instructions, full powers, and letters of credence for the new Minister.[3] "The great object of your negotiation," it was pointed out in these instructions, "is to engage her imperial majesty to favour and support the sovereignty and independence of these United States, and to lay a foundation for a good understanding and friendly intercourse between the subjects of her Imperial Majesty and the citizens of these United States, to the mutual advantage of both nations."[4] In case of a favorable reception, Francis Dana was to sign in St. Petersburg the convention about the adherence of the United States to the armed neutrality, and to reach an agreement about a treaty concerning friendship and trade. (Moreover, apparently, it was not taken into account that the participation of the United States, as a belligerent party, in the league of neutral Powers was scarcely possible at the time, even in a purely formal way.)

Later, in October, 1781, Robert Livingstone, having been chosen Secretary for Foreign Affairs, wrote Francis Dana that the American people entertained the "highest respect" for the Petersburg Court. "They consider the plan of the armed neutrality as the best proof of an enlarged and generous policy" of the Government of Catherine II, and the execution of this plan as an important charter in the liberation of world trade from despotism. In sending information of the decisive victory of the united forces of France and the United States over the troops of Lord Cornwallis in Virginia, and the capture of around 7,000 English soldiers and sailors, Livingstone continued: "You will not fail to make use of this intelligence which must fix our independence not only beyond all doubt, but even beyond all controversy."[5]

That which seemed completely obvious in Philadelphia was far from being recognized at once in the diplomatic chancelleries of monarchical Europe. When in the spring of 1781, Francis Dana acquainted the Comte de Vergennes with the instructions given him, the experienced French Minister at once expressed doubt about the expediency of the trip of the American diplomat to St. Petersburg, inasmuch as Russia still did not recognize the independence of the United States. Vergennes consented to be reconciled to the trip only after it was explained that Dana proposed to put in an appearance at the Tsarist capital only in the capacity of "a mere private gentleman, travelling with a view of obtaining some knowledge of that country."[6] The cautious Benjamin Franklin recommended delaying the trip, and taking counsel in advance with the Russian Minister in the Hague, Prince Dmitry Alekseyevich Golitsyn.[7]

Francis Dana himself preferred, however, to follow the advice of his countryman and defender, John Adams, who was convinced of the contrary. In his opinion, the circumstances for the mission of Dana to Russia were very favorable, and turning to Golitsyn would lead only to unnecessary difficulties and delays. The United States had nothing that it would be necessary to conceal from other Powers. On the contrary, America "has been too long silent in Europe. Her cause is that of all nations and all men, and it needs nothing but to be explained to be approved." Thus, at least, thought Adams himself, and he remarked further that "no measure of Congress was ever taken in a more proper time or with more wisdom, in my opinion, than the appointment of a minister at The Hague and at St. Petersburgh."[8]

Encouraged by the advice of his old colleague, Francis Dana set out on July 7, 1781, from Amsterdam to St. Petersburg, where he arrived on August 27, 1781.[9] The son of John Adams, the subsequently illustrious John Quincy Adams, who stayed in Russia more than a year, went along with Dana in the capacity of his secretary in St. Petersburg.[10]

Some days following his arrival in the Russian capital, Francis Dana made the Marquis de Vérac aware of his mission. The French Minister at once expressed doubt that the Tsarist Government would agree to recognize the representative of a state which, in its eyes, still not did exist politically. Moreover, this step would unavoidably provoke protests of Great Britain, and put in doubt the impartiality of the mediation. A supplementary objection to the establishment of contacts with the Tsarist Government was Dana's lack of knowledge of the French language.[11]

The persistent lawyer from Massachusetts did not want to agree with the conclusions of Vérac, and thought that "to seclude myself in a hotel" would be a betrayal of "the honor and dignity of the United States." Moreover, he was convinced that Catherine II could not propose mediation, and consent to the participation of an American representative at the peace congress, if she did not recognize the political existence of the United States, the independence of which had already been proclaimed on July 4, 1776. Vérac had to explain that in accordance with the Russo-Austrian plan, the negotiations of Great Britain with the rebelling colonists would have to take place without the intervention of the other belligerent parties and the Imperial Courts, if their intervention were not officially requested.[12]

In the end, the American diplomat had to agree with the conclusions of the Minister of the French King, and to refrain from any sort of official representations to the Tsarist Government. Moreover, Francis Dana arrived in St. Petersburg at the time when Panin was already removed from the leadership of the Office of Foreign Affairs. True, he was initially, as is well known, only sent on a three-month vacation, and rumors went about in the capital about his early return. Dana counted precisely on this, when he decided to follow the advice of his French colleague, and not to be in a hurry with an official announcement of his mission. "I am told Count Panin will shortly return to court, and that he has the most favorable sentiments of the United States of any of her Imperial majesty's ministers," Dana reported in his first despatch from the Russian capital in September, 1781."[13]

But nevertheless the hopes for the return of Nikita Ivanovich Panin were not destined to be realized. Aleksandr Alekseyevich Bezborodko* and Grigory Aleksandrovich Potyomkin exerted ever greater influence on defining the course of Russia's foreign policy. The center of the attention of Catherine II's Government was relocated towards the East, and above all, towards the annexation of the Crimea, and interest in cutting short the

---

*TRANSLATOR'S NOTE: A native of Belorussia, Bezborodko acquired military fame as a protegé of Field Marshal Rumyantsev during the First Turkish War (1768-1774). Born in 1746, he became in 1781 the effective head of a Russian College of Foreign Affairs of which Osterman was only the nominal head. He was named Vice-Chancellor in 1784. He survived the change of rulers in 1796, since Emperor Paul named him Chancellor in 1797, and, like Catherine II, loaded him with rewards and honors. He died in 1799.

military activities in Europe and America diminished correspondingly. We must also take into account that English diplomacy exerted all efforts to ward off the establishment of direct
diplomatic relations between the two countries. It had scarcely
just become known in London in the spring of 1781 about the
appointment of Francis Dana to St. Petersburg before the British Foreign Secretary, Lord Stormont, was not slow in advising
Russian Minister Simolin that in England "they are not at all
reassured by this, and think that they would give offense to the
friendly feelings of Her Imperial Majesty for Great Britain if
they suspected even the slightest desire on her part to receive
this new Minister at her Court."[14] Not relying very much, apparently, on just the "friendly feelings" of the Empress, British
Minister James Harris undertook open pressure in St. Petersburg for the purpose of preventing the success of Francis Dana's
mission, warning that in the conditions of the approaching war
with Turkey, it was scarcely expedient for Russia "to approve a
measure which will always arouse the hostility of the English
nation."[15]

After the receipt of news of the conclusion of a preliminary
peace treaty, and the assurance of Pyotr Vasilyevich Bakunin
that "his mission and his person were completely acceptable to
the Empress," Dana decided on February 24/March 7, 1783,
to advise the Russian Government officially of his appointment to the post of Minister of the United States in St. Petersburg.[16] The renewal in March, 1783 of the Russo-Austrian
mediation mission forced Catherine II to put off the granting
of an official audience to Dana. However, at that time, free
access to members of the Tsarist Government was maintained
for him. On April 12/23, in a conversation with Dana, Vice-
Chancellor Osterman advised that until the signing of the definitive treaty of peace, the Empress could not recognize the
American Minister, inasmuch as this would be inconsistent with
the rules of neutrality, and with the role of impartial mediator
adopted by her. "Just as soon as that treaty is completed,"
Osterman stated, "he (Francis Dana) may be assured that then
already no difficulties will stand in the way of carrying on di-

rect communication with him and with his superiors." Osterman pointed out also the necessity of the presentation of a new letter of credence.[17]

The formal motives advanced by the Russian Government encountered the definite objections of Francis Dana. The demand for the presentation of new letters of credence especially disturbed the American Minister. In a lengthy memorandum presented to Osterman on April 27/May 8, 1783, Dana pointed out that the United States had already been an independent and sovereign state for around seven years, and its independence did not flow at all from the recognition of the English King.[18]

The argumentation of Francis Dana, based on the principles of popular sovereignty, could not, it goes without saying, make a special impression (on the contrary, only a negative one) on the Tsarist Government. In the official reply to Dana of June 3/14, 1783, it was emphasized that although the Empress received "with a feeling of satisfaction" news of the despatch of an official representative of the United States, she could recognize him only after the signing of the final peace treaty. Along with this (and this is very important), it was pointed out in the reply that not only Dana, but also all his countrymen who came to Russia "on commercial or other affairs" would encounter "the most favorable reception and the protection of the laws of nations."[19] In essence, this meant recognition *de facto*.

As for the touchy question of the time of the existence of the United States as an independent state from a juridical point of view, the Russian Government preferred to decline to consider "such a delicate matter." Osterman very transparently remarked, "personally" to Francis Dana, "that the less he enters into disputes and discussions, the more pleasant will be his person, and the sooner he will achieve the desired success in this matter."[20] Thanks to the "assurances" given him, Dana promised to await the signing of the final peace treaty.[21]

By an irony of fate, at the same time that Francis Dana was obtaining official recognition in St. Petersburg, they were already reaching a decision in the United States as to his recall. Already on February 26, 1783, Robert Livingstone wrote to the President of the Continental Congress that he did not see reasons for the further presence of Dana in Russia, and did not consider it expedient to have a diplomatic representative in St. Petersburg after the conclusion of the peace treaty.[22] Accordingly, on April 1, 1783, the Congress passed a resolution about the recall of Dana to the United States on the condition that, at the moment of the receipt of the resolution mentioned, he would not be carrying on negotiations with the Russian Government. In this case, the desire was expressed that the negotiations be wound up prior to his return.[23]

As was already noted, at the time of his appointment to St. Petersburg in December, 1780, Francis Dana was empowered to sign a convention concerning adherence to the armed neutrality, and to reach an agreement about a project for a treaty of friendship and trade. In the new conditions, when the independence of the United States was actually secured, and the preliminary peace treaty was signed, they became less in need of quests for new allies, and even feared being drawn into the system of European politics, in particular in connection with proposals about adherence to the armed neutrality made by Holland. The powers of Dana in the part about the conclusion of an agreement concerning the adherence of the United States to the armed neutrality were not renewed, inasmuch as "the true interests of the States requires that they should be as little as possible entangled in the politics and controversies of European nations." Along with this, it was noted in the resolution of June 12, 1783, that on the whole the liberal principles of the league of neutrals were favorable for the interests of all countries, especially the United States, and "ought, in that view, to be promoted by the latter as far as will consist with their fundamental policy."[24]

Having received from the American Congress the order to return to the United States, Francis Dana advised Vice-Chancellor Osterman on July 28/August 8, 1783, of his intention to depart from St. Petersburg. To avoid "misapprehensions" about the reasons for his unexpected departure, Dana considered it expedient to refer to ill health and personal affairs in a letter to Osterman on August 3/14, 1783.[25]

By an irony of history, Dana departed from St. Petersburg on August 24/September 4, 1783, on the next day after the signing of the final peace treaty at Versailles.[25a] Telegraph communications did not exist at that time, and so the Minister did not wait for an official audience with Catherine II. But this, of course, was not the important thing, if one keeps in view the actual reasons for the slight productivity of his mission. After the removal of Panin in the spring of 1781, concerning whose benevolent attitude towards the cause of American independence something was said above, it was not possible, it goes without saying, to count on the success of Dana's mission. Relations with Turkey, and in the first place, the annexation of the Crimea, attracted the basic attention of Russian diplomacy. Catherine II herself was almost not interested in American affairs, and on June 11/22, 1783, she wrote frankly to Baryatinsky, and to Arkady Ivanovich Morkov,* in Paris: "When the occupation of the Crimea is made known to the public, then you may say without attribution in answer to questions put to you, and so in your conversations, while following the reasons laid forth in the manifesto, that Russia has not meddled in recent years in foreign affairs, such as, for example, in the occupation of Corsica [by France in 1768], the recognition of the independence of the English settlements in America, and

---

*TRANSLATOR'S NOTE: Morkov, born in 1747, graduated from the University of Moscow, where, like Fonvizin and Bogdanovich, mentioned in this book, he was considered one of the best students. He was the assistant of Prince D. A. Golitsyn at the Russian Embassy in the Hague during 1781-1783, but failed in efforts to negotiate a peace treaty between the Dutch Republic and Great Britain. Morkov was Russian Minister in Sweden during 1783-1786, but during the succeeding decade, served in the College of Foreign Affairs as the strong right arm of Bezborodko, and of the last of the favorites of Catherine II, Platon A. Zubov. Though disgraced by Emperor Paul, he served as Ambassador to Paris under Alexander I during 1801-1803. He died in 1827.

such like, and that in return for this, she has the right to demand that other Powers not interfere in the acquisition of the Tatar lands by her, and that, while acting unilaterally, and being in close alliance with the Roman Emperor [i.e., Joseph II, the Holy Roman Emperor and hereditary ruler of the Austrian possessions], she did not of course let her ally be disturbed on this occasion."[26]

Francis Dana himself lived in St. Petersburg not only in almost complete isolation from the Tsarist Government, but also from Russian society as a whole, although in the very beginning of the instructions given him by the Continental Congress, it was pointed out that "the great object" of his mission, along with obtaining the support of Catherine II, was "to lay a foundation for a good understanding and friendly intercourse between the subjects of her Imperial majesty and the citizens of these United States, to the mutual advantage of both nations."[27]

For all practical purposes, Francis Dana did little to carry out this important part of his mission. Being in St. Petersburg around two years, he doubtless had the chance to establish ties with those circles of Russian society which could work to some degree for the success of his mission, the more in that, in this regard, the outstanding example of Benjamin Franklin in France was available. Of course, France was on the eve of the Revolution; this was not the serf-holding Russia of the time of Catherine II. It was not possible to count on the special success of the Puritan diplomat. It is just as obvious, however, that Dana was not Benjamin Franklin, and this is why it was more difficult for the obscure lawyer from Massachusetts to penetrate the highest society of St. Petersburg, than for his illustrious colleague, the celebrated investigator of nature and philosophy, to penetrate the Parisian salons. The activity of Dana was made still more difficult in connection with the fact that he was ignorant, not only of the Russian language, but even of the French language, and this alone could not fail already to have the most negative effect during his presence in St. Petersburg.[27a]

But if formal recognition of the United States as an independent state did not take place at that time (after the conclusion of the peace with England, the American Government itself, fearing being drawn into the European system of politics, did not show interest in the establishment of diplomatic relations with St. Petersburg), one may speak with good reason about the *de facto* recognition of the new state, in essence. Giving credence to this are, above all, the above-mentioned reply of the Russian Government to Francis Dana of June 3/ 14, 1783, the practical activity of Russian diplomats abroad, and finally, the official instructions received by them somewhat later from St. Petersburg. Significant in particular is the communication by the Russian Minister in Paris, Baryatinsky, in the summer of 1783 to the effect that Benjamin Franklin made "the first visit to the whole diplomatic corps, and all the Ambassadors and Ministers returned it."[28]

However, all this was to a certain degree only a formality. It is much more important that, as the materials studied by us show, the general position of Russia in the difficult and critical years for the United States of the struggle for its freedom and independence had, objectively, a vital significance for the improvement of the international position of the rebelling colonies, for the diplomatic isolation of England, and, in the end, for the victory of the United States in the struggle against the mother country. A number of documents on the mediation of Russia bear witness already about her effort—given, it is true, very cautious expression—to influence England towards a reconcilation with the rebels, and towards the recognition of their independence. We are not talking, let it be understood, about any sort of "sympathies" of Catherine II and her government for the rebelling colonists, but about *Realpolitik* considerations—the ever growing dissatisfaction with the policy of the British cabinet; the effort of the Empress to play the role of arbiter in European affairs; the understanding of the unavoidability of the separation of the colonies, and even the interest of Russia in the formation of an independent United States; support for the European "balance"; and strengthening of the international prestige and influence of Russia, etc. The proclamation by Russia in 1780 of the Declaration of Armed Neutrality had enormous international significance. This declaration, with its point directed against England, was advantageous for all other countries, and especially for the United States.

Even after the removal of Nikita Ivanovich Panin in May, 1781, and the changing of the general course of the foreign policy of Russia, the Tsarist Government did not give up the idea of exerting itself, in case of cooperation, for the achievement of a reconciliation between England and her rebelling colonies.

Thus, in February, 1782, in transmitting to Vice-Chancellor Osterman "the will of the Most High," the all-powerful secretary of Catherine II, Bezborodko, wrote that while pursuing "a disposition friendly to the Crown of Great Britain," the Empress "would very much desire that the matter between the latter and the settlers in America which have pulled away from her, and which at this time was the only obstacle to a pacification, could be ended by an unimpeded and preliminary agreement between them, and that the current presence in Holland of Mr. Wentworth, as well as of Adams, the emissary of the settlements mentioned, could produce this result." In corresponding instructions to Arkady Ivanovich Morkov in this connection, it was proposed simultaneously to emphasize that he act in this question with extreme caution, "without giving England reason to conclude that the Court here wanted to meddle in the matter with the American settlements."[29]

The defeat of the English troops in America produced in the spring of 1782 the fall of the old Tory cabinet, and the coming to power of the Whig Government of Rockingham and Fox. There did not remain for England any way out except the recognition of the independence of the United States, and an agreement on the opening of peace negotiations. "When the former ministry stated to me, and repeated," reported Russian Minister Simolin from London on June 7/18, 1782, "that the nation would sooner bury itself under the ruins of the state than proceed to the recognition of the independence of America, which Your Excellency will be good enough to remember, it spoke in a high tone, and disposed of the votes of the electors, prior to the catastrophe of the capture of the army of Cornwallis . . . Events in the Chesapeake created a new situation, and caused the resignation of the ministry mentioned. If at that time, the chances for the victory and for the defeat of British arms had been equal, I am inclined to think that the ministry mentioned would have continued still to exist, and would not have given up its plan to subjugate America by force of arms, and for this purpose, to resort to the most extreme measures."[30]

In connection with the preparation of the signing of the definitive peace treaty in Paris in the summer of 1783, the question of Austro-Russian mediation arose anew. On this occasion, there was talk of the purely formal side of the matter—whether the signatures of the Russian and Austrian representatives would be put on the text of the treaty. This procedural matter nevertheless had a vital significance for the United States, inasmuch as from the formal act of the signature of the treaty by Russia and Austria, there flowed official recognition of the independence of the new state by the Governments of both Powers. It is therefore understandable that when the Minister of Foreign Affairs of France, Vergennes, asked the American plenipotentiaries whether the United States did not want to sign the definitive peace treaty with the mediation of the Courts of St. Petersburg and Vienna, they were not slow in responding affirmatively.[31] On the other hand, the English representative, David Hartley, definitely turned down this proposal.

The Russian Minister in Paris, Baryatinsky, reported on this subject to St. Petersburg on August 13/24, 1783: "Yesterday I had a meeting with Franklin; he always converses with me with complete confidence. Between conversations, I offered him my personal felicitations on the subject of the reference made by Adams about their intention to invite us and Count Mercy [the Austrian Ambassador] to the signing of the treaty with England . . . Franklin responded to me: We, of course, would always consider that a special honor had been conferred on us, that the beginning of our independence had been confirmed, and for our part, we will exert all efforts for this, but we are still not sure as to whether we may have the honor, since Mr. Hartley, the English Commissioner, with whom we are now negotiating on this matter, is opposing us on this, referring to the fact that England does not need any sort of mediation."[32]

In the negotiations which Franklin and Adams conducted with Hartley and Vergennes, the French Minister of Foreign Affairs, although he put on the appearance of "a perfect impartiality," was also against acceptance of mediation in the matter, and in the end, the question was laid aside. For the American representatives, it was no secret that this opposition flowed from the effort of England and France to ward off a strengthening of the international position of the United States. "The signature of the two Imperial courts (he is talking of the St. Petersburg and Vienna Courts)," wrote John Adams, "would have made a deep and important impression in our favor upon full one-half of Europe as friends to those courts, and upon all the other half as enemies."[33]

As a result, the Russian plenipotentiaries, Baryatinsky and Morkov, signed only the peace treaties of England with France and Spain.[34] On the final peace treaty between Great Britain and the United States, concluded in Paris on October 3, 1783, their signatures were lacking. Already after the official signing of the treaty, Benjamin Franklin "privately" transmitted its text to the Russian plenipotentiaries, who esteemed it "a duty" to present this document to Catherine II.[35]

In connection with the end of the war in America, Franklin also turned over to Baryatinsky for transmission to Catherine II "a document, the Constitution of the United American Provinces, and a medal struck on their independence."[36] At that time, Dmitry Alekseyevich Golitsyn, the Russian Minister in the Hague, received the stern instruction to refrain from official recognition of John Adams as the American Minister in Holland. When in June, 1784, Adams made to Golitsyn's successor as Russian Minister in the Hague, S. A. Kolychev, as to the other foreign diplomats, a communication about the recognition of the independence of the United States and the signing of the final peace treaty, the Russian diplomat did not shrink from a return visit.[37] Finally, the Government of Catherine II itself gave to Russian diplomats the official order to be guided, in their relations with representatives of the United States, by the generally accepted norms which the other disinterested Powers were following, "the more in that, with recognition of the independence of the American districts on the part of England herself, no one still opposes dealing with them as with the other republics."[38] This meant essentially recognition *de facto* of the United States of America.

5

On the Beginning of Trade Connections
1763-1780

Until quite recently, virtually nothing was known about Russo-American trade connections on the eve of, and during, the War of the American Revolution. It was considered obvious that prior to the Declaration of Independence, trade connections between Russia and America were maintained only through Great Britain, and that only occasional American ships completed rare cruises to the ports of the Baltic Sea through the contraband route.[1] More careful investigation of the archival sources has made it possible to establish that already during 1763-1766, at least eight successful voyages were carried out from America to Russia, while the members of the well known Boston merchant family, the Boylston brothers, demonstrated special zeal in the establishment of direct contacts with Russia. The brig *Wolf*, which belonged to Nicholas Boylston, completed several successful cruises to St. Petersburg, and in 1765, the brig *Hannah*, which belonged to his brother Thomas, was added to it. The Philadelphia ships *Lark, William and Jane*, and several others also took part in the trade with Russia.[2]

The establishment of direct trade connections with Russia, and the open violation of the English navigation acts, was not accidental, and reflected the general discontent of the colonists with the prohibitory policy of the mother country. Already in these years, a significant quantity of hemp, of sail linen, and of iron was sent from Russia to America, *i.e.,* those goods, so to speak, which later became the basis of trade connections between the two countries. It is significant in this connection that on the eve of the War of the Revolution, in 1774, at least three American ships went from St. Petersburg to Boston, Lynn, and

Philadelphia with a cargo of iron, hemp, and maritime tackle. Mention is also made of one Philadelphia ship which tried to acquire rough linen in Hamburg and St. Petersburg in 1775, but so far, there has been no success in finding any sort of reliable reports of sailings of the ships of the United States to Russia subsequently, in connection with the beginning of military operations.

Competent observers point out, however, that the number of French ships which arrived in the port of Petersburg increased by almost five times in 1775, while the export of Russian hemp seemed especially significant. In the opinion of the British Chargé d'Affaires in Russia, this was in the first place the result of the uprising in the English colonies in North America, "which began to receive from France additional deliveries of these goods." Well known are other complaints of British agents in St. Petersburg to the effect that ships under the Dutch flag were being loaded in the Russian capital with hemp, ship masts, and iron, and when they reached the comparative security of the open sea, they changed their flag to the American one. We note in particular that the English Consul in St. Petersburg, Sharp, reported in February, 1777, that a significant part of the goods exported from the Russian capital (hemp, iron, sail linen, etc.) was in reality destined for the British colonies in North America.[3]

Military operations between England and her former colonies led not only to an increase of the export of traditional Russian goods which were used for the shipbuilding industry, but also to an increased demand in Europe for Russian tobacco. Although the tobacco grown in the Ukraine was significantly inferior in quality to the Virginia or Maryland tobacco, a significant quantity of this article reached the European market (above all, in France and Holland) during the period of military operations. If in 1775, only 11,610 pounds of tobacco were exported through the Sound, in the succeeding four years it was a matter, respectively, of 466,787 pounds, 6,229,225 pounds, 5,618,823 pounds, and 5,512,639 pounds.[4] At the end of the war, approximately 2 million pounds of tobacco were exported from St. Petersburg, and 1 million pounds from Riga, mainly to Lübeck and Holland.[5]

It goes without saying that this unexpected increase of the export of Ukrainian tobacco was a purely temporary phenom- enon, and did not have special prospects in the future. The revelation and analysis of reports about the direct trade con- nections between Russia and the rebelling colonies has much greater significance for our theme. An active proponent of, and participant in, these connections was the Russian Consul in Bordeaux, Arvid Wittfooth, who on his own initiative, sent to America some ships under the Russian flag (including *La Marie Elizabeth and La Concorde*). Already in May, 1778, the enterprising Consul sent to the College of Commerce a special report, "On the Advantages of the Establishment of the Trade of Russia with the United States." We must say that the city of Bordeaux served at that time as one of the most important centers for the supply of the rebelling colonies with the goods from Europe needed by them, among which, as is evident from Wittfooth's reports, were also "Russian products." "The United American Provinces," wrote Wittfooth, "have sent here a Con- sul who is stationed here for the direction of the affairs of those provinces. As all goods, and also Russian products, are sent there, trade there would not be disadvantageous if Russian goods were sent there by consignment, and especially sail- cloth, which is bought in great quantities for the American ships, and transported there, about which I have already spoken with the American Consul aforementioned, who also assures that in many cases, they have great needs in America."[6]

Wittfooth's report about contacts with the American Consul in Bordeaux, and about the sending to America of Russian goods, and in particular of sail-cloth, was received in the College of Commerce without any sort of discussion, although formal approval of his proposal was not decided upon without the preliminary consent of the Office of Foreign Affairs. Having heard Wittfooth's report on August 8/19, 1778, by order of Catherine II, the College of Commerce reached the following decision: "As the installation of this Consul from the American settlements in France is a new matter, and Russian merchants have still not had direct trade with the Americans, and moreover, since some sort of difficulties with respect to political matters might perhaps be connected therewith, the College of Commerce may not prescribe anything with respect to the undertaking of this trade to Russian merchants without contact with the College of Foreign Affairs: by virtue of this, an information aide-mémoire is to be sent to that College, with a copy of this, and advice awaited."[7]

So far we have not succeeded in establishing how long the College of Commerce waited for "advice" from the Office of Foreign Affairs, and whether, in general, it received it. Along with this, the correspondence of Arvid Wittfooth with the College of Foreign Affairs makes it possible to reach more concrete judgments about the activities of the Russian Consul in Bordeaux, and the situation which evolved there at the beginning of the 1780's. The United States maintained at that time active ties with France, and, as Wittfooth observed, American ships visited this port often. The Consul reported in December, 1778, that "Russian ships now find a profitable carrying trade in the port here," *i.e.*, the Russian flag "will be respected more than that of any other nation by the English privateers."[8] Respect for the Russian flag grew especially after the proclamation of the February declaration of 1780 about armed neutrality. The insurance offices began, according to Wittfooth's testimony in August, 1780, to insure Russian ships at a rate of 4 to 8 per cent,[9] in connection with which, favorable possibilities for the development of trade widened ever more. Taking advantage of the interest of the French Government in the development of neutral, and especially of Russian, navigation, the enterprising Consul received permission "to send these ships under the Russian flag to the French islands on the same basis that French ships are sent."[10] Later, in January, 1782, Wittfooth reported about Russian ships which were chartered for the transportation of goods to America, and also about the voyage to the "Western Islands [the West Indies]" of two of these ships, the *Graf Osterman* and the *Graf Chernyshev*.[11]

Direct confirmation of the sending of Russian ships to the shores of America was furnished to us also in the very rich collection of the Vorontsov files in the Manuscript Branch of the Leningrad Division of the Institute of History of the Academy of Sciences of the USSR. We are talking of a most interesting report to the College of Commerce of that same Wittfooth of July 30,1782, a passage from which is presented below in the version of that time: "Many Russian ships are here now, of which some are loaded for America, because the Russian flag under present circumstances is much more preferable than that of other nations, and therefore these ships may receive very advantageous contracts, which is the more flattering to me, since a basis was laid by me for this situation, so advantageous for the Russian ships. And I strove as much as I could for this, averting all inconveniences, which were sometimes formidable, seeing to it that the sailors had documents, and watching so that they did not load forbidden goods onto their ships. Although Skipper Brand, who arrived here from St.Petersburg, and having been loaded with salt for America, was captured by an English privateer, it is rumored that he has been set free again, with payment of 1,500 pounds sterling as damages for what happened. The sailor mentioned had all his documents, which I witnessed in appropriate form at the time of departure, because of which I hope that if henceforth the same thing happens to Russian ships, they will be dealt with in England with equal justice."[12]

In evaluating the degree of importance of the reports sent in by Wittfooth, we must take into account the significance, in principle, of the very fact of the establishment of trade contacts between Russia and America in the period of the War of the American Revolution, and of the voyages of Russian ships to the shores of the distant Republic. It is evident also that these trade relations were not an occasional episode, nor a historical curiosity. Already from the contents of the reports of Wittfooth it is clear that they "entered" well into the general international situation of that time, and were, so to speak, quite explicable, and even legal. We recall that the United States desperately needed in these years the establishment and development of all kinds of trade relations with the European countries. At that same time, Russia was actively struggling for the security of the freedom of neutral navigation, and was encouraging the extension of her own merchant marine. The number of Russian ships which sailed through the Sound increased already in 1779 to 62, and the Russian flag took advantage of the ever growing respect of the maritime Powers, and even the proud mistress of the seas was forced to reckon with the head of a league of neutral countries. It is therefore not surprising that the "Russian flag" became in these circumstances "much more preferable than that of the other nations," and that the Russian ships received "very advantageous contracts," including some from Americans, for whom security of communications was especially important.[13]

Trying to prove that the formation of an independent United States would have a pernicious effect on the foreign trade of Russia and of a number of other European states, the British Foreign Office, already in 1777, sent to the foreign Ambassadors accredited to London a special circular letter. In the opinion of the English Government, all diminution of the American trade would unavoidably produce an increase of Russia's trade, which could with success supply Europe with many of the articles that were produced in North America. In the production of naval stores, iron, and other such articles, the Americans were rivals, not only of Russia, but also of Prussia, Sweden, and Denmark. America was now, or would become in the future, a rival of France, Spain, and Portugal also, inasmuch as South Carolina disposed of favorable conditions for the production of wine and fruits. It was still possible at that time "to destroy American navigation, but after some years, it would apparently be impossible already.... The manufacturing, navigation, trade, fishing, and agriculture of America are analogous to those of Europe, which must transform both continents into rivals."[14]

The arguments of the Foreign Office, buttressed by all the power of British arms and propaganda, could not fail to exert serious influence on the diplomats and public opinion of Europe. "The most disinterested and the most knowledgeable people are convinced," wrote the Russian Minister in London, Simolin, in December, 1781, "that the independence of North America will give birth to a new order in Europe, and produce a revolution in the trade of the North, similar to that which the Venetian Republic experienced after the opening of the route around the Cape of Good Hope to the East Indies . . . . The leading merchants of the Russian Company await this revolution with a feeling of bitterness, and some do not doubt that after this independence, whether *de facto* or *de jure*, the trade relations which have existed up to now between Great Britain and the Russian Empire will be severely diminished over a period of some years." After the end of the war the English, in the words of Simolin, "were themselves the first to begin to trade with the Americans in those goods, the trade in which was so far the privilege of Northern Europe, and will extend by all means possible the extraction of their mineral resources, the cultivation of hemp, flax, etc."[15]

Later, in the spring of 1783, Simolin reported that a great part of the London merchants thought "that the use of the resources of North America and the free importation of her goods into Southern Europe will lead in the course of time to a significant diminution of the export of grain and other articles of the Baltic region, and above all, of Russia." The Russian Minister concluded: "Only time will perhaps show whether this supposition is justified."[16]

Fear of the possible competition of American goods on the European market had of course a solid basis. In the Central State Archive of Ancient Formal Acts in Moscow there is preserved a memorandum entitled "Memorandum on the Products of North America Analogous to the Products of the Russian Empire," in which the idea is developed in detail that if America received independence from the mother country, she would very soon be in a position to send to Southern Europe "all naval stores and all those products which at the present time come from Russia and the Baltic countries," and over several years would be transformed into "the greatest trading Power."[17]

On the whole, however, both in governmental circles and in Russian society, already from the time of the War of the American Revolution, the idea was emphasized in the beginning of the advantageousness for Russia of the formation of a new independent state in North America, and the desirability of the development of Russo-American trade relations. We recall in this connection that the leaders of the Office of Foreign Affairs, in the secret report to Catherine II in the summer of 1779, mentioned the advantages of the separation of the English colonies in North America from the mother country, and referred directly, moreover, to the extension of Russia's trade "because England, deprived by the uprising of her settlements of all importation of the products there will now be forced to exchange them for ours, not only for transshipment to other places, but also for her own use." The authors of the report emphasized further "that the American settlements do not otherwise introduce and multiply among themselves the products peculiar to the climate here except because of the burden, designed for them by the British administration, of notable duties on imports from other places, but on the other hand, according to a definition therein in favor of the Americans, with a notable monetary compensation," and they drew the conclusion that in the end, the separation of the colonies from England "not only is not injurious, but may yet be the more useful for Russia in the area of her trade interests" in connection with the fact that in time, "a new direct branch of commerce" would spring up between Russia and America.[18]

Francis Dana, who reported to his correspondents in the United States information about the state of Russsian trade, the growing demand for coffee, sugar, rice, indigo, etc., moved forward as an active propagandist of commercial ties between Russia and America. In a memorandum on the advantages of the trade of Russia with an independent United States, Dana noted in particular that a significant amount of cast iron and steel had always been sent to America via England. After the winning of independence the Americans would naturally buy these goods at cheaper prices directly, in Sweden and Russia. Thinking that in St. Petersburg they were insufficiently informed about the advantages of trade with America, Dana laid forth his views in detail in a letter of April 12/23, 1782 to John Adams, and sent it by ordinary post, expecting moreover (as turned out to be completely correct), that it would be opened and read by the Tsarist authorities.[19]

Trade with America was propagandized in the Russian press, including the pages of a journal of Nikolay Ivanovich Novikov popular with the Russian merchant class, *Supplement to the Moscow News* (1783-1784), and later, in the *Political Journal* published at Moscow University by Professor P. A. Sokhatsky. D. M. Ladygin persistently recommended "the attention and enterprise" of the Russian merchant class to the new market in America in the concluding pages of his book on the *United Provinces* which came out in St. Petersburg in January, 1783.[20] Ladygin's opinion about the expediency of the establishment and development of trade relations between Russia and the United States offers special interest, inasmuch as he relied on the information and experience received by him during the time of his work of many years in the College of Commerce.

For a long time, neither in Soviet nor in foreign libraries, was it possible to find the book of Snell (Shnell), *On the Trading or Mercantile Advantages Flowing from the Independence of the United States of North America for the Russian State*, a detailed review of which was published at that time in one of the periodicals of the 18th century.[21] Only comparatively recently, thanks to the kindness of N. Ya. Krupnikov (Riga), did we receive a photocopy of this rare publication, destined, as is apparent from the introduction, for "the informed public." Its author, the Rector of a gymnasium which existed near the Dom Cathedral in Riga, Karl Snell, wrote: "The peace recently concluded, which proclaimed the independence of North America, is one of the most important events of the state life of our country, and its results will be a great revolution, both in the political world, and in the world of trade."[22] The United States of North America was characterized in the book as "a well organized and comparatively populous state," equal in size almost to Europe, and possessing splendid natural resources. It is not surprising therefore that Snell foresaw "the rapid growth of this happy state," and remarked that it required "no more than one generation, in order to see it deserving respect in all its greatness." Inasmuch as this state would build its future power "principally on trade, for which Nature endowed it with the most desirable gifts, commercial relations with the whole world will take on another form, and a new direction."[23] Moreover, the question arose "whether Russia, as one of the primary trading countries, receives advantages or disadvantages from American independence." Snell concluded: "When you see what an abundance of mast timber and lumber, of hemp, of flax, of pitch, of tar, and of iron the Americans have, it is easy to come to the conclusion that by the sale of these articles, of which the Russian state has so far possessed a monopoly, they will deliver a great blow to Russian trade."[24] But a more careful and detailed survey of the question forced the author to come to a different conclusion. Snell justly remarked that the goods mentioned would still be necessary for a long time to the Americans themselves, and in addition, their quality was inferior to the corresponding Russian products. American masts were more expensive and not as good as the Russian ones. This applied to hemp and flax. As a result, the author of the book pointed out "we will not only keep the old customers, but doubtless will gain new ones," inasmuch as the Americans themselves would increase the importation of Russian flax and hemp, which was necessary to them, not only for the construction of ships, but also for the making of clothing for the Negroes (rough sackcloth). In enumerating the various articles, including iron, which might further the development of trade relations between both countries, Karl Snell expressed in conclusion the hope that "each thoughtful reader" would agree with this, that the independence of America not only would not damage Russian trade, "but on the other hand, will be acutally advantageous to it, will open up new paths for it, will furnish it, as a result of an increase of markets, new strength, new scope. We will welcome our new commercial customers. For my part, I flatter myself with the pleasant hope," remarked the author, "of seeing already this summer the new flag with the thirteen stripes in the harbor of Riga."[25]

Snell's prediction, made on May 6/17, 1783, was already borne out very soon. On June 1/12, captained by Daniel Mc-Neill, a 500-ton American ship dropped anchor in the port of Riga, having come from Lisbon with a cargo of salt, sugar, rice, and brandy. In informing McNeill about the special immunities with respect to the goods being transported by him, Francis Dana expressed the conviction that the Russian Government was disposed to offer "American citizens any reasonable encouragement."[26] In that year, in Riga, and then in St. Petersburg, the enterprising Boston merchant Jeremy Allen visited, sending home a valuable cargo of Russian linen, hemp, naval stores, and iron on the ship *Kingston* under the command of Captain Norwood (officially this ship was registered at the port of Petersburg and sailed under the Russian flag). Having returned to the United States in December, 1783, Allen advertised the wares brought back by him in the pages of the *Boston Gazette,* and also promised to offer interested persons supplementary news on the Russian market.[27]

As a result, in the following year, 1784, already no less than five American ships arrived in the port of St. Petersburg, among which were *Buccaneer* and *Commerce,* which belonged to George Cabot, *Light Horse,* the owner of which was Elias Haskett Derby, and others. The route to the new market was opened; moreover, the leading role in opening it belonged to the traders and navigators of Massachusetts.[28]

Striving for a broadening of the trade relations of the young Republic, the Confederation Government adopted on April 15,

1784 a resolution about the desirability of the conclusion of treaties of friendship and trade with Russia, Austria, Prussia, and other European countries. John Adams, Benjamin Franklin, and Thomas Jefferson were given full powers to begin appropriate negotiations.[29] Accordingly, on September 22 the American representatives sent the Russian Minister in Paris, Baryatinsky, a letter in which they informed him that the American Congress, thinking that trade between the subjects of Russia and the citizens of the United States, "based on the principles of equality, mutual benefit, and friendship, may serve the mutual welfare of both countries," had empowered them on May 12, 1784, to begin negotiations, and to conclude a treaty of friendship and trade with the appropriate Russian representative, if full powers should be given to him for this by the Empress.[30]

On this same day, the secretary of the American "Commission" for the conclusion of treaties of friendship and trade with the foreign Powers, Mr. Humphrey, requested a meeting with the Russian Minister in Paris, Baryatinsky, for the transmission of the letter from the American plenipotentiaries.[31] The meeting took place on September 26. However, inasmuch as "the American Negotiation-Secretary" with "great difficulty explained himself in French," and the Russian Minister "did not apprehend" the English language, their conversation "could not be prolonged." In receiving the letter, Baryatinsky limited himself to a promise to send it to St. Petersburg, and Mr. Humphrey gave him "to understand" that the American plenipotentiaries "flattered themselves" that Catherine II "would be pleased to honor them with a reply."[32]

Insofar as one may judge from the correspondence with Paris for 1784-1785 which was surveyed by us, Catherine II was not "pleased" to give any sort of reply, although Baryatinsky's report, along with the annexed documentation, was stamped "received" on October 9/20, 1784. Some years later, on August 29, 1786, the Secretary for Foreign Affairs, John Jay, stated in Congress that the treaties of the United States with "France, the United Netherlands, Sweden, Russia, and others" foresaw for each of the parties "the right of the most favored nation."[33] What John Jay meant by "Russia" it is difficult to say. (J. Hildt thinks "Prussia," with which such a a treaty was actually concluded on September 10, 1785.) In practice, the trade relations of Russia with the new Republic after the War of the Revolution developed quite normally, without any sort of special limitations, either from the Russian side or from the American side.

In all, according to the calculations of Phillips, at least 19 cruises were completed from 1784 to 1790, inclusive, to the Baltic ports from Salem.   Some of them were direct, but others picked up cargoes at the southern states, or at the West Indies.[34]

More complete, although unsystematic, data may be found in the Russian sources— the "Kronshtadt Reports", containing reports about the nature of foreign ships in the Port of St. Petersburg.[35] Regrettably, for many years the reports did not come down to us, and some of the materials which have been preserved have gaps. Thus, vital lacunae turned up in the reports for 1781-1784, and we did not succeed in discovering therein notations about the American ships.[36] Then among the Kronshtadt Reports for the end of the 1790's was discovered general information about Russian trade over the signature of the President of the College of Commerce, A.P. Vorontsov, referring to the middle of the 1780's. Thus, from information for 1785 it is apparent that in all, 2,145 ships arrived in Russian ports during the year. Of them 640 were English, 100 were Russian, 18 were French, 9 were Spanish, and 6 were American, and also many Dutch, Danish, Swedish and other ships.[37] In the following year, 1786, out of a total number of 2,155 ships, 705 English ones arrived; 107 Russian; 14 French; 4 Spanish; and 10 American.[38]

The foreign trade of Russia at that time was carried on basically through the Port of St. Petersburg, the share of which in the maritime trade of the country amounted to more than 60%.[39] Other Baltic ports (Riga, Reval, and Narva) also had vital significance. Of the total number of 803 ships which arrived in 1787 in the Port of St. Petersburg, 400 were English;

64 were Russian; 17 were French; 5 were Spanish; and 11 were American.[40] In 1790, 932 ships arrived, of which "517 were British alone; 98 were Danish; 22 were American;" etc.[41] Already from these data it is completely obvious that the American ships constituted an insignificant part of the total number of foreign ships which came during those years to Russian ports. Much more vital, however, seems the very fact of their appearance, and the significance, in principle, of the development of the first trade relations with the trans-oceanic Republic. Precisely during these years the Americans first received the chance to become really acquainted with the Russian market, and more or less regular trade relations were established between the two countries. The practical experience of these trade relations also offered evidence that the earlier fears of the possible competition of American goods on the European market turned out to be exaggerated. Objecting to such an idea "of badly informed persons," John Paul Jones, who was in Russia at that time, in a letter to Osterman of January 31/ February 11, 1789, invited the special attention of the Vice-Chancellor to the fact that in all the years since the winning of independence, the Americans had sent to the Russian ports many ships, so as to receive there cargoes consisting at the same time of those goods which Russia was sending to France and England.[42]

The first Russo-American contacts in the area of trade turned out to be quite promising. The number of ships which arrived in Russian ports gradually increased. Thus, in 1792, 24 American ships came to St. Petersburg; in 1795, 42 or 44; in 1798, 39; in 1801, 61, etc.[43]* During the decade 1791-1800 a total of 368 came to Kronshtadt, and according to some data (A. Ya. Dashkov), more even than 500 ships of the United States.[44]

Already in the middle of the 1790's, the importation of Rus-

*TRANSLATOR'S NOTE: As is well known, the United States profited greatly from the fact that it was neutral during most of the period of the wars of the European monarchs against revolutionary France which started in 1792 and ended in 1815. However, it was clear by 1805-1807 that neither the France of Emperor Napoleon I nor Great Britain was willing to respect the rights of neutral commerce.

sian goods into the United States exceeded $1 million in value, and at the turn of the 19th century, reached more than $1.5 million (in 1800—$1,524,995.00).[45] According to the evidence brought forward by the Danish researcher A. Rasch, during the course of 1783-1806 the Americans imported from St. Petersburg 393,460 *puds* of iron, 365,503 *puds* of hemp (and in addition 27,986 *puds* of tackle), 369,365 pieces of sail-cloth, 333,027 pieces of duck, etc.[46] All these goods had a vital significance for shipbuilding, and many American ships which ploughed the sea at that time with unlimited range were constructed with the use of high quality Russian hemp, iron, and sail-cloth.

It goes without saying that in the 18th century, business ties between Russia and the United States were only beginning to develop, and their total extent was relatively small. However, we are concerned not only with the practical significance of the first Russo-American trade relations directly. What is of primary importance, perhaps, is the political significance of the existence of such relations; that the Russians did not fight, but rather traded with republican America! This fact alone embodies the basic difference in the policy of Tsarist Russia toward France and toward America at the end of the 18th century.

PART TWO

Russian Society
and the
American Revolution

RUSSIA'S BENJAMIN FRANKLIN AND HIS ADMIRERS, RUSSIAN AND AMERICAN

MIKHAIL VASILYEVICH LOMONOSOV
1711-1765
Russian Universal Genius,
Founder of University of Moscow.
*A friendly critic of Benjamin Franklin's
theories of electricity.*

GEORG WILHELM RIKHMAN,1711-1753
Professor of Physics, Russian Academy
of Sciences, 1741-1753.
*His electrocution proved the validity
of Benjamin Franklin's theories.*

EZRA STILES, 1727-1795
Pastor, Second Congregational Church,
Newport, R. I., 1755-1778; President
of Yale, 1778-1795.
*He shared an interest in Arctic explora-
tion with Lomonosov.*

6

The Establishment of Scientific and Cultural Relations

In the past, historians of international relations rarely turned to the study of socio-political, scientific, and cultural relations. They investigated minutely the smallest details of the life and activity of leading politicians, generals, and diplomats, of Tsars and Presidents. But in the many-volumed historical collections, very rarely, and only as an exception, can be encountered mention of Euler and Winthrop, of Aepinus and Bond, of Strue and Henry, or of some sort of other scholar who devoted all his life to science and to international scientific cooperation. And one may only regret that the people who took the first steps in the beneficent matter of international scientific and cultural cooperation and took them despite enormous geographic distances, and religious, political, and ideological obstacles, also remained unnoticed, or almost unnoticed, both by contemporaries and by historians. Even such scholars of genius as Benjamin Franklin or Mikhail Vasilyevich Lomonosov* could

*TRANSLATOR'S NOTE: Born in 1711, Lomonosov died in 1765. He was the son of a poor fisherman of Archangel Province, and though he had his early education in Moscow and St. Petersburg, he was at Marburg University in Germany during 1736-1741. He became a member of the St. Petersburg Academy of Sciences upon returning home, and was made a professor of chemistry there in 1745. In 1755, he helped found Moscow University, to which the Soviet Government attached his name. His scientific work included research on the expansion of metals and gases, astronomy, geology, economics, and polar exploration. However, as the author notes, his fame rests even more on his contributions to the development of Russian as a literary language. It is necessary to remember that what is now called "science" was "natural philosophy" in the 18th century, and that most men of learning dabbled in it, usually in amateurish fashion. It was not at all unusual to mix politics with science. For example, Antoine Lavoisier, one of the founding fathers of modern chemistry, lost his head for being on the wrong side in politics during the great French Revolution.

93

scarcely have been able to count on the special attention of later generations, if they had not, at one and the same time, become famous in some areas of the natural and social sciences, in literature, and mainly (as in the case of Benjamin Franklin) in politics and diplomacy.[1]

While evaluating Lomonosov exceptionally highly, Aleksandr Nikolayevich Radishchev,* in a comparison of him with Franklin (while studying the role of the American scholar in the War of the American Revolution) gave preference in this regard to the latter. Thereby he emphasized once more the revolutionary, anti-monarchical slant of his book [*Journey from St. Petersburg to Moscow*]. The well-known Latin motto inscribed under the portrait of Franklin (*Eripuit coelo fulmen sceptrumque tyrannis*) Radishchev translated in a pointed anti-monarchical form ("He who wrested lightning from the heavens and the scepter from the hands of Tsars", although, it would perhaps be more accurate to say "from the hands of tyrants"), and thought this "the very best inscription which a man may see below his picture."[2]

The motto translated is exceptionally clever and conveys precisely the enormous significance of the scientific works of the great American in the area of electricity. Franklin's famous *Experiments and Observations on Electricity Made at Philadelphia*[3] constituted an epoch in science, in a certain sense comparable to the revolutionary overturn which later took place in the area of politics, the war of the North American colonies against England, and the Declaration of Independence adopted in this same Philadelphia. The self-taught man of genius from distant America correctly understood the existence of electrical phenomena and pointed out the way of their further investigation, which his educated colleagues on the other side of the ocean, well armed with the experience and knowledge accumulated by Newton, Huyghens, and Euler, were not able to do.[4]

To be sure, general recognition was far from coming to

*TRANSLATOR'S NOTE: On Radishchev, see Translator's Note, Chapter Eight.

Franklin at once. The Holy Church stubbornly considered the only correct method of coping with lightning phenomena to be bell ringing, which according to its enlightened opinion, allegedly drove away the evil spirits. By an irony of fate, the high and firmly installed church bells were, at the same time, that means of conducting an electrical current badly which turned out to be the most vulnerable to a stroke of lightning, and therefore, ringing the bell during a time of lightning turned out to be a totally dangerous matter. In Germany alone, at the end of the 18th century, 120 bell ringers were killed over 33 years, and 400 bells destroyed.[5] And as if in mockery of the Holy Chruch, the evil spirits, and the Lord God Himself, the majestic shrine of the wise King Solomon in Jerusalem, over the course of many hundreds of years, stood invulnerable to lightning, protected, as it turned out, by polished metal plates which conducted the electrical current well.

Religious prejudices turned out to be far from the only, or even the main, obstacle to the spreading of the new views on the nature of electricity. During the War of the American Revolution, the struggle against the scientific ideas of Franklin and the introduction of lightning rods took on a political character. This became especially obvious in connection with the fact that the English scholar Wilson proposed, in place of Franklin's sharp-pointed lightning rod, his own blunt-ended variant, in order to prevent the flow of the electric charge, which was considered dangerous at that time. Passions ran high in the country, and any unthinking Englishman who furnished his house with a sharp-ended lightning rod, and not a blunt-ended one, was in danger of being reputed politically unreliable.

In our days, these "scientific" disputes seem as deprived of good sense as the famous conflict of the Swiftian heroes as to from which end to break an egg — from the blunt end or the pointed one. Moreover, in the native land of the great satirist [Jonathan Swift], the pointed end of the lightning rod turned out to be dangerous even for the President of the Royal Society and Personal Physician to the King, John Pringle himself. His famous reply to George III to the effect that "he will always to the limit of his strength fulfill the desires of His Majesty, but he is not in a position to change the laws of nature, nor the operation of their forces," cost the stubborn author dearly. John Pringle was dismissed from the office of Personal Physician and President of the Royal Society.

It was easy to remove a Royal Physician from his duties, and even, if necessary, lock him up in jail, but it was much more difficult, of course, to stop the development of science, even if the Holy Church or the King of the greatest Power on earth wanted this very much. *The Philadelphia Experiments* of Franklin, experiments of genius by virtue of their simplicity and clarity, did not remove doubts of the correctness of the conclusion about the identity of lightning and an electrical current, but the lightning rod acted so irreproachably that it could convince anyone, even the most unbelieving skeptic.

In Russia, the experiments of Franklin became known to a wide circle of readers from reports published in the *St. Petersburg Herald* in June, 1752. The newspaper wrote that in Philadelphia, in North America, Mr. Franklin "has been so daring as to try to extract from the atmosphere that terrible fire which so often destroys vast areas," and presented further in this regard a detailed account of his experiments, which were then being repeated in France.[6] "Over the universe the news has spread: Lightning arrows no longer bring dread!" wrote Lomonosov in 1752 in the well known *Letter on the Usefulness of Glass*, and he expressed further the conviction, "that by knowing the laws discovered with glass, we may avert the lightning from our shrines."

News of the "Philadelphia experiments" fell on receptive soil in Russia. Georg Wilhelm Rikhman* was working fruitfully at that time in St. Petersburg in a related area, and constructed in 1745 an "electrical indicator" for the measurement of the

*TRANSLATOR'S NOTE: Rikhman was born at Pernau in Estonia in 1711, and studied at Halle and Jena Universities before attending the academic university of the Academy of Sciences in St. Petersburg, on whose faculty he was named Professor of Physics in 1741. His research was in the areas of heat and electricity. As the author notes, he was a martyr to the cause of science in 1753.

strength of the current in an electrified body. With the aid of a "lightning machine", a metal rod carried up to the roof and attached to an electricity measuring apparatus, Lomonosov and Rikhman investigated the atmospheric electrical discharge. "Mr. Rikhman died a glorious death, doing his duty for his profession. His memory will never die,"[7] wrote Lomonosov about his friend. Entering later into an extensive generalization in the area of electrical phenomena, Lomonosov created an ether concept of electricity, one progressive for its time, which anticipated to a definite degree the development of the field theory in the 19th century.

It is apparent from the collected works of Lomonosov and Rikhman on physics that they highly valued the work of Franklin on electricity, and referred to it more than once. At the same time, basing themselves on their own experiments of many years, they discerned some insufficiences therein, and in their turn, skilfully filled out and developed the ideas of Benjamin Franklin.[8] Many of their works in this area were completed already prior to the publication of *The Philadelphia Experiments*, or prior to the time when they could become acquainted with them, and they differed significantly, moreover, from the ideas developed by Benjamin Franklin.

In refuting unjustified objections on the subject of his famous *Words on Atmospheric Phenomena Arising from Electrical Energy*,[9] Lomonosov emphasized that "many phenomena occurring from electrical energy, of which there is not a trace in Franklin,"[10] were explained by him. In demonstrating the divergence of his theory of the aurora borealis from the "conjecture" of Franklin, Lomonosov remarked: "He tries to draw the electrical matter for the production of the aurora borealis from the tropical zone, while I find sufficient matter in that place itself, that is, in the ether, which is present everywhere. He does not identify its location; I put it in the atmosphere. He does not explain by what means it is produced; I explain it in an understandable form. He does not buttress any conclusion, while I, going beyond this, prove the interpretation of the phenomena."[11]

In pointing out the difference of his theory from the opinions of the American, Lomonosov at the same time emphasized his respect for "the glorious Mr. Franklin," and remarked that "all this is presented here not because I want to put myself ahead of him."[12]

Somewhat later, the new ideas about the nature of electrical phenomena were examined and popularized in Russia in the collected works of Franz Ulrich Theodor Aepinus,* who established a connection "of electrical energy with magnetic energy," and who advanced broadly quantitative calculations in the theory of electricity.[13]

In his major treatise, *Experiment on the Theory of Electricity and Magnetism*, which came off the presses at the end of 1759, Aepinus referred frequently to Franklin, and wrote in the dedication of his book: "The presence in substances of the energy which they call electricity was discovered only recently, and has scarcely yet been sufficiently investigated . . . the theory of this energy presented by Franklin satisfies me to the highest degree. . . . However, I came to the conclusion that I have succeeded in discovering in this remarkable theory some deficiencies; therefore I exerted effort to the end of correcting them, and, with the aid of this correction, of so adapting this theory that it was put into the most complete agreement with the phenomena."[14] The scholar coped most gloriously with the task set. The significance of the works of Aepinus for the development of the ideas of Franklin is sometimes equated even with the significance which the works of Maxwell had in the 19th century for the development of the views of Faraday: in both

*TRANSLATOR'S NOTE: Aepinus was born in Rostock in 1724, and studied at both Rostock and Jena Universities. After service on the faculty of Rostock University, he became a Professor of Astronomy at the University of Berlin in 1755, before joining the Academy of Sciences in St. Petersburg in 1757. Although he acquired fame as an astronomer, physicist, and mathematician, he was active in other areas, arranging the curriculum for the Army Nobles Cadet Corps, and tutoring the future Tsar Paul in physics and mathematics. After helping work out the Declaration of Armed Neutrality in 1780, he served as a member of a commission which vastly improved primary and secondary education in Russia. He retired to Dorpat in Estonia in 1798, and died in 1802.

cases, the experiments and observations of original geniuses received mathematical working out by erudite professional scholar-physicists.[15]

The famous English scholar Henry Cavendish, who, however, not only knew, but also, possibly, even got hold of the book of the Petersburg scholar in the middle of 1766, advanced an almost identical theory of electricity already many years after Aepinus.[16]

The news of the tragic death of Rikhman, during the time of the experiment with the "lightning machine," along with Lomonosov, which was carried out by him in the summer of 1753, made a great impression on Franklin and his colleagues in America. Already on December 13, 1753, in reply to an enquiry of James Bowdoin* from Boston, Franklin confirmed the report of "the unhappy Gentleman's Death at Petersburg," and made the first mention of his name—Professor Rikhman.[17]

TRANSLATOR'S NOTE: James Bowdoin (1726-1790) is best remembered for his role in politics. Born the son of the richest merchant in Boston, he graduated from Harvard in 1745, and thereafter added to his inherited fortune, becoming a large landholder in Maine, then a part of Massachusetts. He was elected to the General Court in 1757, became a member of the Council. An early supporter of the cause of the Revolution, he was removed from the Council by the British, and then was elected to the Continental Congress. He was a member of the Provincial Congress which governed Massachusetts from 1775 to 1780. He also served as president of the state constitutional convention of 1779-1780. Regarded as the spokesman of the propertied interests of his state, he had to fight a bitter political campaign to become the successor of John Hancock as Governor of Massachusetts in 1785. His administration, which lasted until 1787, was marked by Shays' Rebellion, during which Bowdoin upheld law and order. In 1788, Bowdoin helped bring about the ratification of the Constitution by Massachusetts. He published papers in the fields of physics and astronomy, and was the first president of the American Academy of Arts and Sciences, founded in 1780. Bowdoin College in Maine, chartered in 1794, and in operation by 1802, was named in his honor.

John Adams actually did more than did Bowdoin to establish the American Academy of Arts and Sciences in 1780; his local pride had been wounded when he discovered in Europe that Franklin's American Philosophical Society made Europeans think Philadelphia to be the intellectual capital of the United States. Adams was elected President of the Boston Academy in 1791, after Bowdoin's death, and continued to hold that office until 1814. The charter members of the Boston Academy included Ezra Stiles and Francis Dana, the latter America's first diplomatic representative in Russia.

On March 5, 1754, "an Extract of a Letter from Moscow, dated August 23" about the circumstances of Rikhman's death was reprinted in the *Pennsylvania Gazette*, published by Franklin, and simultaneously the conclusion was drawn that everything which took place only confirmed "the new Doctrine of Lightning," in connection with which "many lives" might be saved in the future. "Counsellor Lomonosseu" was named in the account as a participant in the experiment, which, in all probability, was the first mention of the name of the great Russian scholar in the American press. In taking account of the scientific significance of the account of the circumstances of Rikhman's death, the editors of a new collection of the books of Franklin included him in the appropriate volume of their publication, and along with this, expressed the supposition that the concluding paragraph of the account was written by Franklin himself.[18]

To American scholars, and in the first place, to Benjamin Franklin, the works of Academician Aepinus were well known, concerning which they frequently testified in a most flattering way. "Aepinus, a Member of the Academy of Sciences at Petersburg," wrote Franklin on May 29, 1763, "has lately published a Latin Work in 4to. entitled, Tentamen Theoriae Electricitatis et Magnetismi; wherein he applies my Principles of Electricity to the Explanation of the various Phenomena of Magnetism, and I think with considerable Success."[19]

Taking into account the interest which the work of Aepinus could have for American scholars, Franklin sent this work to his steady correspondent, Ezra Stiles,* and requested him to

*TRANSLATOR'S NOTE: Ezra Stiles (1727-1795) was the son of a Congregational pastor in New Haven and graduated from Yale in 1746. An interest in science and law, as well as somewhat shaky religious convictions, kept him from following his father into the ministry until 1755. Meanwhile, he had became a fast friend of Benjamin Franklin. From 1755 to 1778, he was pastor of the Second Congregational Church in Newport, R.I., and in that cosmopolitan city, where he was soon put in charge of the famous Redwood Library, his reputation as a scholar grew apace. He made observations of the comet of 1759 and of the transit of Venus in 1769. He received a doctorate from the University of Edinburgh in 1765 and was elected to the American Philosophical Society in 1768. He promoted silkworm culture, and the

acquaint John Winthrop* with it, the mathematical preparation of whom made it possible to expect that he would value
its contents to the full degree. And actually, Winthrop found
that the book of Aepinus contained "many interesting ideas,"
and that its author was "a person of enlightened ideas, and of a
many-sided and searching mind."[20]

The sensational experiments of Josef Adam Braun** and
Lomonosov on the freezing of mercury (1759) produced an
enormous impression on contemporaries. Benjamin Franklin
thought that "the most remarkable Discovery that has been
made within these three Years, is, that Quicksilver is in reality
a melted Metal; with this new Character only, that of all others
it requires the least Heat to melt it." Franklin wrote that "the
Academy of Sciences at Petersburgh, have found, that by dip-

---

*TRANSLATOR'S NOTE: John Winthrop (1714-1779) was a direct descendant
of the famous founder of Massachusetts, and had two relatives who were elected
to the Royal Society in London, in 1663 and 1734, respectively. He graduated from
the Boston Latin School in 1728 and from Harvard in 1732. In 1738 he became the
second Hollis Professor of Mathematics and Natural Philosophy at Harvard, despite
his shaky religious convictions. His distinguished research in astronomy led to the publication of its results in the *Philosophical Transactions* of the Royal Society in England.
He travelled to Newfoundland to observe a transit of Venus, and introduced calculus
at Harvard. He sturdily supported Franklin's theories of electricity. Elected to the
Royal Society in 1766, Winthrop was also elected to the American Philosophical Society in 1769, and subsequently awarded doctorates from Edinburgh and Harvard. He
inspired the establishment of the American Academy of Arts and Sciences, though he
died before he could become a member. He was an ardent patriot during the Revolution, and a counsellor and friend of Washington and Franklin.

**TRANSLATOR'S NOTE: Born in Germany in 1712, Braun came to St. Petersburg
as a member of the Academy of Sciences in 1746. He published *De insigni viribus tel-
luris mutationibus* in 1756. *De atmospherae mutationibus praecipuis earumque prae-
sagiis* in 1759, and *De admirando frigore artificiali quo mercurius est congelatus* in
1760. He died in 1768.

---

spiritual welfare of the numerous black slaves in Newport. He protested the removal
of deistical books from the Yale Library. He helped the Baptists of Rhode Island establish Rhode Island College, now Brown University. A supporter of the Revolution, he
found it expedient to flee from Newport in 1776, because of the danger of a British
occupation, and eventually accepted the presidency of Yale in 1778. He found that
"the Diadem of a President is a Crown of Thorns," and arranged for state aid to and
partial state control of Yale. He permitted the appearance of a dancing master at Yale,
and in 1790, because an abolitionist.

ping a mercurial Thermometer into repeated cooling Mixtures, and so taking from the Mercury the Heat that was in it, they have brought it down some hundred Degrees … below the Freezing Point, when the Mercury became solid, and would sink no lower; and then the Glass being broke, it came out in the Form of a silver Bullet, adhering to a Wire which was the slender part that had been in the Tube. Upon Tryal it was found malleable, and was hammered out to the Bigness of a Half Crown; but soon after, on receiving a small Degree of Warmth it return'd gradually to its fluid State again."[21]

A report of the experiments on the freezing of mercury appeared in the *Works* of the London Royal Society (1760), and then was put in a popular English yearbook for 1762, the *Annual Register*. Precisely from this latter publication the discoveries of the Petersburg scholars became known in America. In the papers of Franklin's friend mentioned above, Ezra Stiles (later President of Yale College), an extensive extract about the experiments on the freezing of mercury, which were carried out during the heavy frosts in Petersburg in December, 1759, has been preserved.[22] Initially, Stiles did not succeed in repeating the Petersburg experiments, and in May, 1765, he decided to address himself to Joseph Adam Braun with a special letter.[23] Already earlier, in February, 1765, taking advantage of the services of Franklin, he attempted to establish scientific contacts with Lomonosov. The corresponding letter of Stiles in the Latin language, addressed to "the Reknowned Mr. Lomonosov, Citizen of Petersburg in Russia, and Member of the Petersburg Academy of Sciences" is also preserved in the Franklin papers in the archives of the American Philosophical Society.[24]

"I have had occasion to read in a London newspaper of October 29, 1764," wrote Stiles to Lomonosov, "that you, believing in the possibility of the discovery of a route from Russia to America via the sea covered with ice, have prepared two ships which, after wintering in Kola, are to be sent, in the course of the following spring, to the Pole, and will undertake a detailed study of the northern regions. This is a very laudable plan and worthy indeed of an investigator of nature! In my turn, I deeply believe that the polar regions and the arctic seas, to the extent of the distance from the shores, are lighted either by the aurora borealis or by the tropical sun...."[25]

The inquiring American was compiling at that time tables of temperature observations, and in this connection, turned to Lomonosov with the request that he send to him, or to Franklin, "all information with respect to magnetism and temperature, registered or assumed, in the polar lands and oceans," and also "reports about the readings of the thermometer in some places of the Russian Empire," which he lacked. Stiles requested in particular that "such observations be made in Petersburg, Moscow, Kazan, and Tobolsk, and even in Archangel, Kola, Kamchatka, and Selenginsk."

Referring to possible correspondence of Franklin with Aepinus and Braun, Stiles requested his famous friend to become an intermediary in the forwarding of the message to St. Petersburg, or, in any case, to supply him with an account of the polar expedition of Lomonosov, if the latter should be carried out.[26]

Eufrosina Dvoichenko-Markov, exceptionally precise and careful in her judgments, is on this occasion somewhat hesitant about a categorical conclusion that "Franklin carried out this instruction."[27]

In a letter of reply to Stiles on July 5, 1765, Franklin reported that very recently he had sent Lomonosov the enclosure destined for him, but that the Russian scholar was then already not among the living. Lomonosov died on April 4/15, 1765, and this completely excluded the possibility of the timely receipt by him of the message from Stiles and Franklin. It is quite probable that Franklin, upon learning of Lomonosov's death, might in general have refrained from forwarding the letter to St. Petersburg, and that this led to its being preserved in his files in the archives of the American Philosophical Society in Philadelphia.

But if Franklin and Stiles did not succeed in establishing direct contact with Lomonosov, in the light of certain data it may be confirmed quite definitely at the present time that they knew about the work of the Russian scholar, and valued it highly. They were advised also about some other work of Russian scholars. From the letter of reply to Stiles of July 5, 1765, mentioned above, it is clear that Franklin was interested in the Russian geographical discoveries, and was advised about two expeditions to the northwestern shore of America, and also about unsuccessful attempts to proceed across the Arctic Ocean. Precisely in this connection, Franklin attributed great significance to the new polar expedition, and pointed out that "Lomonozow will set the matter right."[28]

Until recently there were serious doubts of the existence of correspondence of Franklin with the members of the Petersburg Academy of Sciences, Braun and Aepinus, about the possibility of which Stiles made mention. The compilers of a new basic collection of the works of Franklin, in a special note on this subject, authoritatively observed that "there is in fact no evidence of any such correspondence."[29] Meanwhile, in the archives of the Pennsylvania Historical Society we have succeeded in discovering a letter of Franklin to Aepinus completely unknown earlier. Taking into account the exceptional significance of this document as the earliest letter of the great American to his colleague, the full text of it is presented below:

London, June 6, 1765.

Sir,

When I was in America the last time, I received there your splendid work on the theories of electricity and magnetism which, as I understood, you did me the honor of sending me. I read it with endless satisfaction and contentment, and request you to accept my best expressions of gratitude and congratulations, which you actually deserve from the whole Republic of Letters. Along with this letter I take the liberty of sending you my slight work which has still not been published, but which is to appear in a forthcoming volume of the *Works* of the Royal Society. Please accept it as a modest token of the great respect and esteem with which, Sir, I am your most obedient and humble servant.

Benjamin Franklin.[30]

The major treatise of Aepinus, *Experiment on the Theory of Electricity and Magnetism,* produced such a great impression on Franklin that even seven years later he wrote to his friend, the French scholar Barbeu Dubourg:

"A powerful magnetized apparatus may magnetize millions of steel bars without transmitting to them any part of its own magnetism, while only bringing into action the magnetism which existed in these bars."

"I am chiefly indebted to that excellent philosopher of Petersburg, Mr. Aepinus, for the hypothesis, which appears to me equally ingenious and solid. I say chiefly, because as it is many years since I read his book, which I have left in America, it may happen, that I may have added to or altered it in some respect; and if I have misrepresented anything, the error ought to be charged to my account."[31]

Thus we see that Benjamin Franklin himself adopted an attitude of great respect towards the works of the Russian scholars, and recognized that he owed much "to that excellent philosopher of Petersburg Mr. Aepinus."

In his turn, Dmitry Andreyevich Golitsyn, the Russian Minister in the Hague during the War of the American Revolution, who himself published interesting works in this area, valued exceptionally highly the work of Franklin on the theory of electricity. "Mr. Franklin," wrote Golitsyn in a work printed in the Works of the Petersburg Academy of Sciences in 1777 "was the first to find that two forms of electricity—positive and negative—exist."[32] Being one of the sincerest admirers of the famous American, Golitsyn considered it possible in January, 1777, to turn to Benjamin Franklin with a letter for which, as he noted, "love of science and sincere interest in its progress" gave him the right. "Who better than You, Sir, would be able to decide if the ideas which I have proposed of positive and negative Electricities and the force of attraction of the Poles are correct or not...," wrote Golitsyn, and then he described in detail his experiments in the area of atmospheric electricity.[33]

It is impossible not to consider as quite a bold step on the part of the Russian Minister in the Hague the direct approach to Franklin, who was at that time the representative of the rebelling colonies in Paris, and who had not yet received official recognition even from the French Government; such license could not meet with the approval of the Tsarist Court in St. Petersburg.

The available materials as a whole do not leave doubt of the fact that the famous "Philadelphia experiments" of Franklin not only became well known in Russia already in the middle of the 18th century, winning the most flattering evaluation in scientific circles, but, what is especially important, received further sharpening and development in the works of Russian scholars, among whom must be put in the first rank the names of Lomonosov, Rikhman, and also Aepinus and Golitsyn.

Mutual interest in investigations undertaken, and the first occasional connections, expressed principally in mutual acquaintance with investigations in the area of physics, and also of geographic discoveries, prepared the ground for the establishment of official contact between the American Philosophical Society,[34] founded by Benjamin Franklin in 1743, and the Russian Academy of Sciences in St. Petersburg, in the early 1770's.

In connection with the issuance at the beginning of 1771 of the first volume of the *Works* of the American Philosophical Society,[35] it was decided to send it to all the most important foreign "philosophical" institutions, on the list of which, drawn up on February 22, 1771, figured the "Imperial Society of St. Petersburg."[36] From the official inscription on the *Works*, it is apparent that the "American Philosophical Society, found in Philadelphia, sincerely desiring to work together with the Imperial Society in St. Petersburg ... requests that it accept this volume as the first result of its labors in this New World." The *Works* of the Society were forwarded to Benjamin Franklin in

London for transmission to the various European scientific institutions. A suitable occasion for contact with the Petersburg Academy of Sciences presented itself in the summer of 1772, during a visit to London of one of the members of the Academy, Timofey Ivanovich von Klingshtedt,* to whom Franklin entrusted on July 31, 1772 a copy of the *Works,* with a personal inscription. Baron Klingshtedt, although only after some delay, transmitted this volume to the Academy in the summer of 1774, about which there is a corresponding memorandum in the protocols of the conference of August 22/September 2, 1774,[37] and he himself, already earlier, on January 15, 1773, on the recommendation of Benjamin Franklin, was elected the first member of the American Philosophical Society from Russia.[38]

Subsequently, in the *Academic News,* issued "by the St. Petersburg Imperial Academy of Sciences," there appeared a translation of the basic content of the *Collected Works of the American Scholarly Society, Established in Philadelphia for the Increase of Useful Knowledge. Volume I, 1769-1770.* Among the translated materials, the reader found "Disquisition on the Physical State of North America," an article of Hugh Williams on comets, and others.[39]

Curious scientific contacts between America and Russia arose in the later 1780's, on, so to speak, the highest level, through Catherine II, Washington, Franklin, and Lafayette. These contacts were the result of the interest which the Russian Empress showed at that time in the preparation of a comparative dictionary of all the languages of the world. It is not appropriate, of course, to accuse Catherine II of bad conditions for the scientific work: at her beck and call was a myriad army of bureaucrats of all ranks within the country, ready to satisfy any of her orders and even whims. There is no reason to be surprised therefore that linguistic material in abundance came to

*TRANSLATOR'S NOTE: Von Klingshtedt was active in the work of the St. Petersburg Free Economic Society, publishing numerous articles in the *Works* of that Society on economic questions. He also translated the celebrated *Nakaz* of Catherine II into German.

St. Petersburg from all corners of the huge empire. Somewhat more complicated was the matter of the receipt of information from America. But here too the problem was settled quite simply for the Tsaritsa. It was enough for Catherine II to inform Lafayette about her project for the latter to turn immediately to George Washington and Benjamin Franklin directly. "Enclosed I send you a vocabulary," wrote Lafayette, "which the Empress of Russia requests may be filled up with Indian words. You know her plan of a Universal Dictionary. . . . Your commissioners for Indian affairs, Colonel Harmar and General Butler, will be able to superintend the business, which it is important to have well done, as the Empress . . . sets a great value upon it."[40]

In their turn Washington and Franklin, trying to satisfy this request as fully as possible, made contact with a number of persons in the United States capable of obtaining a selection of the materials necessary for Catherine II.[41]

Already in April, 1787, Franklin was able to return to Lafayette the "vocabulary" of Catherine II, filled with "words in the Delaware and Shawnee languages."[42] Later, at the beginning of 1788, Washington, who expressed his heartfelt desire that the project of the Empress "to form a universal Dictionary may be attended with the merited success,"[43] sent analogous materials for Catherine II.

Thus was carried out, to express oneself in contemporary language, the first scientific exchange between America and Russia at the highest level. The materials about it have already been published recently, but, as sometimes happens, they were practically lost in the midst of the documents without number in the many-volumed collected works of Washington and Franklin. They apparently seemed to researchers of too little significance to devote serious attention to them, and they cited them quite rarely. Meanwhile, contemporaries, and above all, Washington himself, looked on this matter — and, it is necessary to say, not without foundation — as an important step towards a rapprochement between the nations. It is impossible not to recall in this connection the remarkable words of the

Founder of the American state, written by him in this same letter of his to Lafayette, in which he forwarded the material about the languages of the Indians to Catherine II: "To know the affinity of tongues seems to be one step towards promoting the affinity of nations. Would to god, the harmony of nations was an object that lay nearest to the hearts of Sovereigns; and that the incentives to peace (of which commerce and faculty of understanding each other are not the most inconsiderable) might be daily increased! Should the present or any other efforts of mine to procure information respecting the different dialects of the Aborigines in America, serve to reflect a ray of light on the obscure subject of language in general, I shall be highly gratified."[44]

Washington expressed further the desire that the project of Catherine II "might, in some measure, lay the foundation for that assimilation of language, which, producing assimilation of manners and interests, should one day remove many of the causes of hostility from amongst mankind."[45]

These dreams, of course, had an abstract quality at that time, but nevertheless, the first practical step, carried out with the intimate participation of Franklin and Washington, as a boon for the development of linguistics both in Russia and in America, was not in vain. The materials received from the United States were used in part for the second edition of the universal comparative dictionary,[46] which in turn then exerted a vital influence on philological investigations in the United States. Already, in collecting materials for Catherine II, the Americans showed themselves thereby attracted to the comparative study of the Indian languages. Later, Barton, Hekevelder, Schultz, and several others prepared in America dictionaries of the various Indian tribes on the model of the Russian dictionary.

The important American philologist and Vice-President of the Philosophical Society, Peter S. du Ponceau, frequently noted this circumstance later. "Comparative linguistics, as a science, was born in Russia," wrote Du Ponceau, and he pointed out further that Catherine II already had first realized its significance.[47]

In connection with a review of Russo-American scientific and cultural ties in the 18th century, it is impossible not to invite attention to the correspondence and personal acquaintance of Benjamin Franklin with Princess Yekaterina Romanovna Dashkova,* who was the Director of the Petersburg Academy of Sciences during 1783-1796, and President of the Special Russian Academy founded on her initiative in 1783 for developing the Russian language. The first exchange of letters and meetings between Franklin and Princess Dashkova took place in Paris in the winter of 1781.[48] Later, Franklin sent Princess Dashkova the second volume of the *Works* of the American Philosophical Society, in connection with which the Princess expressed gratitude to him in a letter of August 30, 1788.[49]

---

*TRANSLATOR'S NOTE: Princess Dashkova was born in 1743 and was the daughter of Count Roman Illarionovich Vorontsov and the niece of Vice-Chancellor Mikhail Illarionovich Vorontsov. Her husband, Brigadier Prince Mikhail Ivanovich Dashkov, died in 1764, but she lived on until 1810. Her formal education was limited to foreign languages, dancing, and painting, but extensive reading, especially in Bayle, Montesquieu, Boileau, and Voltaire not only made her a remarkably well informed woman for her time, but also accounted for her friendship with the future Catherine II (who was 13 years older), before the latter's accession to the throne. Because of her uncle's high position, Dashkova was *au courant* of the great affairs of state when Empress Elizabeth died, and though only 18 at the time, played a leading role in the palace revolution of 1762 which seated Catherine II on the throne. She is credited, *inter alia,* with having won over Nikita Ivanovich Panin to the overthrow of Peter III. However, her friendship with Catherine soon cooled, and she spent the years from 1769 to 1772 in Germany, England, France, and Switzerland, becoming acquainted with Voltaire and Diderot. She was abroad again between 1775 and 1782, enrolling her only son in Edinburgh University, meeting William Robertson and Adam Smith, and travelling as far south as Italy. After her second return home, her relations with Catherine II improved, leading to the important appointments mentioned by the author. However, Catherine eventually turned against her again when she arranged a performance of Knyazhnin's play "Vadim" at the Russian Theater, and in 1796, Emperor Paul removed her from all her positions and exiled her from St. Petersburg. She declined reappointment as Director of the Academy of Sciences upon the accession of Emperor Alexander I in 1801. Meanwhile, after her appointment to that post in 1783, she had stepped up the Academy's instructional program, pushed forward translations of important foreign literary works into Russian, provided a vehicle for the publication of the important Russian authors of the day, and arranged for the publication of a new and improved Russian dictionary. She wrote some literary pieces herself, and published those written by Catherine II.

On April 17, 1789, on the proposal of Benjamin Franklin, Princess Dashkova was unanimously elected a member of the American Philosophical Society, and on May 15, an appropriate certificate was sent to her. "In striving to serve the interests of the Society by drawing the leading scholars into it," it was pointed out in the certificate, "they elected Madame Princess Dashkova, President of the Imperial Academy of Sciences in St. Petersburg, as a member of the aforementioned Philosophical Society . . . "[50] Princess Dashkova became the first woman member and the second Russian member of the American Philosophical Society. On August 18/29, 1791, A. Yu. Kraft officially reported the election of Yekaterina Romanovna Dashkova while presenting to a conference of the Academy of Sciences a copy of the certificate, "signed in his own hand by the famous Doctor Franklin," as "evidence of the high and flattering evaluation of the literary services of the Princess on the part of the most remote scientific institutions."[51]

Later, referring to the circumstances of her election, Princess Dashkova herself wrote in her memoirs: "He [she is talking about Franklin] bears me enough friendship and esteem to propose me as member of the respected and already famous Philosophical Society of Philadelphia. I was unanimously elected. I have already received the diploma and since that time the Society has never failed to send me all its published works."[52]

Already in the years of the War of the American Revolution, American scholars showed an ever growing interest in the achievements of Russian science, in connection with which, it would be desirable to quote the words of the Vice-President of the Philosophical Society, Dr. Thomas Bond, from his speech to the jubilee meeting of the Society on May 21, 1782: "If we direct our attention to the countries of the Old World and the New, then we discover that the most significant mark of their character, a mark which guaranteed them recognition abroad, was their love of literature, art, and science. Russia, which already some years back was almost unknown in Europe, has risen to world greatness like the morning sun. She bor-

HANDS ACROSS THE SEA: RUSSIAN MEMBERS OF AMERICAN LEARNED SOCIETIES 1775-1783

Above: PRINCESS YEKATERINA ROMA-NOVNA DASHKOVA, 1743-1810.
Director, Russian Academy of Sciences, 1782-1796; Member, American Philosophical Society, 1789.
Her intimate friendship with Benjamin Franklin promoted the cause of Russo-American understanding.

At Right:
LEONHARD EULER, 1707-1783.
Member, Russian Academy of Sciences, 1727-1741; Berlin Academy, 1741-1766; Russian Academy of Sciences, 1766-1783; American Academy of Arts and Sciences, 1782.
A cosmopolitan mathematics genius in a century of cosmopolitan culture.

rowed the interests of scholars in the whole world, and gave all possible encouragement to the various branches of literature, so there is something common and similar as between Russia and America, as far as improvements effected, and unexpected greatness, are concerned. I cannot refrain from a sincere recommendation to the Society that it exchange knowledge with the learned people and institutions of this outstanding country. Science is in the care of universal friendship. It does not know that which is hostile and odious. It does not wage war with anyone. It exists in everything in the world, and the path of friendship which it opens is opened for all humanity."[53]

When the American Academy of Arts and Sciences was founded in Boston in 1780, one of its most distinguished foreign members became the famous Leonhard Euler.* Officially the election of Euler is dated January 30, 1782, but there is reason to think that this event took place even somewhat earlier. In any case, there is preserved in the protocols of the conference of the Petersburg Academy of Sciences a memorandum of February 29/March 11, 1782 which reads: "The Secretary (at that time this was the son of Leonhard Euler, Johann Albrecht Euler) opened a package addressed to the

*TRANSLATOR'S NOTE: By birth, Euler was Swiss, being born the son of a Calvinist pastor in Basel in 1707. He studied at Basel University under the famous mathematician Bernoulli, whose two sons were lured to the new Russian Academy of Sciences in St. Petersburg in 1725, after which, they persuaded Euler to join them in 1727. He was in the Russian capital from 1725 to 1741, and soon acquired fame through his prodigious publication of mathematics articles (in Latin). He also made great contributions to marine science. Two of his sons, Johann Albrecht (born 1734) and Karl (born 1740) eventually became members of the Academy on the strength of their father's reputation, while a third son, Christopher (born 1743) eventually became a Lieutenant General in the Russian Army. However, Euler himself was lured away to the Berlin Academy by Frederick II of Prussia. He was in Berlin from 1741 to 1766, and while there engaged in academic disputes over problems of mathematics with Leibniz, D'Alembert, and one of the Bernoullis. He also was involved in engineering works for Frederick II and did work on problems of physics. Quarreling with Frederick II, he returned to St. Petersburg in 1766 and remained there until his death in 1783, just after his election to the Boston Academy. Though almost blind, he continued his prodigious publication of books and articles and scientific letter writing with the aid of assistants subsequently famous in their own right.

Imperial Academy of Sciences which contained a letter of the Academy of Arts and Sciences recently founded in Boston in America, to Mr. Euler, Sr., of June 1, 1781, signed by the Corresponding Secretary, Joseph Willard. This Society, only just formed, elected Mr. Euler, Sr. to the ranks of its members and requested him to transmit to and publicize in the Imperial Academy of Sciences its charter, drawn up on a printed sheet entitled: An Act for the Founding and Establishment of a Society for the Support and Encouragement of the Arts and Sciences."[54]

In making such a fortunate choice, the Boston Society of Arts and Sciences demonstrated its respect for the best achievements of the Petersburg Academy, with which contacts were established immediately after its founding. Regrettably, I have not succeeded in finding in the archives of the Academy of Sciences of the USSR any sort of supplementary materials relating to this election. And investigations of the authors of the basic guide to the manuscript materials of Euler were not crowned with success.[55] At that time, it was known from the notes of Eufrosina Dvoichenko-Markov, published in 1965, that on August 22, 1782, at a session of the American Academy of Arts and Sciences, Euler's letter of reply about his acceptance of membership in the Boston Academy was read.[56] The American scholars were undoubtedly well informed of Euler's scientific services; the library of the Boston Academy, according to its first manuscript catalogue, had eleven works of the great scholar (17 volumes).[57]

The ties of the American Academy of Arts and Sciences with Russia were not limited to this. The Boston scholars showed significant interest, in particular, in the study of Siberian wheat; William Gordon presented special remarks on this subject on August 22, 1781, and on November 14, 1781, at a session of the Academy, a letter of Daniel Little and Caleb Gannet about the time and the circumstances of the appearance of Siberian wheat in America was read. Later, on May 29, 1787, in connection with the publication of the first volume of the *Works* of the Boston Academy,[58] it was decided to send it to various "literary societies," among which was mentioned the "Imperial Academy in Russia." The receipt of these *Works*, along with the letter of Joseph Willard of September 25, 1787, is confirmed in the official publication of the Petersburg Academy. Some time later, the receipt of news from Boston of the death of the first President of the American Academy of Arts and Sciences, James Bowdoin, was reported in this publication.[59]

And the election of the first American scholar who was given the honor of entering the ranks of the foreign members of the Petersburg Academy of Sciences turned out to be extremely fortunate. He turned out to be none other than Benjamin Franklin. As it was recorded in the protocol of the conference of November 2/13, 1789, Princess Dashkova, in reading the records of the Academy, "discovered with surprise that the famous Franklin is not numbered among the foreign members. . . . His candidature, on the proposal of Her Serene Highness, was put to a vote, after which this respected and famous scholar received all affirmative votes and was elected unanimously."[60]

In a well known letter to Benjamin Franklin of November 4/15, 1789, written in English, Yekaterina Romanovna Dashkova remarked: "Having always supposed, and even cherished the idea, that you were a member of the Imperial Academy of Sciences, which is at St. Petersburg under my direction, I was greatly surprised, when, reviewing the list of its members some days ago, I did not find your name in the number. I hastened therefore to acquire this honor for the Academy, and you were received among its members with an unanimous applause and joy. I beg you, Sir, to accept of this title, and to believe that I look upon it as an honor acquired by our Academy." In ending the letter, the Princess pointed out that it gave her the greatest satisfaction to present to Franklin "a token of my regard and veneration" and that "I shall always recollect with pride the advantage I had to be personally noticed by you."[61]

In sending Franklin a certificate about his election as a foreign member of the Petersburg Academy of Sciences, "the

Permanent Secretary of Academy Conferences," Johann Albrecht Euler, wrote with complete justification that although the Academy was "one of the last to show this official mark of its respect, it has not failed for more than four decades already to admire his rare services more than those of any other Academician."[62]

The election of Franklin as a foreign member of the Petersburg Academy not only reflected respect for services to science, but also was recognition of his extensive political, social, and literary activity, which already had served recently as the object of the serious and ever growing attention of Russian society. Franklin became the first American author whose works were translated into the Russian language.[63] The well-known *Poor Richard's Almanack* (or Rikhard, as he was called in the Russian press), first published in 1784, enjoyed special popularity in Russia, and thereafter was many times republished in several variations.[64]

Franklin first began to publish his almanack already in 1732 under the pseudonym of Richard Saunders. Franklin filled in the little spaces between remarkable days in the calendar with "proverbial sentences, chiefly such as inculcated industry and frugality." In the words of Franklin, "it being more difficult for a man in want to act always honestly," as reads one of these proverbs, "it is hard for an empty bag to stand upright." "These proverbs," wrote Franklin in his autobiography, "which contained the wisdom of many ages and nations, I assembled and formed into a connected discourse prefix'd to the Almanack of 1757, as the harangue of a wise old man to the people attending an auction."[65] The clear, simple, and pointed proverbs reflected the ideals of the rising bourgeoisie, and enjoyed enormous success. In America and Europe, they brought out ever newer and newer editions of the almanack, which became the book of reference of the third estate. In the "preface of the authors" of the Moscow edition of the *Wisdom of Rikhard* in 1791, the necessity was pointed out "of spreading true foundations for wise conduct in the course of life, and developing a taste for civil and moral virtue in that valuable class of the people without which we would have deficiencies in almost everything."[66]

Another well-known work of Franklin, his autobiography, which came to light in a French translation in 1791, enjoyed great popularity in Russia.[67] It is notable that this book at once aroused a lively response in Russia on the part of one of the most important writers of that time, Nikolay Mikhailovich Karamzin,* who wrote in a special review in the journal published by him: "Everyone reading this comment on a worthy book will be impressed by the wonderful tale of a human destiny. Franklin, who wandered into Philadelphia along the streets in a thin coat, without money, without acquaintances, not knowing anything except the English language and a poor typographical trade—this Franklin, after several years, made himself well known and honored in the two parts of the world, humbled the pride of the British, gave freedom to almost all America, and enriched science with great discoveries!"[68]

Some years later, *Selections from Franklin's Writings*, dedicated to various moral virtues and the status quo of the day, was published in a journal under the innocent title of *Pleasant and Useful Pastimes*,[69] and received extensive publicity, for that time, in the most varied circles of Russian society.[70]

The modest outward appearance of Franklin, who turned up in the splendid Parisian salons in a simple brown suit, with smoothly brushed hair, and not in the powdered wig which European custom decreed, produced an unforgettable impression on contemporaries.[71] This was, so to speak, a living model of the moral rules and virtues, about which he wrote so clearly and beautifully in his collected works. The impression

---

*TRANSLATOR'S NOTE: The principal period of the career of the great Russian littérateur and historian, Nikolay Mikhailovich Karamzin (1766-1826) came after the period covered by this book. It is therefore enough to note here that his favorable comments on Franklin in 1791 were made at a time when the eventual excesses of the French Revolution had not yet caused him to adopt the extremely conservative views reflected in his great masterpiece, the *History of the Russian State,* which was written during the reign of Emperor Alexander I.

was strengthened by the completely unusual, and even exceptional, destiny of the American, who by his very nature vividly
symbolized the superiority of modesty, talent, and work over
riches, rank, and idleness. "Having emerged from the poverty
and obscurity in which I was born and bred, to a state of afflu-
ence and some degree of reputation in the world," wrote
Franklin with pride in his autobiography, ".... the conducing
means I made use of ... my posterity may like to know ... "[72]

It seems quite probable that the personal acquaintance of
Denis Ivanovich Fonvizin with Benjamin Franklin in Paris is to
some degree reflected in connection with the creation of the
character of Starodum in the undying comedy of the 18th century, *Nedorosl*. There is no reason to doubt either the serious
attention on the part of Lyev Nikolayevich Tolstoy to the legacy
of Franklin.[73] However, this is already too remote a subject for
our theme to dwell on it in any sort of detail.

In summary, from the time of the War of the American Revolution, the loftiest opinion about the leaders of the young republic which defended its freedom in a struggle against a mighty
mother country was emphasized in the Russian press. This
opinion did not change later, in the 1790's, in the period of the
extreme reaction, reinforced by fear of the French Revolution.
It was characteristic, in particular, that in 1790, T. Voskrensensky
published in Tobolsk a speech of Condorcet in which was
contained an exceptionally high evaluation of the services of
Benjamin Franklin and Leonhard Euler.[74] (Although the names
of these two scholars were not mentioned, the text of the
speech did not leave the slightest doubts as to whom the author
had in mind.) In the following year, in 1791, there could be
read in the *Moscow Journal* the lines "To the Current Century," in which were given an evaluation of the basic achievements of an 18th century nearing its end:

> Oh century of splendor, wisdom, and invention!
> Permit a speck of dust before you,
> At the place where sacrifices are brought,
> To honor you with reverence!

What century had achieved such radiant glory?
In you depraved morals were reformed;
In you a free path was opened to the shrine of the Sciences;
In you were born Voltaire, Franklin, and Cook,
the Rumyantsevs* and the Washingtons;
In you the laws of Nature became known.[75]

The first contacts between Russia and America were established and developed, despite the enormous geographical distances, the religious prejudices, and the political obstacles. The lofty spirit of internationalism in science, which has taken on such a splendid form in our days in the solution of the mysterious secrets of the nucleus of the atom, in the joint Soviet-American Soyuz-Apollo space program and in many other areas, found expression in the 18th century in the development of the original foundations of the theory of electricity. And it is especially pleasant to us in this connection to invite attention to the fact that at the source of the first contacts between Russia and America two great names shine with a bright, undimmed light—Mikhail Vasilyevich Lomonosov and Benjamin Franklin, illuminating the best traditions of the past and serving as a symbol of the future.

*TRANSLATOR'S NOTE: Although these lines were written by the great Russian historian Nikolay Mikhailovich Karamzin, it is doubtful that the coupling of Washington's name with that of General-Field Marshal Count Pyotr Aleksandrovich Rumyantsev (1725-1796) was very apt. A true professional soldier whom Suvorov regarded as his teacher, Rumyantsev cut his military teeth during the Russo-Swedish War of 1742-1744, and went on to become one of the great Russian commanders of the Seven Years War (1756-1763). However, he won his greatest fame during Catherine II's First Turkish War of 1768-1774, when he led the Russian Army across the Danube. Washington, on the other hand, was the sort of general who lost most of his battles but won his war, because he possessed statesmanlike qualities of which Rumyantsev was in short supply.

7

The American Theme in the Russian Press of the 1770's and 1780's

The War of the American Revolution, in the graphic expression of Karl Marx, "sounded the tocsin for the European bourgeoisie."[1] Precisely in America, in the course of the War of the Revolution, arose "the idea of a great united democratic republic . . . and the first impulse was given to the European revolution of the 18th century. . . ."[2]

Of course, the Russia of the second half of the 18th century was neither pre-revolutionary France, nor industrially developed England nor bourgeois Holland (the Republic of the United Provinces). The capitalistic structure was only beginning to develop in Russia, and there still was no "third estate" as such in the country. It would therefore be an obvious exaggeration to speak of a straight and direct influence of the War of the American Revolution on the revolutionary movement in Russia. Along with this, it would be profoundly mistaken to suppose that the development of Russia proceeded in any sort of completely exceptional, special way, outside the mainstream of world progress, that Russia did not in general enter into the realm of "western civilization," etc. By virtue of a number of objective reasons and favorable circumstances, the course of the War of the American Revolution of 1775-1783 could receive in the Russian press, if not a fuller reflection, then in any event a much more correct and impartial one, than did the events of the Great French Revolution of 1789-1794 subsequently.[3] We must take into account moreover the sharp difference between the general position of the Tsarist Government with respect to the United States during 1775-1783, and the one with respect to revolutionary France during 1789-1794;

120

the special features of the internal development of Russia in the corresponding years; and finally, the eccentricity of the methods of administration employed by Catherine II herself in the various periods of her reign.

In principle, of course, the revolutionary American War for Independence and the bourgeois revolution in France of the 18th century, as phenomena of the same type, had to provoke a sharply negative reaction of the ruling classes both of Russia and of the other feudal-absolutist states of Europe. In practice, events in America affected the interests of England above all, took place somewhere far across the ocean, and, it seemed, did not offer any sort of real threat to the existing order. On the other hand, the threatening events of 1789-1794 in France (not to speak of the fact that by their character they were much more radical than the American ones), took place, not somewhere on the outer edge of the world, but in the heart of Europe, and created, in the eyes of the European monarchs, a direct threat to the existing order.

For an understanding of the causes of the more or less objective evaluation of the events of the American Revolution in the Russian press, we must take into account the preservation in the 1770's and 1780's of some remnants of the "liberalism" of Catherine II, who tried in such a way to conceal the ugly forms of the system of serfdom in Russia. In extending protection to the men of the European Enlightenment, Catherine II hoped to strengthen her position within the country, and to elevate her international prestige. Correspondence with the most important philosophes was used by the Russian Empress for the broadcasting of reports favorable to her, and for the strengthening of her authority in European public opinion. And after the uprising of Pugachyov was ended, the ties with the men of the European Enlightenment continued further, albeit with "legislative pranks," as Catherine herself called them. Voltaire regularly corresponded with the Empress up to his death in 1778 "on the insights and the style of the Sovereign." Still more lively and prolonged (up to 1796) was the correspondence of

Catherine II with the French critic Baron Melchior Grimm,* who belonged to the circle of the Encyclopaedists. Grimm was not only a constant correspondent, but became in essence a confidant and agent of Catherine II abroad, with whom the Empress took counsel on the most varied questions, and to whom, moreover, she furnished material support.[4]

Representatives of the highest aristocracy did not lag behind the "enlightened" Tsaritsa. Catherine II invited Diderot and D'Alembert to St. Petersburg; Grigory Grigoryevich Orlov and Kirill Grigoryevich Razumovsky** invited the philosophe-exile Rousseau. The Tsaritsa read with delight Montesquieu's *The*

*TRANSLATOR'S NOTE: Like his sometime friend, Jean-Jacques Rousseau, Fréd-éric-Melchior Grimm was a cosmopolitan West European drawn to residence in Paris during the apogee of the Enlightenment. Unlike Rousseau, however, Grimm lived to witness the great French Revolution, and had to spend the last 15 years of his life in his native Germany. Born at Ratisbon in 1723, he was educated at the University of Leipzig, and came to Paris as the tutor of the children of Count von Schomberg. Later he attached himself there to the household of the Prince of Saxe-Gotha, and with Rousseau's help eventually became the secretary of a nephew of the Marshal de Saxe. By the time rivalry for the affections of Madame d'Epinay had ruined his friendship with Rousseau in 1753, he had acquired a reputation as a literary correspondent of six rulers, who showered gifts upon him. In addition to Catherine II, these included King Gustaf III of Sweden and King Stanislaus Augustus of Poland. The Free City of Frankfort appointed him its Minister to the French Court, and he eventually became a Baron of the Holy Roman Empire and a State Counsellor of the Russian Empire. The sixteen volumes of his correspondence constitute a history of French literature between 1752 and 1790. The praise of Voltaire had earned him his repute as a critic, and he was the friend of Diderot. Fleeing from Paris in 1792, he went to Gotha. Both Catherine II and Paul I used him as a diplomat representing Russia at the petty Courts of Upper Saxony. He died in 1807.

**TRANSLATOR'S NOTE: Count Kirill Grigoryevich Razumovsky (1728-1803) was the last Hetman of the Zaporozhe Cossacks, and the younger brother of a particular favorite of the Empress Elizabeth. During 1743-1745, he was sent abroad by that brother to obtain a Western education. He studied with the famous Leonhard Euler in Berlin and then at Göttingen, before visiting France and Italy. When he returned home, Elizabeth made him President of the Academy of Sciences at the age of 18, and in 1750, the post of Hetman of Little Russia (*i.e.*, the Ukraine) was revived for him. However, Elizabeth came to dislike his independent ways and clipped his wings. Though he supported the accession of Catherine II in 1762, that Empress decided to abolish the post of Hetman of Little Russia in 1764. Appointed a General-Field Marshal thereafter, Razumovsky lived quietly for the rest of his life at Moscow and at Baturin in the Ukraine.

Spirit of the Laws; Count Pavel Sergeyevich Potyomkin*
translated Rousseau; Princess Yekaterina Romanovna Dashkova printed quotations from the book of Helvétius, *De l'Esprit,*
in the newspaper *Innocent Exercises.* Being in Paris, the Princess was not laggard in becoming acquainted with Benjamin
Franklin, in dining with the Abbé Raynal, and in receiving "the
whole of society," including Diderot, at her home in the evening.[5] Finally, Prince Mikhail Mikhailovich Shcherbatov,** who
was critically disposed with respect to the Court of Catherine
II—and this is especially important—stated directly to the
French Chargé d'Affaires in Russia that he was a republican,
and a decided proponent of the independence of America.[6]

We must not exaggerate too much, it goes without saying,
the enlightened "pranks" of the Empress Catherine. Attraction
to the Western Enlightenment was in the final analysis only
an external one: when a matter concerned Russia, the attitude
of the Empress changed abruptly. With bitter irony, Alexander
Sergeyevich Pushkin remarked later on this subject: "Catherine
loved the Enlightenment, but Novikov, who spread the first
rays thereof went from the hands of Sheshkovsky to prison,

*TRANSLATOR'S NOTE: Count P. S. Potyomkin (1743-1796) was a kinsman of
the more famous Prince Grigory Aleksandrovich Potyomkin-Tavrichesky. Though a
part-time literary figure after graduation from Moscow University, Potyomkin also had a
military and administrative career. He helped save Kazan from Pugachyov, and was
thereafter active in promoting Russian expansion in the Caucasus region, serving as
Governor-General of Saratov and the Caucasus during 1784-1788, and then, during
1788-1796, as Governor of the Caucasus. Though he performed well on the battle-
field during the Second Turkish War and the Russian invasion of Poland in 1794, his
career was under a cloud after the death of his famous kinsman in 1791, because a
Persian prince had been murdered in his province.

**TRANSLATOR'S NOTE: Though hostile to the Court of Catherine II, Shcherbatov
was an ardent defender of the special privileges of the nobility. Born in 1733, he retired from the Semyonovsky Guards Regiment in 1762, and subsequently represented
Yaroslavl on Catherine II's Legislative Commission. Though he was active in the College of Commerce during Catherine's reign, and became a Senator, he is best remembered for his amateurish efforts to write a history of Russia. The 14th and 15th volumes
of his work, which brought it up to the year 1610, were published posthumously. Despite the numerous errors in his work, it prepared the way for Karamzin by making
available new source materials not hitherto used, and was notable for its 18th century
anti-clerical viewpoint. Shcherbatov died in 1790.

where he was located up to her death. Radishchev was sent to Siberia; Knyazhnin died under the birch rods, and Fonvizin, whom she feared, would not have escaped this same fate, had it not been for his being extraordinarily well known."[7]

Nevertheless, to some degree the liberal "pranks" of the Empress created some legal possibility of the spreading of the advanced literature and revolutionary ideas in Russia, which was used very well by the Russian men of the Enlightenment. One may judge already about the degree of the acquaintance of the Russian reader with the ideas and literature of the Western Enlightenment by the fact that in the years of the reign of Catherine, around 60 individual works of Voltaire, principally the major ones, were translated, and some of them went through several editions.[8]

It is of course impossible to compare the popularity of Franklin in Russia with the popularity of Voltaire, and the degree of American influence, in comparison with French influence, was not great at that time. Nevertheless, we think that there exist sufficient reasons to suppose that Russian society (in any case, the educated part thereof) was informed quite satisfactorily about the situation in North America and the character of the events which took place there in the 1770's and 1780's. At the disposal of the reader were a number of books in the Russian language (not speaking even of a variety of foreign publications), a great quantity of magazine articles, and finally, extensive and varied material about events in America systematically printed in the pages of the *Moscow News* and the *St. Petersburg News.*

We must keep in mind that the American theme was not completely new for the Russian reader of the last quarter of the 18th century. To some degree or other, the theme of America, the history of its discovery and colonization, had attracted the attention of various levels of Russian society earlier. It is sufficient to remember that Mikhail Vasilyevich Lomonosov referred to this theme in various aspects and in a variety of connections. Widely known also were the verses of Aleksandr

Petrovich Sumarokov,* "On America" (1759), inspired by aroused sympathy for the Indians:

> The Europeans touched dry land,
> Whither boldness had led them,
> They want to purify the souls of mortals
> And kill their bodies.[9]

The question of the appearance of the first inhabitants in North America interested Artemy Vorontsov.[10] Finally, in 1765, one of the first detailed books on North America was published.[11]

This listing could, it goes without saying, be continued: towards the middle of the 1770's, the first reports were already accumulating, and there existed some literature (although very limited) about America. However, only after the beginning of the War of the American Revolution, and as a result of this war, is a serious and ever growing interest in America to be first discovered in Russian society, and the possibility appears of speaking about the real knowledgeability of the Russian reader concerning American events. Moreover, not only did the amount of literature about America grow, but the American subjects themselves which had been touched upon earlier more or less infrequently now sounded a completely different note, and were filled (indirectly, but sometimes directly also) with a new, revolutionary content. The exciting news from across the ocean caused the Russian reader to take an attitude of interest towards the most varied compilations about America, even those which did not at first glance have direct relevance to events in progress.

At the end of the 1770's the *History of America* of the im-

*TRANSLATOR'S NOTE: Sumarokov was born in 1718 and died in 1777, and, like Lomonosov, was one of the literary luminaries of the reign of the Empress Elizabeth. He was relatively well educated in the Nobles Army Cadet School, and became in time a protegé of the powerful Razumovskys. He wrote poetry, songs, and plays, and did much to develop a taste for the theater, opera, and ballet among the Russian upper classes during the time of Elizabeth.

portant English historian William Robertson, published in England in 1777, received significant publicity. *Academic News*
printed in 1779-1780 *An Account of the History of America,
Compiled by Mr. Robertson, Historiographer of His Majesty
the King of Great Britain.*[12] We must note that Ivan Bogayevsky
rather expounded than translated the basic content of Robertson's book, which offered for the Russian reader special interest "with respect to the center of the attention of Europe, which
is directed towards the affair that is now taking place in the
American settlements which have broken away from England,
and which are opposing so stubbornly the forces of Great
Britain . . . "[13] Somewhat later, in 1784, the collected works
of Robertson came out in a different edition in the translation
of A. I. Luzhkov.[14]

It is notable that in the year of the end of the War of the
American Revolution, *i.e.*, in 1783, the first book of a Russian
author specially devoted to the new state, the United States,
saw the light of day in St. Petersburg. This was D. M. Ladygin's
small work of a reference nature, which gave the reader a
general picture of the history of colonization and the contemporary situation in the former English settlements in North
America which had proclaimed their independence.[15]

In this same year, the American theme was especially richly
presented in the publications of Nikolay Ivanovich Novikov,*

*TRANSLATOR'S NOTE: Novikov (1744-1818) is generally regarded as having
been one of those two Russian literary figures (the other being Radishchev) whose
persecution at the hands of Catherine II during the years of the French Revolution
indicated that the seed of the desire for such a revolution in Russia had already taken
root. He was born at Tikhvin near Moscow, educated in the gymnasium attached to
Moscow University, and served in the Guards Regiments, subsequently becoming a
member of Catherine's Legislative Commission. During 1769-1774, he published a
series of satiric journals in which serfdom was attacked. However, Novikov was no
Pugachyov, and relied on the ameliorating effects of education, rather than on revolution, to bring about improvements. He also rode the horse of Russian patriotism hard.
Active in Russian Masonry during 1775-1779, he embarked upon the extensive publishing career described by the author of this book in 1777. As early as 1789 he was
deprived of the use of the press of Moscow University, and from 1792 to 1796 was
locked up in Schlüsselberg Fortress. Though Emperor Paul set him free, neither Paul
nor his successor, Alexander I, would allow Novikov to resume his career as a publisher. Nevertheless, that career was an inspiration to Radishchev, Fonvizin, Krylov,
Pushkin, Herzen, Belinsky, Chernyshevsky, and Dobrolyubov.

RUSSIAN
SYMPATHIZERS
WITH THE
SPIRIT OF '76

DENIS IVANOVICH FONVIZIN, 1744-1792
Literary Giant of the 18th Century
Benjamin Franklin served as a model for
one of the best known characters in his
plays.

NIKOLAY IVANOVICH NOVIKOV
1744-1818
Editor, *Moscow News,* 1779-1789. *He*
made literate Russians aware of the
deeper significance of the American
Revolution.

ALEKSANDR NIKOLAYEVICH
RADISHCHEV, 1749-1802
Author of "Freedom" and of *Journey*
from St. Petersburg to Moscow.
"Oh unyielding warrior,
You are and were invincible,
Your leader is Freedom, Washington."

who brought out in particular, the books of J. B. Bossiev [16] and F. V. Taube [17] in Russian translation. We must invite attention to the fact that already, in the very name of Taube's book, the year of the proclamation of the independence of the United States, 1776, was emphasized, and the correctness of the reasons which produced the war in North America was pointed out. Regrettably, the author of the book was not consistent, and in the introduction, described the "dispute between England and her American settlements" as "contrary to nature." However, in the text itself, the reader found the following stirring lines: "Freedom—this is the noblest natural right of the reasonable being! It peopled these great lands (he is talking about the English settlements in America) and made them mighty, rich, and courageous . . ." [18]

The acquaintance of the Russian reader with the foreign literature about America was not limited, it goes without saying, to translations only. We must take into account that many of the best foreign books about America, for reasons of the censorship, did not appear at that time in the Russian language. However, the educated circles of Russian society were well advised about their contents, ordered them from abroad, and read them in the original. As a characteristic example in this regard may serve the famous collected works of the Abbé Guillaume-Thomas-Francois Raynal,* *Histoire philosophique*

---

*TRANSLATOR'S NOTE: The author of this book may be overly generous in dealing with Raynal, though he scarcely exaggerates the sensation which the *Histoire des deux Indes* produced when it first appeared. Born in 1713, Raynal lived on until 1796. Originally a teacher at an obscure Jesuit college, he came to Paris in 1747, but having been discovered in the practice of simony, he abandoned the vocation of priest and entered journalism in 1748. His early historical works, published between 1748 and 1763, ranged from the mediocre to the poor, though they brought him money and the attention of Madame Geoffrin, Helvétius, and Holbach. His method of writing the *Histoire des deux Indes* between 1763 and 1770 was to pick the brains of others (though he visited England, Holland, Russia, Germany, and Switzerland, he never visited America). Diderot later claimed that he had written a third of Raynal's book, and at least half a dozen other major writers contributed. This was why Raynal failed to publish the first edition in his own name in 1770, though he did claim credit for the much revised Geneva edition published in 1780. Though pronounced a literary disaster by Voltaire, the first edition became famous because of its attacks on the reigning European monarchs; it was officially condemned by the Parlement of Paris in 1779.

et politique des établissements et du commerce des Européens dans les deux Indes,[19] published many times in the 1770's, and supplemented in 1780 with chapters about the American Revolution. The unusual variety of the subjects touched upon, the political realism, the criticism of the feudal-absolutist structure, and the unmasking of the colonial policy of the European monarchs, in conjunction with the splendid literary skill of the author, put Raynal's *Histoire des deux Indes* in the ranks of the most popular works of the European Enlightenment. In the many-volumed work of Abbé Raynal, the reader found, alongside the propaganda of the American Revolution, a merciless unmasking of the system of serfdom in Russia. And although Raynal could, of course, be mistaken in details, his passionate criticism of the system of political and civil slavery sounded an audacious call for the violent overthrow of the old order.[20]

It is not surprising therefore that advanced social circles of Russia and the Tsarist Government took completely different attitudes towards the book of Abbé Raynal. Catherine II received the chapters about the American Revolution already in the summer of 1780, and remarked in a letter to her constant correspondent, Baron Melchior Grimm, that "the American record is filled with declarations in which there is too little that

---

Before bringing out the second edition of the book under his own name in 1780, Raynal did extensive research to eliminate some of the errors of the original. Louis XVI had the revision burned by the public executioner in 1781 because of its anti-clerical passages, after which Raynal fled to Germany, hoping to become the protegé of Frederick II of Prussia. However, Frederick was bored by him, and he went on to St. Petersburg to meet a reluctant Catherine II. He was allowed to return to France in 1787, but declined a chance to be elected to the Estates-General in 1788-1789. To the dismay of the Left in the French National Assembly, he had decided by 1791 that the French Revolution had gone too far. He might have lost his life during the Reign of Terror had he not been put down by both the Girondins and the Jacobins as a senile old man who had entered his second childhood. Even so, his rather considerable fortune was confiscated during the Reign of Terror. After the Thermidorean Reaction, he was back in the good graces of the Government again, and was about to be elected to the new Institut de France when he died in 1796. Posterity has not endorsed his own feeling that he deserved a place alongside Montesquieu, Voltaire, Diderot, and Rousseau as one of the major figures of the Enlightenment.·

is reasonable and too much that is unbecoming impertinence," and that she had "less time than ever before for almost useless reading."[21] All the same, she found the time for the reading apparently, since in a letter of April 1/12, 1782, Catherine II again made mention of "the empty idle talk of Abbé Raynal against Us," and some days later, with obvious irritation already, she added in her native tongue that Abbé Raynal *quackt und lügt*.[22]

The Russian public evaluated quite otherwise the collected works of the Abbé Raynal. It rallied, in particular, to the opinion of a leading littérateur, the editor of *Academic News*, Pyotr Ivanovich Bogdanovich,* who made mention of the translation of Raynal's book made by Ivan Parfinovich Khmelnitsky. Bogdanovich remarked that "nowhere is it possible to extract such disinterested and such fundamental information about such subjects as in the magnificent philosophical and political history of the settlement and trade of Europeans in both Indies, which was translated into the Russian language by Ivan Parfinovich Khmelnitsky," and he expressed the conviction that the book "without a doubt will be published in the world for a prolonged time."[23] The translation of Raynal's book did not succeed in being published "for a prolonged time" for fully understandable reasons. And a number of other attempts to bring about the publication of Raynal's book in the Russian language in the 18th century suffered failure. We note in particular that in the summer of 1787 an unknown translator reported through the *Moscow News* that "the philosophical and political history of the settlements and trade in both Indies" was being translated, and that it was already translated completely; however, nothing is also known about the subsequent fate of this translation.[24]

But if the publication of the translation of Raynal's book

*TRANSLATOR'S NOTE: Bogdanovich published mostly unexceptional travel books, grammars, and the like during a fifteen-year literary career starting in 1781, and was editor of the *New St. Petersburg Herald* during 1786. He was ordered to take up residence in his native Poltava in 1796 by Emperor Paul, and never allowed to return to St. Petersburg.

could be forbidden, and even confiscated, and the copies which had already come out could be burned, as the Government of Louis XVI did in France in 1781, it was much more difficult to stop the spread of revolutionary ideas.

To some degree, the news of the prohibition of Raynal's book drew the additional attention of readers thereto, and served its popularity, and the punitive measures of the French authorities were little effective. "Almost no one came to the destruction of this forbidden book, and the author was given means to depart for England," reported the *St. Petersburg News* in the summer of 1781.[25] As a rule, the French original of Raynal's collected works (sometimes in several editions) was present in all the large book collections of Moscow and St. Petersburg, and it could be obtained in the free market. Thus, for example, on November 13/24, 1781, an announcement was placed in the *Moscow News* that in St. Petersburg "at the merchants Kurtener, Reinberg, and Company" subscriptions "to the collected works of the glorious Abbé Raynal" were being opened.[26]

Approximately at that same time, a still more interesting announcement with regard to the possibility of ordering a collection of American legislative acts could be read in the newspapers: "They write from Philadelphia on July 28 that recently, in that city, by decision of the American Congress, there was printed a collection of the various acts of that Congress with regard to the new administration of the thirteen United American Provinces, *i.e.*: (1) the constitutions of the various independent states in America; (2) the Declaration of Independence of the aforementioned states; (3) the Articles of Confederation between these states; (4) the treaties concluded between His Majesty the King of France and the United American States. This collection consists of 226 pages in 8-v folio, and those interested may order it from Holland."[27]

On the whole, the possibilities of becoming acquainted with the best foreign publications widened ever more for the Russian reader in these years. The number of book stores grew sharply: if only one book shop existed in St. Petersburg in 1768, then thirty years later, 29 were already opened. In Moscow, at the end of the 18th century, 20 book stores already existed, and in the provinces, 17.[28]

Despite all the significance of book literature in the formation of the picture of the Russian reader about America and the events which took place there, this was not the only source, or even the main source, of information. Much more important were the extensive materials published in the Russian periodical press of that time. Precisely the periodical press, in part journals, and newspapers especially (the *Moscow News* and the *St. Petersburg News*) were at that time the best source of information of the Russian reader about events in America, and precisely in them do we find the most important materials about the course of the revolutionary American War for Independence.

Current information about the most important events in America which most of all interested the reader of the time naturally got into the book literature with great delay.[29] The periodical press disposed of the great possibilities in this regard. The American thematics attracted the attention of the most varied journals: among them may be noted the journal close to academic circles, the *Collection of Various Compilations and Novelties*, published by Ippolit Fyodorovich Bogdanovich[*] in 1775-1776, the moderately liberal *St. Petersburg Herald* of G. L. Branko, which brought out in 1778-1781 the *Academic News*, edited by Pyotr Ivanovich Bogdanovich, and finally, the especially Novikovite *Supplement to the Moscow News* (1783-1784).[30] Later, in 1786-1787, significant material on the United States could be found in the monthly *Mirror of the World*, and in the 1790's, in the *Political Journal* published at Moscow University by Pavel Afanasyevich Sokhatsky.[**]

---

[*]TRANSLATOR'S NOTE: A poet and civil servant, Bogdanovich was born in 1743, attended Moscow University after military service, worked in the College of Foreign Affairs during 1763-1766, and at the Russian Embassy in Saxony during 1766-1769. Attached thereafter to the Department of Heraldry, he joined subsequently the Archives Department, of which he was head from 1788 to 1795. He died in Kursk in 1802. Though only his first narrative poem, *Dushenka*, had enduring literary value, he belonged to the literary circle of the Princess Dashkova and wrote plays for the Hermitage Theater.

It is notable that already in the first number of Ippolit Fyodorovich Bogdanovich's *Collection of Novelties*, which came out
in the fall of 1775, it was noted that the "American colonists,
being long discontented with the orders of the English Parliament, do not want to be subject to the English any longer. With
a strong armed hand they are defending their rights and freedom, and this defense is hopefully much exhausting the Kingdom. England must suffer much damage in her internecine
war, and in the sort of one in which the opposite side is basing
its efforts on justice."[31]

In a subsequent *Collection of Novelties*, they systematically
made surveys of foreign information, in which a prominent
place belonged to news about the uprising which had begun
in the North American colonies of England. Although on the
whole, English reports predominated in the journal, in some
articles the reader was acquainted with materials from French
and even American sources. [32]

In 1781, *Academic News* put in "A Description of the Countries Engaged in War," in which basic attention was devoted
to the war of the United States and England, and Catherine
II and the system of armed neutrality were extolled throughout.[33] In this same year, the editor of the journal, Pyotr Ivanovich Bogdanovich, published over a series of six numbers an
extended article "On America,"[34] based apparently on a number of French compilations, and in particular, on Raynal's
book.

The *St. Petersburg Herald* of G. L. Branko usually informed
its readers of events in America in the division "Survey of
Foreign News." The texts of the convention of Russia with
Denmark, Prussia, and Sweden about armed neutrality, and
also numerous reports about the internal situation in Great
Britain, were printed in the newspaper. Material about the
individual military battles was also put in.[35]

But if current reports in the journals about the War of the

TRANSLATOR'S NOTE: Born in 1765, Sokhatsky was a Professor of Aesthetics
and Ancient Languages at Moscow University. He lived until 1809, and was a prolific
writer.

American Revolution bore to a certain degree an occasional character, and were published irregularly (and the very time of the publication of the majority of the journals was often limited by some years, and in some cases, even months), then the newspapers of both capitals, beginning with 1775, the *St. Petersburg News* and the *Moscow News,* put in systematically enormous material, which gave a quite full picture of the course of military operations, the general international situation, and the internal situation of the rebels.

Soviet researchers, first A. I. Startsev, and then M. N. Shprygova,[36] have already drawn attention to the rich materials published in the Russian periodical press in connection with the War of the American Revolution, which vitally facilitates our task. It is true that their valuable investigations are not lacking in some insufficiences and gaps. Thus, for example, if Startsev, in our opinion, mistakenly denies the vital differences in the positions of the Moscow and St. Petersburg offices, and does not identify the especially Novikovite decade (1779-1789), Shprygova begins an investigation only with 1779, thus leaving the preceding years outside the field of her attention. Meanwhile, it is clear that use of the material of 1775-1779 would make it possible to define more clearly, and to analyze, that new thing which Novikov later introduced, beginning with 1779 as editor of the *Moscow News,* and at the same time not to denigrate the significance of the preceding period.

In connection with a general evaluation of the contents of both Russian newspapers (there were no other newspapers in the country except the *St. Petersburg News* and the *Moscow News*), we must take account of the fact that although the one was published by the Academy of Sciences, and the other by Moscow University, both were official, government organs (and not private publications like many foreign newspapers), which unavoidably put a definitely official stamp, both on their contents, and also on their form. The editors of the St. Petersburg newspaper naturally encountered special difficulty in this regard. (During 1776-1782, the well known littérateur of the time of Catherine, Ippolit Fyodorovich Bogdanovich, mentioned above, edited it.)[37]

It is impossible not to invite attention once more also to a single peculiarity of the Russian press of that time: in connection with a look at the newspapers and journals of the 18th century, the absolute predominance of translated material at once strikes the eye. *Hamburg Correspondent (Staats- und Gelehrte Zeitung der Hamburgischen imparteiischen Correspondenten)*, in particular, served as the basic source of the foreign information of the Petersburg newspaper. For a contemporary investigator, it often seems difficult to define where he is dealing with the text of an author, and where with a translation; how to separate the author from the translator; and what is original and what is borrowed. The predominance of translated literature was not of course unusual: that about which, in the Russia of serfdom, it was impossible to write in one's own name, it was possible to express in a veiled form, in the name of a foreign author. Already the choice of the theme itself, and especially the choice of material for translation, made it possible to judge, in a number of cases, about the general direction of some printed organ or other, and the opinions of the editor or the translator.

Both Russian newspapers devoted significant attention to events in America already prior to the beginning of the open armed struggle of the North American colonies of England against the mother country. The materials put therein led the reader directly to the idea of the seriousness of the conflict of England with her American settlements, and the unavoidability of an armed collision. Thus, in a report from London of January 20, 1775, after mention of the irreconcilable position of Lord North's Government, it was pointed out: "From the following it may easily be concluded that an internecine conflict must inevitably be expected: since troops consisting of 3,000 men in Ireland have been ordered to prepare on ships for a voyage to America, and in addition to this one other regiment of light dragoons has received the same order." And further: ". . . All information, all signs, and all dispositions point to their subduing the Americans. . . ."[38]

To the degree of the intensification of the conflict, and especially after the beginning of the open armed struggle of the North American colonies of England against the mother country, information about events in America became ever more regular and abundant. The basic information, it is true, continued to come from English sources. (Reports from London, as a rule, devoted at this time and often wholly to events in America, were printed in almost each number.) Along with this, the reader found on a number of occasions materials about events in America in reports from Paris, and also from American sources (already in 1775 reports from Boston, Philadelphia, etc. are encountered). As a rule, the material in the Moscow and St. Petersburg newspaper corresponded (up to the end of the 1770's); however, in Moscow, these reports were published after some delay, and sometimes also in abbreviated form.

Much attention in both Russian newspapers was devoted already to the first news about the beginning of military operations. With June, 1775, previously unknown geographic names — Lexington and Concord, where sounded the shots which announced the beginning of the war of the English colonies in North America for independence — appeared in the pages of the newspapers. In a report from London of May 29, 1775, published in both the *St. Petersburg News* and the *Moscow News*, it was noted: "There was received from the courier who arrived here yesterday from America, from General Gage,[39] the news that the enmity between the royal troops and the inhabitants of Boston at last reached the point of real hostile actions."[40] A short description of the battle "not far from the village of Concord" followed later. Both newspapers made mention some days later of the battle of April 19 at Lexington.[41] Finally, a detailed description of the battles at Concord and Lexington, from official English sources, was placed in the *St. Petersburg News* of June 30/July 11, 1775. This was a report "from Vitegal" (*i.e.*, Whitehall), of July 10, 1775, in which the Americans were called no less than "rebels," and their "inhumanity and barbarism" is depicted everywhere. It is also noted in the report that the Court of London "is inclined to engage 10,000 German troops and send them to Boston."[42]

Later some materials appeared about the activity of the Second Continental Congress, and in particular, it was reported that the Congress had declared the independence of the colonies from England. (The text itself of the Declaration of Independence, like other documents of the American Revolution, was not published.) In the reporting of events in America, an effort to adopt a free and independent position also appeared, concerning which the following report offers evidence: "The war in America has divided, not only the English nation, but also all Europe, into two camps: one decides in favor of the Court of London, and the other moves forward for the Americans. It is not our business to establish a consensus in this great dispute; our duty requires only that we present solely the simple facts, in order that readers may themselves, to the extent of their enlightenment, find the best side for their prejudices and inclinations." In leaving it to the reader himself to make up his mind about what was happening in North America, the newspaper presented further news about American events, beginning with 1763, and ending with the proclamation by the colonies of independence from England in 1776.[43]

On the whole, of course, reports from English sources predominated at this time in the newspapers, which naturally gave a slant unfavorable to the rebelling colonists to the general tone of the information about events in North America. Along with this, they could not fail to express the class sympathies of the ruling circles, which viewed the rebelling colonists as "insurrectionists" against a lawful monarch. The actions which the patriots were forced to take against the internal enemies of American independence, the open partisans of the English King, who were called Tories and Loyalists, also provoked special disgruntlement. In the fall of 1776, the *St. Petersburg News* printed in this connection a report in which it was pointed out: "The provincials or the rabble there . . . all steal and pillage, and now many distinguished families have left there completely ruined."[44] We note, however, that even from these words penetrated with fierce class hatred of the rebels the thoughtful reader could draw his own conclusions about the character of the events which were transpiring in America, where the war was being waged, not only for independence, not only against a foreign enemy, England, but also against the supporters of the old colonial regime within the country, against the "distinguished families," against the Loyalists connected with the English Crown.

In general, the reports about events in America gave the Russian reader considerable food for thought. Despite the falseness of official English accounts about the course of military operations, the general impression often turned out to be not at all favorable to the British Government. It was possible to read in the newspapers that "all America has taken up arms" and that "the royal troops are reduced to extremities, apparently."[45] The reader learned about the extensive discontent of the people with the policy of the Tory cabinet of Lord North, about the protests of the English merchants in connection with the war in America, about the differences within the Government itself, etc. Thus, in a report from London of June 20, 1775, it was said: "By reason of the extremely critical circumstances in which all England now finds itself, secret councils are being held unceasingly at the Court, and the Court sees more each day, from hour to hour, that the great part of the people are extremely discontented with the conduct of the ministry in the condemnation of America. Now the Dublin petty bourgeoisie are taking counsel among themselves about the despatch to the King of deputies with a representation relating to American affairs, about which something was heard earlier already: since it is experiencing complete ruin from the complete cutting off of trade with America. In this same direction, the London petty bourgeoisie also will have a meeting on the 24th of this month in the City Hall; the merchants trading in America will also soon do the same."[46]

As if generalizing the varied material about events in America, both newspapers printed the following report: "Much news has come from America, but news whose contents are almost always the same. It announces the unanimity of all the settlements, the establishment of an American force against the royal troops, the complaints of General Gage that the whole country is being armed against him, that the capability to act has been taken away from him and from the royal troops, and that they are giving him no food supplies, although the whole country overflows with them."[47]

The English Government and the conservative press strove persistently to present the rebelling colonists as "insurrectionists," "insurgents," and "bandits." Meanwhile, the Russian reader learned that the representative of these "rebels" in France was the "glorious Doctor Franklin," whose name was well known to all the world already since the middle of the 18th century. But if they knew about him earlier above all as an outstanding man of learning—the inventor of the lightning rod—now he personified independence from England to advanced public opinion. With the end of 1776 and the beginning of 1777, the name of the "glorious Doctor" is not absent from the pages of both Russian newspapers. The reader learned interesting details about his arrival, first in Nantes, and then in Paris, and about his acquaintance with the leading Frenchmen of the Enlightenment, and the visit to him of the aged Voltaire; about the secret negotiations with the French Government; and finally, about the conclusion of the Franco-American treaty of 1778, the recognition of Franklin in the capacity of official respresentative of the "American United Settlements," and the triumphal reception at Versailles.[48]

After becoming acquainted with these materials, the observant contemporary could naturally draw his own conclusions about the American "insurrectionists". In the final analysis, despite the falsehood of the official English bulletins, the truth about the actual course of the war in America became well known to Russian society in one way or another, and reports about the biggest defeats of the royal troops took on an especially sensational character in this connection. Thus it was, for example, when on December 29, 1777/January 9, 1778, the *St. Petersburg News* published the news of the capitulation of the royal troops under the command of General Burgoyne at Saratoga in the fall of 1777. In this report, not only were the military operations which ended in the shameful capitulation of "General Burgon" set forth in detail, but it was also noted that the members of the English Parliament were led by this news "to the same sort of astonishment as were the Roman senators upon the receipt in the Senate of the news of the defeat suffered at Cannae."[49] The mention of Cannae gave the reader a sufficiently clear and convincing picture of the degree of the catastrophe which overtook the English, and also about the strength and the resourcefulness of the American troops.

The reporting of the concluding phase of the War of the American Revolution in the Russian press was connected with the activity of the illustrious Russian man of the Enlightenment of the 18th century, Nikolay Ivanovich Novikov.[50] In the spring of 1779, Novikov signed a contract by which the university press was rented to him for a period of 10 years (from May 1/12, 1779 to May 1/12, 1789). Along with the press, the publication of the *Moscow News* came under his control. With the appearance of Novikov, a brilliant new period, a genuine flowering of the newspaper and of all the Moscow press as a whole, began. Novikov himself, being sprung from a poor noble family, did much for the destruction of the class, closed-caste nature of Russian culture. At that time in Russia there was only just beginning to be developed "a middle class between the nobleman and the peasant . . . the people who everywhere constitute the true permanent basis of the state. Novikov came from the ranks of this class . . . He first created a circle of educated young people of the middle level, separate from the upper class circle."[51] According to the testimony of Karamzin, Novikov "traded in books, as a rich Dutch or English merchant trades in the wares of all lands; that is, in wisdom, wit, and far-sighted thought."[52]

The energetic and talented man of the Enlightenment reorganized the Moscow newspaper in a radical way; drew new
collaborators into its publication, above all from the ranks of
the alumni of the university—L. Ya. Davydovsky, P. S. Lik-
honin, A. F. Malinovsky, A. A. Petrov, N. Ye. Popov, D. Ryka-
chev, and M. Stepanov;[53] significantly broadened the foreign
information; and also added a number of supplements. From
1780 to 1789 the *Economic Store* came out under the editorship of A. T. Bolotov; in 1781, the *Moscow Publication*; and in
1783-1784, the famous *Supplement to the Moscow News*,
into which important political articles were inserted.

As a result of the changes effected by Novikov, the popularity of the newspaper sharply increased; the number of
readers and subscribers grew many times; and not unusually,
already at the end of 1781, the editor himself could note with
satisfaction the benevolent reception and the approval of the
official public, how it "approved the *Moscow News* presented
to it in a completely new form, in contrast to the earlier *Moscow
News*."[54] Confirmatory in this connection is the evidence of
Karamzin, who remarked that prior to Novikov, "no more than
600 copies of the Moscow newspapers were circulated,"[55] but
that with his appearance, the newspaper became "infinitely
richer in content . . . The number of subscribers increased
yearly, and ten years later, reached 4,000." Special interest
attaches to the remark made in this connection by Karamzin,
that "many noblemen still do not resort to the newspapers,
and even ones in a good situation, but at the same time, the
merchants, the petty bourgeoisie, love to read them. The poor-
est people subscribe, and the most unlettered desire to know
what they are writing from foreign lands."[56] It is difficult to
suspect Karamzin of hostility towards the nobility, and therefore
his testimony about the social status of the readers of the
Moscow News acquires additional value. Not only the not so
"enlightened nobles" read Novikov's newspaper, but even the
merchants, petty bourgeoisie, representatives of various classes,
people of varied material condition and cultural level, read
it.

Amongst the extensive and varied foreign reports of the *Moscow News*, the reports connected to some degree or other with the war which England was waging against her former colonies in America, and now also against France and Spain, occupied a place which was anything but obscure. From the beginning of 1780, abundant information was printed in the newspaper about all the increasing difficulties of England, about the open discontent in the country with the policy of the conservative cabinet of Lord North, which was stubbornly insisting on the continuation of the American war, and in particular, about sharp representations which were being made by the representatives of the Whig Opposition in Parliament. In the newspaper, one was often able to encounter the names of the glorious Whig orators, and above all, that of Charles James Fox. On January 8/19, the *Moscow News*, in informing its readers in detail about the representations of the leaders of the Opposition, mentioned the statement of Fox to the effect that in the chronicles of England, "one could not find a more unhappy and a more repellent war for England than the present one."[57] On the whole, during 1780-1782, the Moscow newspaper (sometimes even in contrast to the *St. Petersburg News*) wrote much about the strengthening of the Opposition in the English Parliament, about the serious condition within the country, about the increase of the national debt, loans, and imposts, about the presentation by various groups of the population of petitions with the demand to cut short the war in America, and conclude peace.[58] An important place was reserved also for the situation in Ireland, where the inhabitants were "exasperated," and where "respect for the British Parliament" was steadily being diminished.[59]

By putting in vivid and varied material about events in Europe and America, *Moscow News* not only did not now yield pride of place to the newspaper of the capital, but in a number of cases took issue with it in the best sense. Thus the *St. Petersburg News* devoted much attention to the news of the military failures of the American troops, to the serious internal situation of the rebels, to the discontent of the soldiers in Washington's

Army, who were allegedly stating that "it might be better to obtain bread under one king than under a large number of sovereigns," etc.[60] The newspaper wrote about the representations of the inhabitants of Philadelphia against the power of Congress, and about the fact that complete anarchy reigned in the city—the sad result of "the insurrections and disorders."[61] The tone of the *Moscow News* after the arrival of Novikov became ever more objective and even favorable to America. According to many reports of the newspaper, the impression was implanted in the reader of the nearness of the complete victory of the rebels. Thus, on March 25/April 5, 1780, in a report from Pennsylvania, the *Moscow News* noted that "the taking from the English of Rhode Island, which was serving them as a haven in America, shows their weakness, and forecasts the complete cleansing of America of the English."[62] A little later, the newspaper wrote that the American people "were never so united as now," that the army was in good condition, and that its "numerical strength is reaching 35,000 men."[63] In the fall of 1781, there could be read in the pages of the *Moscow News* a passionate speech of one of the supporters of the cause of American independence, the Dutch Stadtholder, who called for an offensive against England. "The strivings of all Europe," remarked the author of this speech, "are turned towards America. May policies be instructed by this great change, and may they assure themselves that the independence of the Americans is the stumbling block on which all the forces of Great Britain will crumble away."[64]

At the end of 1782 and the beginning of 1783, the *Moscow News* printed extensive information about the actual end of the war in America, the conclusion of the preliminary agreement, and the recognition of the independence of the new state by the English King.[65]

On the whole, the material of the *Moscow News* offers evidence of the obvious pro-American sympathies of its editor. Characteristic in this connection is the reprinting by Novikov in September, 1782, of the fable "Titmouse in the Field" from the French journal *Courier de l'Europe*, which referred "to

England and to her former American settlements." The idea of this fable came down to this, that having once got free, the titmouse already did not return to its master, although the latter promised to let it go at will. To the servants of the master sent to it, the titmouse stated: "It is your fate to suffer under his power, but I take delight in independence." Commenting on the fable, the newspaper remarked that its contents "advance toward the truth."[66] Thus approval was given to the freedom-loving idea propagandized therein, to the legality of the right to freedom and independence.[67]

Finally, the publication in the pages of the *Moscow News* of a series of short biographies about "the glorious people of the present century" offers special interest. It is important to note that along with the outstanding Frenchmen of the Enlightenment (Montesquieu, Voltaire, Rousseau, and others), the *Moscow News* published "notes" on Washington, Adams, Franklin, Raynal, and Lafayette. About Raynal, for example, one could read that "he taught the nations to give thought to their most important interests." About Lafayette it was said: "This young hero is one of those great minds who open a new path for themselves. He was the first, overcoming all obstacles, who proceeded to the distant field where glory greeted courage. . . ." Adams was characterized as the first "talent" of American freedom, a decisive supporter of the republic. "The simplicity of his external appearance is joined to the sharpness of his thought, which, having striven solely towards a republic, did not lose at all its passion, which is capable of being expressed with agreeableness and precision; like an army going against the enemy, he no less observes the laws of tactics."

The most important were the passionate descriptions of Franklin and Washington. In the "notes" about Franklin, it was pointed out that "in some ages he would be honored as a demigod. Electricity is transforming all physics; the English settlements are transforming all politics. Franklin was the prime mover in connection with both these important changes, and thus merited for himself the two best places on the part of posterity." In a detailed description of George Washington (or

Vasginton, as they called him in the Russian press), at the heart of the matter was put a harmonious concept of revolution, the necessary condition of which was the unity of the people and its leaders. "General Vasginton," it was pointed out in the "notes," "was needed very much for the changes which took place in America." A revolution could not be successful "when the people are indignant," and its leaders "do not nourish in themselves that same spirit of freedom with which he was inspired," and equally when "the leaders stir up the people to revolt," but "it does not foresee for itself such advantages from it as they expect . . . But when the people and its leaders are both guided by the same spirit, and are set on fire by those passions, then the first agitation effects a complete change; in such an event, the whole nation constitutes one solid block, which exerts all its weight and greatness, which no one is able to withstand."[68]

So the obvious conclusion from this "note" comes down to this, that the guarantee of the success of a revolution is the unity of the people and its leaders, in the face of which no obstacles can stand.

The publication of such materials in the pages of the *Moscow News* was doubtless a very daring step on the part of Novikov: to write about a revolution (even one which took place somewhere very far across the ocean) and its leaders was not so simple in Russia at that time. And one can only admire the dexterity with which Novikov took advantage therefore of the legal possibilities which opened before him, as an editor. A wise and cautious editor, Novikov avoided any sort of open incitement to revolution in his own name. But already, the very choice of a theme, the selection of published information, and in some cases too, the character of the editor's personal notes, offered evidence of the obvious pro-American sympathies of the Russian man of the Enlightenment. Novikov forced the reader to think, to compare what was read about foreign events with the Russian reality, and to draw his own conclusions. He did not comment too often in his own name, but the material published by him usually spoke sufficiently clearly and convincingly on its own. Moreover, in some cases, the commentaries were given, so to speak, at second hand, not directly, and presented through another person. As an example of such eccentric "second hand" commentaries on events in America the article "Discussion about War" in the *Moscow Monthly Publication* of 1781, which developed on a theoretical level the idea of just and unjust wars, could serve in particular. In connection with all the "unfortunate results produced by war," the author of the article thought it legal "to resort to arms when necessity requires this," when the war is "a just defense of the oppressed against the unjust oppressor." As the author remarked, "the good flowing from a just war and one founded on truth, outweighs the evil produced by the latter."[69] In analyzing the events of the War of the American Revolution which were taking place before his eyes, the objective reader could not fail to arrive at the idea of its legality and justness—the abundant material published in the Novikovite publications convinced him all the more of this.

In the course of 1783, both Russian newspapers printed detailed reports connected with the end of the War of the American Revolution, and the signing of the appropriate peace treaties. It is significant that if in St. Petersburg, only a short summary of the peace preliminaries was published, *Moscow News* printed in March, 1783, the texts of the corresponding documents "in all their amplitude."[70] In October, 1783, a report about the signing in Paris of the final peace treaty between England and the "United American Districts" appeared.[71]

Reports about the victorious completion of the War of the American Revolution were received sympathetically by Russian readers, and aroused in them a heightened interest in international politics, and in the first place, in American thematics. The constant concern of Novikov about the spreading of information about foreign events caused him to undertake in 1783 the publication of a special political journal, *Supplement to Moscow News*, which gained popularity at once among the widest levels of Russian society. "The Russian merchant class," wrote Novikov, "can derive excellent advantage from these *Supplements*, since from the reading thereof, it acquires sufficient news about all wares and goods, in what places it is possible to receive them in great quantity, and with great advantages over other cities."[72] With the very first number of the *Supplements*, Novikov began to publish a most far-reaching treatise, "On Trade in General."[73] The interest of the leading Russian men of the Enlightenment of the 18th century in trade was not accidental. The boisterous development of trade at that time was one of the most important signs of the establishment of new capitalistic relationships, which were ripening in the vitals of the old feudal structure.

Very remarkable also was the heightened attention of the author of the treatise to Holland, and to the republican form of government in general. "The freedom acquired by Holland during the war against its oppressor, Philip, King of Spain, was the principal cause of its rapid growth."[74] "This republic," emphasized the author of the treatise in another place, "had in itself the true source of its wealth; it found credit among its own citizens, since trade was engrossing its efforts uninterruptedly."[75] It is also characteristic that in this article the sympathies of Novikov already at the very beginning of the conflict are clearly on the side of the rebelling North American colonies: "North America is in a state of revolt; these taxes were too burdensome for it, and unjust."[76]

Sizeable, interesting, and varied material was published by the new journal in connection with the victorious completion of the American war. In particular, the biography of George Washington, containing an enthusiastic evaluation of the leader of the rebelling colonists, was printed. In the opinion of the author of the article, the outstanding heroes of the past could not compare with Washington, since "he founded a Republic which probably will be a haven of freedom, one banished from Europe by luxury and corruption."[77]

The publication of the *Supplements to the Moscow News* and the character of the materials published therein could not fail to arouse the disquiet of the Tsarist authorities. Having learned that Novikov was printing in the *Supplements to the Moscow News* "an abusive history of the Society of the Jesuits," Catherine II ordered "such types of printing" forbidden, referring to her protection of this Order.[78] The *Supplements* were published by Novikov for just two years (1783-1784); however, already during this short time period, a series of articles specially devoted to America was published in the journal.[79]

Reporting in detail on the War of the American Revolution and its results, Novikov did not leave without attention some negative aspects of American reality also. In this connection, the publication by Novikov in 1784 in the *Supplements to the Moscow News* of an article on "The Idea of the Slave Trade," which belonged to the pen of a defender of American slavery, has special interest.[80] Praising the odious institution of the slave trade, the author of the article stated hypocritically that as a result of the "slave trade," the Negroes were drawn away from their ignorance, and "transformed into the best men," and moreover still, it seems, they were enlightened with "the very best religion" (!?). In publishing this article in his journal, Novikov simultaneously put in a special note in which he condemned slavery in a decisive way, and refuted the pharasaical arguments of its defender. "We reported this letter," wrote Novikov, "solely because of the fact that it was written by a right-thinking observer. Although we have not put forth a preliminary defense of the slave trade, we do not however agree with it, since it is based on many false conclusions . . . The excuse that in Europe, we commit similar injustices, that much good is done by means of the slave trade, which without it would have to be stopped—all these excuses are not taken into consideration in the court of justice and humanity, and still do not prove the justice of the right of property of white men over their black brothers."[81]

By putting in this remark, Novikov opposed to the views of the American slave trader his own view—the view of the advanced Russian man of the Enlightenment of the 18th century. The irreconcilable position of Novikov with respect to American slavery is quite understandable: already the yoke of serfdom was too heavy in Russia, and the Russian people had to suffer too much therefrom, for it to be possible to observe with indifference the spread of slavery wheresoever, including America. By denouncing American slavery, Novikov at the same time, although indirectly—but quite unequivocally—protested also against serfdom in Russia, which also could in no way be justified before the "court of justice and humanity."

In ending the survey of the attitude of the Russian press towards events of the American Revolution, it is impossible not to invite attention to the evaluation in the newspapers of the uprising of Daniel Shays (September, 1786-February, 1787). Both in the *St. Petersburg News* and in the *Moscow News*, they reported in February-April, 1787 about the uprising in a malevolent way, on the whole. The newspapers wrote about the "anarchy and confusion" in America, about the sending of government troops against the "insurrectionists," etc. On April 24/May 5, 1787, the *Moscow News* reported, not without some satisfaction, that "the disturbance in the province of Massachusetts is happily subdued, and now they are trying only to capture the main instigator of that Shire."[82]

It was of course impossible to write objectively about an uprising of the poor in a country which had lived through the peasant war of Yemelyan Pugachyov. This was precisely the main reason for the unanimity of the Moscow and St. Petersburg newspapers in the report of the uprising of Daniel Shays. It is also possible that Novikov himself was not in general inclined to depart from the official viewpoint in this question, inasmuch as the Russian man of the Enlightenment was not a supporter of the revolutionary overthrow of the existing order, a supporter of a peasant war, etc. He sympathized with the War of the American Revolution, but this, it goes without saying, did not mean at all that he had to sympathize with an uprising directed against the power of the bourgeoisie, which had been confirmed in America.

On the whole, the documentary material surveyed by us offers evidence of the mistaken nature of the idea spread at that time to the effect that the events of the American Revolution were reported in the Russian press exclusively "from the English viewpoint," or reflected the Loyalist position.[83] There is no reason either to speak about the isolation of Russia from the influence of the most important international events, about her "apartness" from the mainstream of the development of European civilization, etc. Although in a significantly muffled way, the sounds of the "tocsin" of the American Revolution of the 18th century were heard in Russia with sufficient attention, and, what is most important, were received very sympathetically by the advanced circles of Russian society.

The serious interest of the Russian reader in events in America was not an accident, nor a paradox. The sharpest class contradictions of Russian reality, the most savage yoke of serfdom, which combined with new bourgeois forms of exploitation in connection with the capitalistic accumulation of the economy, which was beginning to arise in the vitals of the feudal order, the mighty wave of the elemental peasant movement, which was not dampened down even after the fierce suppression of the uprising of Pugachyov (1773-1775)—all this created objectively a favorable basis for the spread of libertarian ideas. We must also keep in view that if in the condition of autocratic Russia, it was impossible to speak of the right of the Russian people to change the political regime in their country, then by virtue of certain favorable circumstances, it was possible more or less to write objectively about the right of the American people to freedom and independence, and about the experience of its successful revolutionary war against England.

The publication in the Russian press, and above all in the publications of Nikolay Ivanovich Novikov, of the most abundant material about the revolutionary American War for Independence, acquired in the conditions of the autocratic-serfdom order in Russia a special meaning and significance. The reading of the varied reports about the successful military activities of the rebelling colonists against the royal troops, the very fact of the victorious climax of the revolutionary War for Independence, and the establishment of a republican state in America

—all this naturally led the Russian reader to thinking about his motherland, forced him to take a critical look at the reality which surrounded him, to compare republican America and autocratic-serfdom-ridden Russia.

Thus, the material about the War of the American Revolution published in Russia, in accordance with its objective content, took on, to a certain degree, a revolutionary political meaning.

8

A. N. Radishchev and America

Toward you my soul is inflamed.
Toward you, reknowned land, it strives,
Where freedom lay bent, trampled by oppression.
You are exulting! While we are suffering here! . . .
We too are thirsting for the very same;
Your example has revealed the objective.
I have not earned your glory.
Permit, if my spirit is not subjected,
That your shore hide at least my ashes![1]

In these excited lines, Aleksandr Nikolayevich Radishchev*
expressed his delight at the War of the American Revolution,
and drew revolutionary conclusions for Russia. Radishchev,
more deeply than anyone else in Russia, was able to read the
meaning of the War of the American Revolution, to make profound theoretical enrichments on the basis of his analysis. His
collected works—the ode "Freedom" belongs by right to the
number of the most outstanding products of European literature of this time—were dedicated to one degree or another
to the American Revolution.[2]

---

*TRANSLATOR'S NOTE: Radishchev has been regarded, *inter alia* by Vladimir I.
Lenin and Joseph V. Stalin, as the first true Russian revolutionary. Born in the Kuznetsk
District of Penza Province in 1749 into a family of the nobility, Radishchev attended
the *gymnasium* attached to Moscow University from 1756 to 1762. From 1762 to
1766, he attended a very exclusive school, the Corps des Pages in St. Petersburg. From
1766 to 1771, he was one of eleven young noblemen sent to Leipzig University. In
addition to law, he studied medicine, history, natural sciences, literature, philosophy,
and foreign languages there. He was much influenced, in the formation of his world
outlook, by Voltaire, Helvetius, Diderot, Rousseau, and Mably. He secured a position
with the First Department of the Senate upon his return to St. Petersburg. His first
literary endeavor was a translation of a work of Mably, and in his commentary he gave
evidence of anti-autocratic views.

Now, after a number of interesting and detailed investigations by our literary historians,[3] historians, and philosophers, it is easy to write about; everything, so to speak, goes without saying. But once there was a time when the idea of connection between the ode "Freedom" and the American Revolution seemed scarcely less than a fantasy; the salutation of Radishchev to the "promised" land was interpreted by readers and historians of literature as a salutation to revolutionary France.[4] Only on the basis of a detailed analysis of the text of the ode, and of its juxtaposition with the development of historical events and with the literary materials did V. P. Semennikov establish a direct connection between these lines and the War of the American Revolution. He investigated in particular the influence on Radishchev of Raynal's compilation about the American Revolution.[5] His conclusions were developed and refined by many other investigators.

Any pedant, in analyzing the text scrupulously, begins perhaps to emphasize some sort of "borrowing" by Radishchev from Raynal, or another Western author. There is nothing more

---

Service on the staff of the 9th Finnish Division during the suppression of the Pugachyov uprising (1773-1775) made Radishchev more aware of the dimensions of the problem of serfdom in Russia. Thereafter he established contact with other opponents of serfdom and autocracy: Fonvizin, Novikov, I. A. Krylov, F. V. Krechetov, and F. O. Tumanovsky. He published various literary pieces in the 1780's; the ode "Freedom" was written in 1783. Another important piece was the article "Conversation About What a Son of the Fatherland Is," published in December, 1789, after the outbreak of the French Revolution, and penetrated with revolutionary patriotism.

His most famous literary work, *Journey from St. Petersburg to Moscow*, an all-out attack on serfdom, was also finished in 1789, some 650 copies being privately printed. It created a sensation in 1790, and Catherine II said that Radishchev was worse than Pugachyov. He was arrested and confined in the Petropavlovsk Fortress, and his book was suppressed. Catherine II commuted his death sentence to penal exile in Siberia.

While in Siberia, Radishchev continued his literary career. Tsar Paul permitted him to live in the vicinity of Moscow. In 1801, Tsar Alexander I permitted him to return to St. Petersburg, and appointed him a member of a commission to reform the law code. His agitation for thorough-going reforms influenced I. P. Pnin, V. F. Malinovsky, A. R. Vorontsov, V. N. Karazin, and M. M. Speransky, but earned him a warning from the chairman of the commission, Count P. V. Zavadovsky, that he might be sent to Siberia again. Despairing of any chance that Alexander I would really effect major reforms, Radishchev committed suicide in 1802.

absurd and more dangerous than such a primitive viewpoint. Of course, by analyzing the collected works of Radishchev, and indeed, of any other Russian or foreign author, it is always possible to uncover traces of a "Western" or an "Eastern" influence to some degree or other.[6] Radishchev himself referred more than once to, and cited, American legislative acts. A new generation of Russian revolutionaries, the heirs of Radishchev, the Decembrists, also took advantage of the experience of the American Revolution of the 18th century. And, let us say, with the constitutional acts of the United States, one can clearly discover a certain similarity in Decembrist Nikita Muravyov's project of a constitution.[7] The plan of our work compels us, naturally, to invite attention precisely to this side of the question; however, we are very far from drawing any sort of conclusions on this basis about the "derivative nature" of Radishchev or Muravyov, about "borrowings" from a western source, etc.

Yes, Radishchev, and later the Decembrists and other Russian revolutionaries, were acquainted with the ideas, events, and basic documents of the American Revolution, and to a still greater degree, of the French Revolution. But this was not their shortcoming, but their merit. They were all highly cultured and widely educated people who moved in step with their time, who sought out contemporary advanced literature. Thus, in defending his viewpoint as to the necessity of civil liberties, and in particular, of freedom of the press, Radishchev revealed a thorough acquaintance with the history of the question, as to which, for example, the section on "the origins of censorship" bears witness. For confirmation of his viewpoint, he refers to experience, and to documentary materials which relate to the most varied epochs and countries; beginning with hoary antiquity, he analyzes the history of ancient Greece and Rome, and turns to materials on the history of the German states, England, France, Austria, Denmark, Spain, and finally, America.

It was quite natural, therefore, that a presentation of the question was given by Radishchev on a high contemporary

level, and there was no need for him to conceal recently discovered truths. While publishing his collected works and pro-
jects and relying above all on the experience of Russia, on
Russian reality, Radishchev took advantage of the achievements of other peoples. The Russian liberation movement was
not developed in some sort of special, specific, exclusive way
outside of the mainstream of world progress. The Russian
revolutionaries valued and studied the experience of other
peoples. Their views were advanced for their time, and their
collected works took account of the best that had been created
before them by the world revolutionary movement. Yes, Radishchev glorified the American Revolution, and rejoiced in it:
"You are exulting! While we are suffering here! . . . ," exclaimed
Radishchev, joining the Russian and American experience together in only just one line. "Your example has revealed the
objective," — here is an example of insistent, sincere internationalism, and at the same time, of patriotism. "What sort of
patriotism?," the skeptic-pedant may remark, as if, at the conclusion of the 46th strophe, the talk is to the effect that Radishchev is dreaming of the "shore" of America covering his
"ashes." It is impossible, if you please, to reply to this better
than did Radishchev himself in the following, 47th strophe:

But no! Where Fate decreed that I be born,
Let my days end there too.

The poet sees with joy the succession between his first
"prophecy" of freedom and a future generation of Russian
revolutionaries:

Yes, young man, hungry for glory.
You will come to my shabby grave,
In order to declare with feeling:
This one, who was born,
Carrying gilded chains,
Was the first to prophesy freedom for us.[8]

As for Raynal, Radishchev knew of course his *L'histoire des deux Indes* (like many other of the best collections of advanced people of this time), and even himself gave testimony at the judicial investigation: "I may consider this book as the beginning of my wretched condition." We must not, however, take this remark literally. Radishchev was making a statement about this at a judicial investigation in which it was in his interests to emphasize the widely known collection of the western revolutionary man of the Enlightenment for the purposes of self-defense, and also in order to lead the investigation, if not down a false trail, then in any event down a secondary trail.

Radishchev not only understood many of the special characteristics of the American Revolution, but was able to express their essentials skilfully, briefly, and feelingly. Radishchev was able to see, for example, with exceptional perspicacity the just character of the War of the American Revolution, and to evaluate the superiority of the new, people's army over the old, "unfree" troops of the feudal states. We cite as an illustration the well-known 34th strophe of the ode:

> Look at the boundless field,
> Where an army cleansed of brutality stands.
> It is not cattle which has been herded here against its will,
> It is not the dice which bestow courage,
> It is not the mass which fights by the book.
> Every warrior appears the leader here,
> He seeks a glorious death.
> Oh unyielding warrior,
> You are and were invincible,
> Your leader is Freedom, Washington.

We invite special attention to the two lines:

> It is not cattle which has been herded here against its will,
> It is not the dice which bestow courage . . . .

How much scorn for the old army, for its unfree organization, and for militarism in general there is in these few, sparse words! And further:

Every warrior appears the leader here. . . .

It is obvious that Radishchev was able to understand correctly the main peculiarity of the American Army, founded on completely different, progressive for that time, principles of organization.

On the basis of the analysis of the 34th strophe, V. P. Semennikov was drawn to the conclusion to the effect that the ode was written around 1781-1783, because something is said about the War of the American Revolution therein as a fact which has already taken place, or in any case, is a contemporary one, and Washington still emerges as the leader of an army.[9]

Actually Radishchev was writing about the War of the American Revolution in the present tense, as if it was already in progress, but V. P. Semennikov, and following him, many other investigators, did not invite attention to the following, 35th strophe of the ode, which, to all appearances, also must be related to America, and which pictures the triumph of a republic which has received freedom:[10]

The shrine of the two-faced god is closed,
Everyone has abandoned violence;
This god of triumph has appeared among us
And sounded a happy bugle.

We recall that the shrine of the two-faced god Janus, according to established practice, was opened in time of war, and closed after the advent of peace. In the given instance, "the shrine of the two-faced god is closed," i.e., the war is finished, and "everyone has abandoned violence" — the time of triumph has arrived: "this god of triumph has appeared among us." Finally, in the address to the "promised land" cited above

(46th strophe), Radishchev exclaimed: "You are exulting!" (*i.e.*, the United States is exulting). Therefrom it is apparent that the ode "Freedom" (in any case, the strophes cited) was not written during, but after the end of the War of the American Revolution, most likely immediately after news of the conclusion of peace. (The preliminary agreement between England and the United States was concluded on November 30, 1782, and the final peace was signed at Versailles on September 3, 1783.) Most likely of all, it was written immediately after the publication in the newspapers of the news of the victorious completion of the War of the American Revolution. Speaking in favor of this supposition is the unusual freshness of the impression of the events depicted, not yet darkened by anything. Since Washington appears in the ode as still the Commander-in-Chief—the "chief" of the revolutionary army, it could not have been written in the 1790's, inasmuch as at that time, he had already become President of the new state. (We do not even speak of the fact that in the 1790's, the events of the War of the American Revolution were already pushed into the background by the Great French Revolution of 1789, and it is difficult to suppose that Radishchev would not even have mentioned them.) Moreover, it is sometimes recalled that Radishchev read the ode "Freedom" to his friends in the middle of the 1780's.[11] Finally, the very word "freedom" in the lexicon of the 18th century meant in the first place independence, political freedom (*i.e.*, it had a somewhat different meaning from "abstract freedom"), which also connects the ode to the liberation struggle of the United States against England.

In speaking of the general contents of the ode "Freedom," we permit ourselves some modernization of terminology, and note that Radishchev moves forward as a supporter of that agrarian order which we now call the American, or free farmer, means of the development of capitalism in agriculture. Radishchev revealed the superiority of the free labor of the farmers over the slave labor of the peasant serf:

But the spirit of freedom warms the field,
The field grows fertile in an instant, without tears,
Everyone sows for himself, reaps for himself.

Radishchev depicts the happy life of the free ploughman, comparing it with the heavy burden of the Russian peasant serf (see strophes 31, 32, 33). For the freed ones, "labor is happiness . . . ," writes Radishchev, and he firmly believes that a time will come when the Russian peasant will find the happiness of free labor on a free soil and in a free country. The belief of the poet in the future Russia and the Russian people was unshakeable. If Raynal looked upon the breakup of the Russian Empire as an enormous "happiness," Radishchev saw in this only the first stage of a revolution which would be crowned with the formation of a republic based on the principles of federalism:

From the depths of an enormous heap of debris
Little luminaries will appear;
Their steady helmsmen will
Adorn friendship with a garland.
They will steer the bark for the benefit of all.[12]

"Oh day! Most chosen of all days!," Radishchev cried out in conclusion, greeting the time of the coming revolution.

Radishchev also turned more than once to American thematics in the text of *Journey from Petersburg to Moscow;*[13] moreover, in each case he revealed himself well informed and possessed of a clear understanding of the substance of the matter. The question of freedom of the press was developed by him in a most detailed way. "The American governments adopted freedom of the press among the very first legislative acts, confirming civil liberty," wrote Radishchev, and he subsequently brought forward characteristic quotations from the constitutional acts of Pennsylvania, Delaware, Maryland, and Virginia, in particular: "The people has the right to speak, to write, and to publicize their ideas; consequently, freedom of the press must never be made difficult" (from the Pennsylvania constitution of 1776, Art. 12, the declaration—"bill"—of rights.) "Freedom of the press is the greatest bulwark of the freedom of the state" (from the constitution of Virginia, Art. 14), and others.[14]

The ideas of Radishchev about freedom of speech and the press, the quotations from the constitutions of the various American states brought forward by him, have enormous interest. Their significance increases still more if it is taken into account that these quotations, to all appearances, were the first official American constitutional materials which appeared in the Russian language. As a practical example, in characterizing the democratic tenor of society in America, Radishchev produced an incident in connection with the important leader of the war for independence, John Dickinson (Pennsylvania), who came forward with a refutation of an unjust criticism directed at him. "The very first magistrate of the state [he is talking about Pennsylvania]," wrote Radishchev, "came down into the arena, published his defense in the press, justified himself, refuted the conclusions of all his enemies, and shamed them. . . . An example for posterity of how one ought to take revenge when someone accuses someone publicly with a printed charge."[15]

While glorifying political freedom in the United States, Radishchev did not at the same time hesitate to condemn severely the negative aspects of American reality. He criticized social injustice angrily, he denounced Negro slavery and the extermination of the Indians with indignation: "Having sacrificed the Indians at one time, malicious Europeans, preachers of peace in the name of a God of Truth, teachers of meekness and love of mankind, engrafted on the branch of the violent murder of the conquerors, the cold-blooded murder of slavery, the acquisition of the unfree for sale. These were the unclean sacrifices of the sultry shores of Niger and Senegal. . . . They till the rich fields of America, while abhorring their labors. And we call a country of devastation blessed because of the fact that its fields do not grow thorns, and their fields abound with varied crops. We call blessed a country where a hundred proud citizens wallow in luxury, and a thousand do not have certain subsistence, nor their own shelter from heat and cold."[16]

In connection with a review of the attitude of Radishchev towards America, one must run across some one-sided opinions. Some authors concentrate attention only on the negative aspects in the characterization by Radishchev of American society, while others, on the contrary, are inclined to deprecate the significance of the critical remarks, and to highlight only the positive evaluations by Radishchev of the American Revolution. Regrettably, such a specialist in this question as A. I. Startsev did not escape a certain one-sidedness. He knows well of course the negative attitude of Radishchev towards slavery in America and the extermination of the Indians, and even makes mention of his basic remarks in this respect. However, he tries here to show that these remarks relate "to America outside the United States," *i.e.*, above all, to the countries of Latin America. He argues this idea along with this, that two American themes existed in the literature of the 18th century: a new one connected with the revolutionary war for independence, and a second, traditional one, connected with the conquest of America and the extermination of the Indians.[17]

These views have a certain validity. It may be considered established that the condemnation of slavery and the extermination of the Indians by Radishchev was extended not only to the United States, but also to all America as a whole, especially, when Radishchev writes about sugar, coffee, and indigo (*i.e.*, goods chiefly of Latin American origin), which were still not drained of "the blood, sweat, and tears which washed them in connection with their cultivation."[18] But in the final analysis, this viewpoint seems not completely convincing to us. In the first place, the outstanding leaders of Russian culture, not only prior to Radishchev (Sumarokov, Novikov), but also after him (Pushkin, Chernyshevsky, and others), sharply condemned the slavery of Negroes and the extermination of the Indians in America, including, of course, North America; moreover, it is completely obvious that in the 19th century, the talk was above all about the Indians and slavery in the United States.

Thus, if one speaks already about tradition, then it would scarcely be just to separate the viewpoint of Radishchev from the views of other leaders of Russian culture. Further, if one is still to be objective, then why must we relate all the positive remarks of Radischev solely to the United States, and the negative ones mainly, and even exclusively, to Latin America? Is it not rather more correct to relate the remarks about America above all to the United States (although some of them were related, it goes without saying, to Latin America too), since at the end of the 18th century, basic attention was riveted precisely on the new republic in North America?

Finally, the decisive condemnation of Negro slavery and the extermination of the Indians does not at all offer evidence of some sort of malevolence of Radishchev towards the United States. On the contrary, precisely because Radishchev valued so highly the achievement of the American Revolution of the 18th century, he condemned with such anger the preservation of an ugly trace of the Old World in the new republic.

It would be profoundly mistaken to survey these or other phenomena of Russian culture and the Russian liberation movement only as the result of West European or American influence. But it would be just as incorrect to think that the development of Russian society went forward by some sort of exclusive, isolated route, outside the connections with world progress. Russian society as a whole, and especially its advanced portion, not speaking even of such leaders as Novikov, Fonvizin, or Radishchev, followed attentively the development of a revolutionary movement in the West, and was very fundamentally acquainted with the events and the ideas of the American Revolution.

Of course, the voice of Radishchev in the 18th century could not be heard by wide strata of the Russian people. Frightened by the awesome events of the revolution in France, Catherine II locked him up in a fortress, and then sent him to Siberia.

The Tsaritsa stated "with passion and feeling" that Radishchev was "a rebel worse then Pugachyov" and pointed out moreover to his secretary, Aleksandr Vasilyevich Khrapovitsky,* that passage at the end where he praises "Franklin as a prime mover, and represents himself as such."[19] However, history has its laws which were not subject either to the Tsaritsa or to her true subjects. And now, almost two centuries later, what is still important is not that about which the "great" Empress spoke and wrote, and what was indisputably brought about by her armies of official and unofficial servitors, but that about which our first Russian revolutionary, poet, writer, and thinker, Aleksandr Nikolayevich Radishchev, thought, wrote, and dreamed.

It may be said without exaggeration that through an analysis in depth of the events and ideas of the American Revolution, through the wealth of ideas and the clarity of presentation, the appropriate places in the ode "Freedom" and the *Journey from Petersburg to Moscow* of Radishchev may be related to the most outstanding responses in the contemporary world literature on the American Revolution of the 18th century. It is also in character that Radishchev, on the most important question of the liberation movement, adopted a most consistent position for this time, and was, so to speak, in the avant-garde of world revolutionary progress.

---

*TRANSLATOR'S NOTE: Khrapovitsky (1749-1801) started his career as a civil servant on the staff of Field Marshal Count K. G. Razumovsky, after which he served on the staff of the Senate before becoming Secretary to the Empress in 1783. He was her confidential advisor, particularly in the area of economic affairs. A minor literary figure, Khrapovitsky left behind a diary, correspondence, and memoirs, all of which are important sources for the later period of the reign of Catherine II.

9

The Participation of Natives of Russia in the War of the American Revolution

The question of Russian participants in the War of the American Revolution, and even simply the question of Russian people who were present in America in the 1770's and 1780's, has still not been the subject of a special investigation. The only exception is the interesting and eccentric figure of the Russian traveller and littérateur Fyodor Vasilyevich Karzhavin (1745-1812). Already in 1875, N. P. Durov published in the pages of *Russkaya Starina* an emotion-laden autobiographical sketch of Karzhavin, embellishing it with a beautifully argued elucidation, and with supplementary things; however, this slight piece was practically lost in the pages of the esoteric historical publication.[1]

Comparatively recently, Karzhavin has again interested several scholars simultaneously. Historical-philological studies written by Academician M. P. Alekseyev, by A. I. Startsev, and by Eufrosina Dvoichenko-Markov are in press.[2] Although these investigations facilitate very much the task confronting us, the very character of the materials which have been preserved, their discontinuous character, and their fragmentary nature, do not make it possible, on a number of occasions, to reach completely definite conclusions, and to show sufficiently fully and clearly Karzhavin's role in the tempestuous events in America in the 1770's and 1780's.

Finally, in 1967, there came to light a special book about the American journey of Fyodor Vasilyevich Karzhavin written by Y. I. Rabinovich. With respect to documentation, he added comparatively little to the already known facts about the arrival of Karzhavin in the United States, but he was distinguished by excessive boldness in the conclusions. In the pages of Rabinovich's book, Karzhavin looked, if not precisely like a second Radishchev, then in any case like an active revolutionary man of the Enlightenment, and "a direct participant in the revolutionary-liberationist struggle in America and Europe."[3] Although the author's enthusiasm and some exaggerations lower the value of the investigation carried out by Rabinovich, we must take it that only as a result of the publication of his work has the reader received in full measure a picture of the impressive life and travels of this eccentric, bold, and talented man.

Fyodor Vasilyevich Karzhavin was born into the family of a rich Petersburg merchant, received a most splendid European education,[*] and a life experience rare in diversity, going, as he said, "through fire, water, and earth." Not without some basis, although also with obvious exaggeration, Karzhavin wrote that "he traversed three-quarters of the world," and even considered himself scarcely "less than Christopher Columbus." Fate clearly turned out to be unjust to this courageous and capable man with a multi-faceted education: in his life there were too many abrupt reversals, serious deprivations, and family irregularities, and too little of the most ordinary simple human joys. A clearly very superior person, he could not find his proper place in the Russia of serfdom, and was forced to roam for many years through various countries. "It would be better for me to be a shoemaker," wrote Karzhavin in anger, "instead of learning, and then using up my life in vain."[4]

The motives which inspired the actions of Karzhavin cannot always be established with sufficient assurance. He himself usually referred only to the very best circumstances. It is difficult to say how justified this was. In any case, this was easier, and in the main, safer. "In compliance with Your permission, I

[*]TRANSLATOR'S NOTE: After his studies in Paris, Karzhavin at a very early age lived in Moscow, teaching French at an Orthodox seminary and serving on the staff of the architect responsible for the buildings of the Kremlin. He abandoned this work in 1773, when only 18, to set out on his travels.

departed for foreign lands," Karzhavin informed his father in September, 1773, "not for the sake of a need of the latter, but solely so that You be left in peace."[5] From his autobiographical sketch we learn that Karzhavin, being in Paris, "thought of alleviating his lot by marriage at the beginning of 1774, but did not find real peace ... in a state of matrimony."[6] The maiden Charlotte Rambour, although she was a poor orphan, turned out to be quite capricious, judging by her correspondence.

An early misunderstanding with the wife, and material difficulties, forced Karzhavin to seek happiness beyond the sea. Informing his father in May, 1775, about his intention "to go rambling to Martinique and Saint-Domingue (Haiti)" on commercial business, Karzhavin wrote: "Although I had carried on American business interests with correspondents there, consisting of granulated sugar ... cotton stuffs, and coffee, it is far out of sight, however, and it is best to make a visit."[7] Only quite unobtrusively, as if accidentally, does he make mention, moreover, of the beginning of uprisings there "of no little importance."[8]

In September, 1776, Karzhavin went to the island of Martinique. His great American journey, which continued until 1788, had begun. During that period he visited the United States several times: initially, at the climax of the war for independence—from May, 1777 to January 25, 1780; and the second time, while finding himself on a Spanish ship in the port of New York from May 12 to June 11, 1782; and then, after the end of military operations already, from September 4, 1784 to April, 1787. The factual side of the complex and prolonged journey of Karzhavin is at the present time quite well known, above all from his autobiographical memorandum presented in 1788 to the College of Foreign Affairs.

The reliability of the reports submitted by Karzhavin is completely confirmed by the documents found among his papers, and in particular, by several passports issued to him by various official persons: by the French Minister in the United States, A. Gérard, on February 27, 1779; by the Consul in Massachusetts, J. de Valnier, on March 13, 1779; by the Consul in Virginia, Chevalier d'Anoumereau, on January 8, 1780; and by the Vice-Consul in Virginia, M. Austerre, on April 15, 1787, and others.[9] As Eufrosina Dvoichenko-Markov demonstrated, the contents of the autobiographical memorandum of Karzhavin tally with the American materials, including reports of the local press.

But if the purely external, chronological side of Karzhavin's journey is more or less established, and does not arouse special doubts, then the matter of an explanation of the motives of his actions, and the degree of his participation in the American events of that time, is much more complex.

"In their struggle for independence, representatives of almost all the European nations helped the Americans: The Frenchman Lafayette, the German Steuben, the Pole Koscziusko, and others ..., but there is not known to the American historians a single Russian who took part in the revolutionary war in America,"[10] remarks Eufrosina Dvoichenko-Markov, and she strives to show further that Karzhavin was such a Russian.

Arriving in America, Karzhavin actually found himself in the thick of revolutionary events. But of what sort was his personal role in these events? What political views did he hold? On which side were his sympathies? To answer these questions turned out not to be simple. "That which is known to us of the political views of Karzhavin," wrote A. I. Startsev, who is well acquainted with the documentary materials, "is insufficient to characterize him as a supporter of the bourgeois revolution." At first glance, this assertion may seem quite convincing. On a number of occasions, Karzhavin actually gave harsh testimony about the American administration as "unsteady and powerless," and, in justifying himself to his father, he mentioned that "the Karzhavins were never Pugachyovs." Along with this, the same A. I. Startsev could not fail to recognize that it is necessary to accept Karzhavin's assurances, made in official documents and censored letters, "with account taken of all the circumstances which required of him confirmation of his reliability."[11]

It is true, of course, that "the Karzhavins were never Pugachyovs," but they also were not the usual Tsarist humble subjects. And it is no accident that they called the Karzhavins "a family of free thinkers."[12] Already in 1755, a political report was submitted to the Secret Chancellery on the Karzhavin brothers (the father and uncle of Fyodor Vasilyevich Karzhavin), in which they were accused of atheism, and criticism of Tsarist officials, and of the Empress Elizabeth herself.[13]

While refraining from final conclusions, we will attempt nevertheless to collate and analyze all the totality of facts and circumstances connected with the life and activity of Karzhavin himself. It is known, for example, that he was very close to the famous architect V. I. Bazhenov, and through his literary activity, turned out to be connected with Nikolay Ivanovich Novikov.[14] Among the papers of Karzhavin can be encountered the text of the "Marseillaise," a quotation from his own verse forbidden by the censor, one penetrated with hate of the "proud magnates" and sympathy for the poor,[15] and on the margins of books read by him, "seditious" commentaries.

He expressed open sympathy in his printed works for the enslaved Negroes and Indians, published an epitaph of Benjamin Franklin, and called Montesquieu the "glorious lawgiver," etc.[16] On the other hand, in the memorandum given by him to the College of Foreign Affairs, and also in letters to his father and wife, he strongly emphasized the commercial motives of his activities.

Quite naturally, the question arises: if Karzhavin showed a very significant interest in commercial affairs, would there have been any necessity for his abandoning Russia, and betaking himself beyond the sea to an America plunged into war? In this case, his dispute with his father, who devoted all his life to commercial affairs, who built up an active foreign trade, and who even presented the Government with a special memorandum on the extension "of Russian commerce in the European states," would seem completely unjustified.[17]

In explaining the reasons for his trip from the island of Martinique to the United States, Karzhavin writes: "Desiring to double my capital in the light of the then critical circumstances of the New England trade, I entered into partnership with a Creole (Monsieur Lassere); we sent a great ship to America; I invested my total wealth in it, and myself departed on that ship on April 13, 1777."[18]

In what sort of condition was this "New England trade" in which Karzhavin took part? Its nature can scarcely arouse special doubts. At that time, the island of Martinique had been turned into an important base of supply of the rebelling colonists. True, in his letters to his father, Karzhavin submitted a completely innocent list of goods transported (wine, molasses, salt—he was silent about military supplies), but along with this, he reported that the ship sent out was armed, and that he himself empowered the captain "to act like a naval commanding officer on that ship." The measures of precaution taken turned out to be far from excessive, as subsequent events showed. "We were," wrote Karzhavin, "*nolens volens* in a battle between an English privateer and a Philadelphian merchantman-privateer, in which the latter also lost their boat."[19] The dangerous enterprise turned out well in the end. In a thick fog, the ship on which Karzhavin found himself was able to slip away from the English frigate, and to reach the shores of Virginia. This fact is confirmed by a report of the *Virginia Gazette* of May 16, 1777, about the arrival of a ship from the island of Martinique with a cargo "of powder, arms, salt, etc."[20]

Referring to his stay in Virginia, Karzhavin remarked that he was busy with trade in various cities and settlements over the course of 22 months. Using the American sources, Eufrosina Dvoichenko-Markov invited attention to the fact that he was connected with a Captain Laporte (in 1779, he lived at his house in Williamsburg), and possibly, took part in the creation, on the initiative of the latter, of a French military detachment from among the inhabitants of Martinique and Saint-Domingue.[21]

Karzhavin's return journey to Martinique turned out very unsuccessfully. "Upon the very departure from Virginia in February, 1779," the ship, with "a rich cargo," was captured by the English. "Thinking of discovering assistance in Boston, and filled with a Russian never-say-die spirit," Karzhavin, "to the surprise of all my acquaintances," set out on foot on the distant journey "with a pack on my shoulders." In 23 days, "with a passport of the French Minister and Consul," he reached Boston. However, he did not succeed in achieving any success in his business, and he was forced to return to Philadelphia: "Suffering the greatest need, I was blind for two days from the reflection of the sun's rays on the snow-covered fields, and in danger both from the English and from the Americans themselves."[22]

In depicting expressively the misadventures of his American journey, Karzhavin was unusually chary in political judgments. In his papers there are no sort of direct testimonies about political sympathies for the rebels, and still less about participation in military activities. Nevertheless, individual occasional remarks made in passing or even between the lines make it possible to judge as to his attitude towards the struggle of the Americans for freedom and independence. Referring to his presence in America, Karzhavin wrote his wife in anger: "I lost three years, 2 ships, and everything that I had in New England, and I risked my life more than 20 times in the course of this period . . . and I see no end to this serious situation. What is the cause of all this? Everything is due to one fateful 'no' said by the one who wanted to be Mademoiselle Lamy (the name under which Karzhavin lived in France) and did not agree to become Madame Karzhavina. But farewell to all proud dreams of happiness! Remember, poor Lamy, that you have lost her proud heart for long, that you are nothing but an unhappy druggist, and brew your medicines for the brave men who will take revenge on your enemies, the English, for your ruin. . . ."[23]

Thus it turns out that for Karzhavin, the English were the enemy and the Americans were brave soldiers for whom, using his medical knowledge, he brews medicine. A quite definite conclusion about the sympathies of Karzhavin can be drawn also on the basis of his cautious autobiographical memorandum, in which he reported the following about events in Virginia in 1779: "The English, under the command of Goridzh (he is talking about the Virginia Loyalist John Goodrich), arrived in Chespek Gulf (*i.e.*, Chesapeake Bay) and delivered themselves over to plunder and destruction along all the rivers." We learn further that Karzhavin helped the French merchant Venelieu "to transfer goods by water into remote forests where we hid so long as the enemy did not leave."[24]

The most important and interesting evidence of the close ties of Karzhavin with the rebelling colonists and their leaders is the project of sending him to St. Petersburg with a special diplomatic mission from the Congress of the United States. In remembering about this, Karzhavin wrote to his relatives in Russia on September 1, 1785: "Six or seven years ago, I was living at the cost [*i.e.*, at the expense] of the Virginia Government for 6 months in Williamsburg, with the intention of being sent to the Russian Sovereign from the American Congress with a public character, at that time when they were sending Doctor Franklin to the French King as Minister Plenipotentiary. But military circumstances, some changes in American affairs, and the fear that I was not in good graces there, and the apprehension of the Russian Minister Panin, should I, a Russian person, be sent to his Sovereign in a public capacity from a foreign Crown, etc., caused me to prefer to return to Martinique on the 74-gun French ship *Le Fendant*."[25]

The testimony of Karzhavin seems very unexpected, and at first glance may seem even improbable. There is no confirmation of this report in the historical literature.

Nevertheless, there are no reasons to deny the reliability of the news brought forward by Karzhavin. First of all, we shall try to pin down its dating. We find in the autobiographical memorandum of Karzhavin that he sailed "on the 74-gun French ship" which the Marquis de Vaudrieul commanded on January 25, 1780, "in little York," and after 20 days, arrived "in Martinique, enduring a salvo of the whole English fleet before entry into the harbor."[26] Thus, the discussion of the question of sending him to St. Petersburg took place, according to all appearances, at the end of 1779 and the beginning of 1780 (in any case, no later than January 25, 1780.) We must take into account that at that time, the question of a diplomatic mission to Russia still was not settled (the candidacy of Francis Dana received the approval of the Continental Congress in December, 1780.) A. I. Startsev advanced a more or less probable theory, noting that in a preliminary way, Karzhavin's candidacy could have been discussed in the circle of his Virginia acquaintances, who included a Professor "of the College of William and Mary," Carlo Bellini (a constant correspondent and close friend of Thomas Jefferson). The possibility is not excluded that Bellini proposed Karzhavin's candidacy to Thomas Jefferson, who was Governor of Virginia during 1779-1781. A. I. Startsev also invited attention to the fact that in 1778, a close friend of Bellini, the Italian doctor and agronomist F. Mazzi, was sent to Europe by the Virginia authorities to carry out financial-diplomatic instructions.[27]

After arriving in the United States already after the war for independence, Karzhavin again based himself in Virginia (at first in Smithfield, and then "in the Virginian capital," the city of Williamsburg). "Lastly, having made his way to Virginia, he practised medicine there, he engaged in business, and was a translator of the Anglo-American language at the chancellery of the French Consulate," Karzhavin wrote about this period of his life, in a biographical entry inserted in the form of an educational translation in one of the specialized philological compilations.[28] Here he had every chance to reestablish and broaden his ties with the leaders of the American Enlightenment, and above all, with Carlo Bellini. It is notable that Karzhavin dedicated one of his books, published in 1789, to "Mr. C. Bellini, Professor of Vilyasberg University in Virginia."[29] In his dedication he invited Bellini "to accept these lines as a sign of the close tie existing between proponents of the true faith [literally, vrais-croyans], despite the shoreless seas which separate them."

Later Karzhavin definitely rejected a charge of sympathy with the ideas of "freedom and equality." It is known, for example, that in a letter of April 27, 1797, to his wife from St. Petersburg, he emphasized especially: "I do not know why Madame is disposed to attribute to me sympathy for freedom and equality, since if this were so, I would never have left America; I could have become a professor there like Mr. Bellini, and everyone there knew and loved me."[30]

While rejecting the charge of sympathy for revolutionary ideas, Karzhavin contradicted himself when he remarked that everyone in America "knew and loved" him. If the "rejection" of Karzhavin is fully accepted, then his friendship with and ideological closeness to Bellini become completely inexplicable. The contents and friendly tone of their correspondence also become inexplicable. A letter of Bellini to Karzhavin from Williamsburg on March 1, 1788, in which mention is made of the federal constitution adopted by the Philadelphia convention in 1787, offers special interest in this connection. From this letter it is clear that in the circle of the Virginia acquaintances of Karzhavin entered such well known persons as the future President of the United States, James Madison,* and one of the most educated representatives of the American Enlightenment, Professor James Wise "of the College of William and Mary."[31]

*TRANSLATOR'S NOTE: While the possibility that Karzhavin knew James Madison of Orange County, Virginia cannot be excluded, the Russian traveller almost certainly was better acquainted with a cousin of the future President of the United States who had the same name, James Madison of Augusta (later Rockingham) County, Virginia, who served as President of the College of William and Mary from 1776 to 1812. James Madison of Augusta County was of course present in Williamsburg during both of Karzhavin's visits to Virginia, the one of 1777-1780, and the one of 1784-1788. The future President, on the other hand, was not in Williamsburg during a part of 1777-1780, though as a member of the House of Delegates he did come there at regular intervals during 1783-1786, before proceeding to Philadelphia to play his major role in the constitutional convention of 1787. Unlike the future President, who graduated from Princeton, James Madison of Augusta County graduated from William and Mary in 1771, and then studied law under George Wythe. He became a Professor of Natural Philosophy and Mathematics at the college in 1773, and in 1775 went to England for further study and ordination in the Church of England. Newly returned, he supported the patriot cause and was not only elected President of the college in 1776, but also chaplain of the House of Delegates in 1777. A fighting parson, he organized his students into a militia company, and saw action during the War of the Revolution. In 1779, he helped draw the boundary between Virginia and Pennsylvania, and received a D.D. degree from the University of Pennsylvania in 1785. Thomas Jefferson was his friend, and he cooperated in the reorganization of William and Mary while Jefferson was Governor of Virginia. During the British invasion of Virginia, his college buildings

Thus, the circle of Karzhavin's American and Russian friends testifies quite definitely as to the direction of his views and sympathies. While still quite young, Karzhavin was brought up in Paris under the watchful eye of Dmitry Alekseyevich Golitsyn, and lived in his house. In Russia, as has already been noted, he maintained throughout all his life a friendship with V. I. Bazhenov, and was published in the publications of Nikolay Ivanovich Novikov. In America, James Madison and James Wise were among the number of his acquaintances, and Carlo Bellini became an especially close friend. In this connection, the fact that Karzhavin — sprung from a "family of free thinkers" and a representative of the Russian "third estate" — turned out, during the revolutionary war of the United States for independence, to be from the very beginning connected with the American-French side, seems fully justified and natural.

In the formal sense, it is difficult to call Karzhavin's American journey successful. "The gods named by the Romans *Paupertas* and *Necessitas* constantly pursued Karzhavin, and he did not even succeed in getting together money for the return trip, in connection with which, he had to turn to the Russian Embassy in Paris, to N. K. Khotinsky, through whom was finally received the necessary 1,200 livres."[32]

At that same time, his role in the establishment of the first direct Russo-American ties, and above all, cultural contacts, seems quite vital. The practical activity of Karzhavin, his literary works, the extensive and varied circles of acquaintances, etc. —

---

were used successively by the British and Franco-American forces, and he had great difficulty keeping his college going in the wake of the end of hostilities, after the Franco-American victory at Yorktown in 1781. At one point, he served as a temporary Professor of Political Economy, and used Adam Smith's *Wealth of the Nations* as a textbook. John Tyler, a future President of the United States, was one of his students, and admired him extravagantly. Much of Madison's time between 1785 and 1814 was consumed by his efforts to reorganize the disestablished Episcopal Church in Virginia, though he was regarded widely as a free thinker. He went to England again in 1790 to be consecrated by the Archbishop of Canterbury as the first Episcopal Bishop of Virginia, but over the next thirty years, his church declined in Virginia, because it was associated with the British colonial regime. It seems reasonably clear that if Karzhavin knew Bellini and Wise well, he must have known this James Madison also during 1784-1788.

all this was doubtless a means of mutual acquaintance with the conditions of life in both countries, exchange of experience, and the development of interest on the part of both. It is impossible not to take into account also that Karzhavin was the first Russian person who, on his own initiative, undertook a trip to America and lived in the United States for a significant period of time, both in the years of the war for independence, and also after its completion.

During the time of his presence in the United States, Karzhavin was doubtless able to become acquainted with the conditions of life in America in detail, and profoundly. According to his own words, he "learned the enormous country, and learned it well." The precision of the information brought forward in Karzhavin's autobiographical memorandum, the numerous details, and especially, the chronological data, make it possible to suppose with assurance that he kept a brief diary while in America. It was not accidental, apparently, that diary notes, in particular for March-August, 1782, are included among his papers. It is interesting also that Bellini made mention of "Karzhavin's North American diary" in a letter of March 1, 1788. The former was interested in whether the reading public would soon be able to become acquainted with it. Regrettably, the public never saw Karzhavin's special book about his American trip, and the fate of his diary notes remains unknown.

Along with this, quite unexpected and often even curious observations, directly connected with his American trip, may be met in Karshavin's literary works, including the manuscripts. Thus the reader found among the educational materials a general description of the American traveller: "One of our fellow countrymen, a curious and knowledgeable man, set out in 1776 across the Atlantic Ocean, and, directing his course to the southwest, came ashore in the West Indies . . . Therefrom he continued the journey to the continent of America, and did not return to his fatherland before 1788. . . This Russian is the first person of our people who went to live in those distant countries at the age of twelve [Karzhavin's boyhood schooling in Paris], and who had to look at them with observant eyes. . . ."[33]

It is striking also that Karzhavin signed the introduction to one of his books: "A Russo-American."[34]

Having become acquainted with the contents of this book, the reader found in the explanation of one of the tables interesting details about the American trip of Karzhavin, from which it is clear that in 1785 a work was published by him in Virginia "in the Anglo-American language" under the title of *The Virginian Fortuneteller*. The reader learned further that the table introduced into both books was copied "from the 19th number of the *Havana News* of 1783, published in Havana, the capital city of the island of Cuba, which is in the Gulf of Mexico, where Fyodor Karzhavin then lived."[35]

Offering special interest is the definite condemnation of Negro slavery by Karzhavin, which was so characteristic of advanced circles of Russian society of this time. In that same book of his, which, judging by its theme, would seem very far from politics, and, according to the words of the author, seemed "an innocent vehicle for people not wanting to be occupied with something better in a time of boredom," may be encountered angry lines vis-à-vis Negro slavery and its defenders. "All the African and American shores," remarked Karzhavin, "groan from the inhumanity with which the sugar entrepreneurs deal with the black-colored peoples."[36]

The democratism of Karzhavin, and his sympathy for the Negroes and the oppressed Indians of America, was also made clearly evident in his description of the so-called "wild" peoples. "I lived for twelve years in various districts of America, both cold and warm," wrote Karzhavin, "and was away from the fatherland 28 years in all. . . . I saw most of the peoples who did not live as we do, nor as the other Europeans do; I saw wise people, I saw stupid people; everywhere I found people, but nowhere a wild one, and I recognize that I did not find one wilder than myself."[37]

Already these brief remarks, dropped by the author as if accidentally, shed a quite definite light on his views. It becomes understandable why this superior and exceptionally educated man did not find a place for himself in the Russia of serfdom.

Having lived for a long time in Western Europe and America, and not belonging to the noble class, Karzhavin seemed politically unreliable in the Russia of serfdom, and clearly, frequent assurances of loyalty did not help him. Even his wife put little faith in these assurances, not to speak of the Tsarist officials. It is not surprising therefore that a petition to the College of Foreign Affairs "to be at a post in foreign lands"[38] was not granted, and prior to his death in 1812, Karzhavin did not cease to struggle with life's misfortunes.

The manuscript and printed remains of Karzhavin have become in recent years the object of an all-sided detailed investigation. Far from everything in these remains seems clear, and far from everything retains artistic and perceptional value. Much of what Karzhavin wrote had an accidental or abstract character, and makes practically no sense to the contemporary reader. At the same time, it has been established that his philological observations had significant value for his time. The works on the theory of architecture and also the expressive and original drawings of Karzhavin have no less significance. His literary collected works also deserve special attention. A graduate of the University of Paris, "a wanderer over the face of the earth," Karzhavin, in the words of Academician M. P. Alekseyev, "made not a little difficulty for his homeland as 'a privileged pupil approved by Moscow University', a translator and compiler, and it was not his fault that he did less than he wanted and could do."[39]

The fragmentary and indefinite nature of the reports which have come down to us still do not make it possible to draw a sufficiently full and clear picture of the first Russians in America. Nevertheless, it can already be said now with sufficient assurance that in the 18th century, there were those who preceded and followed Karzhavin. References are encountered in the American literature to a certain Charles Thiel, a physician from St. Petersburg, who arrived in Philadelphia already in 1769. Calling 'himself Charles Cist,* the enterprising doctor

*TRANSLATOR'S NOTE: Charles Cist (1738-1805), though born in St. Petersburg, was of course of German origin. He derived his American last name from the initials

soon was a success in the publishing business. However, his fame is connected chiefly with the fact that he was one of the first who understood that coal could be used as a fuel.[40] The fate of another Russian wanderer—the Nizhne-Novgorod artisan Vasily Baranshchikov, who turned up at the beginning of the 1780's in America, on the island of St. Thomas, which belonged to Denmark—was fantastically complicated.[41]

Among the participants in the War of the American Revolution was the Estonian nobleman Gustaf Heinrich Wetter von Rosenthal (1753-1829). In an illegible Gothic script, *Report on the Wetter von Rosenthal Family,* which is preserved in the historical archives of the Estonian Soviet Socialist Republic in Tartu, it may be read that in 1775 he left Europe "so as to take part in the liberation struggle of the young American republic against England." We learn further that in America the young Gustaf Heinrich "became the adjutant of J. Jackson, a major, and a Knight of the Order of the Cincinnati," and even "was acquainted with Washington."[42]

It may be established from reference works that G. H. Wetter von Rosenthal (in America he was known as Lieutenant John Rose) served from 1777 as a military doctor, and in 1781-1782, was the adjutant of General William Irvin, with whom he continued to correspond after departing from the United States in April, 1784. Wetter von Rosenthal received tracts of land in Ohio and Pennsylvania from the Federal Government for participation in the war for independence; however, he

---

of his full German name—Charles Jacob Sigismund Thiel—and apparently came to Philadelphia in 1769 because of trouble in connection with service as a Court physician for Catherine II. Having learned medicine at the University of Halle, he soon found a congenial life in the large German community of Pennsylvania. His Philadelphia printing firm published Thomas Paine's *The American Crisis* in 1776. After the Revolution, Cist published the *American Herald* and the *Columbian Magazine,* and in 1792 was one of the organizers of the Lehigh Coal Mine Company. He was threatened with mob violence when he tried to market his coal. During the administration of President John Adams (1797-1801), he was appointed the Public Printer of the United States, but returned to Philadelphia from Washington when Jefferson became President in 1801.

lived in his native land up to his death in Reval on June 26, 1829.[43]

In the United States, they called Wetter von Rosenthal "the only Russian who took part in the war for independence on the side of the Americans."[44] However, this assertion seems not completely accurate, since the detailed information about Karzhavin has been presented above. Moreover, the possibility is not excluded that in a future investigation, information will come to light about other Russian participants in the events of 1775-1783. We note in particular that Karzhavin mentioned in his diary (a note of May 29, 1782) that he met one Russian, a native of Reval, among the German soldiers in America. Some days later (on June 2) he defines more accurately that the name of the Russian soldier was Zakhar Bobukh ("Zakhar Ivanov, son of Bobukh"). At one time, reported Karzhavin, "he did much diamond work on clothing for the Sovereign Catherine the Second and for the Counts Orlov, and in place of a reward, was forced to flee from Russia."[45]

The fate of the Russian craftsman in diamond work, possibly like that of some other unsung wanderers, has remained unknown. Then the life and activity of another person, who belonged in his origins to the highest Russian aristocracy, and who came to reside permanently in the United States at the end of the 18th century, produced a great impression on contemporaries, and on later investigators. This was none other than the son of the Russian Minister in the Hague during the Revolution, Dmitry Alekseyevich Golitsyn, who came to Baltimore in 1792 under the name of Augustine Smith. Relinquishing his high position and princely title, young Dmitry Golitsyn became a Catholic missionary—"Father Augustine"—and founded in a remote part of Pennsylvania, some 200 miles from Philadelphia, the settlement of Loretto, where his monument is now preserved. Several special works in the German, French, and English languages are devoted to the life and activity of "Father Augustine," and there is no necessity of dwelling here at length on the details of his unusual career.[46]

It seems obvious however that, given the choice of America as the locale of his life, the American sympathies of his father exerted an influence on young Golitsyn to a certain degree. It is also striking that Dmitry Alekseyevich Golitsyn furnished his son with letters of introduction to George Washington and John Adams.

In directing attention to the first Russian travellers and settlers in the United States in the 18th century, we do not wish to exaggerate their number and significance. However, it is clear from the preliminary information already brought forward by us, and in the first place, from the materials about the participation of emigrants from Russia in the War of the American Revolution (including Karzhavin and Wetter von Rosenthal) that this question deserves special study. It is possible that interesting findings may await the persistent investigator in the future.

Conclusion

In concluding the investigation of Russia's position in the period of the American Revolution of the 18th century, one should emphasize that aside from the subjective sympathies of the Tsarist Government, the actions undertaken by Russian diplomacy in the for the United States difficult years of struggle for freedom and independence, had objectively a vital significance for the improvement of the international position of the rebelling colonists for the isolation of Great Britain, and, in the final analysis, for the victory of the young republic. In particular, the proclamation of the Declaration of Armed Neutrality by Russia, which received the official approval of the Continental Congress of the United States in October, 1780, had great international significance.

In proclaiming the Declaration of Armed Neutrality, the Russian Government in essence defended (it goes without saying, by virtue of its own interests) one of the principles in the name of which the Americans were fighting. The common interests of both Powers in the defense of the rights of neutral navigation became a lasting foundation of their relations of goodwill subsequently. Many years later, on July 22, 1854, the American Secretary of State, William L. Marcy, and the Russian Minister in Washington, Baron E. Stoeckl, signed an official agreement about the rights of neutral ships at sea, at the basis of which were put the principles of the Declaration of February, 1780.[1]

The array of documents on Russia's peace mediation during 1780-1781 bears witness to her efforts, expressed, it is true, very cautiously, to incline England towards peace with the rebels, and the recognition of their independence. We are talking, it is understood, not about some sort of "sympathies" of Catherine II and her Government for the United States, but first of all about considerations of *Realpolitik*—the ever growing discontent with the policy of the British cabinet; the effort of the Empress to play the role of arbiter in European affairs; the understanding of the unavoidability of the separation of the

"American settlements"; and even the direct interest of Russia in the formation of an independent United States. Although the peace mediation of Russia was not crowned with success, the very fact of the advancement by Nikita Ivanovich Panin of a concrete plan of peace mediation, and the subsequent moves of the Russian Government in favor of the conclusion of peace, could not fail to facilitate the opening of direct negotiations, and the final peace settlement, during 1782-1783.

A special feature of this investigation has been not only the survey of diplomatic relations proper, but also the study of the commercial, social-political, scientific, and cultural connections. In the past, the historians of international relations very rarely turned to this side of the problem. At the center of their attention were only the inter-state, and first of all, the diplomatic relations, the activity of famous politicians and generals, Tsars, Kings, and Presidents. Thereby a principal element was left out of the history of international relations—the people, and, moreover, the people in the form of its most educated and active representatives—the scholars, the social activists, the literary people. Meanwhile, the very history of the relations between America and Russia was opened in the middle of the 18th century by direct and indirect contacts between Benjamin Franklin and other American scholars and their Petersburg colleagues—Mikhail Vasilyevich Lomonosov, Georg Wilhelm Rikhman, Josef Adam Braun, and Franz Ulrich Theodor Aepinus.[2]

At the beginning of the 1770's, official ties were established between the American Philosophical Society in Philadelphia and the Academy of Sciences in St. Petersburg. Soon after the formation of the American Academy of Arts and Sciences in Boston, the famous Leonhard Euler was elected a member thereof (1781). Catherine II termed Aleksandr Nikolayevich Radishchev a rebel worse than Pugachyov, and in this connection, invited attention to the fact that he praised Benjamin Franklin. Meanwhile, not long before this, the Imperial Academy of Sciences in St. Petersburg elected the great American to the ranks of its honorary members (November, 1789).

The first direct trade connections between America and Russia were established already in 1763-1766, when American ships, despite the prohibitory policy of the mother country, completed at least 8 successful cruises to St. Petersburg. In the course of the war for independence, individual ships under the Russian flag sailed to the shores of America via Bordeaux, and beginning in 1783, the merchant ships of the United States were visiting Russia ever more frequently.

At the end of the 18th century, some dozens of American ships came annually to Petersburg, and although on the whole, the extent of the first trade connections was still as always not very great, the very fact already that they traded with republican America, at a time when they were fighting with France at the end of the 18th century, offers evidence of the important difference between the French policy, and the American policy, of Tsarist Russia.

In principle, of course, the War of the American Revolution of 1775-1783 and the French Revolution of 1789-1794, as phenomena similar in character, provoked a sharply negative reaction of the ruling classes, both of Russia, and also of other feudal-absolutist states. But this was only in principle. In practice, by virtue of concrete objective reasons and circumstances, about which something was said in detail in the appropriate chapters, the general international situation added up very favorably for the United States (in contradistinction to France). Events in America affected above all the interests of Great Britain, which could not fail to make her European competitors rejoice. Moreover, these events took place somewhere very distant, beyond the ocean, and did not, it seemed, present any sort of serious threat to the status quo, whereas the great revolutionary storm of 1789-1794 broke out in the very heart of Europe, and created a real perspective of the downfall of the old order and of the entire feudal-absolutist structure.

We must take into account also the emergence of a reaction inside the United States after the end of the war for independence, which found expression in the suppression of the uprising of Daniel Shays (1786-1787), and the coming to power of the Federalists (presidencies of George Washington, 1789-1797, and of John Adams, 1797-1801). It is significant in this connection that in the spring of 1799, as a result of unofficial negotiations between the Russian and American Ministers in London, Semyon Romanovich Vorontsov and Robert King, the question of diplomatic relations and the conclusion of a trade treaty was settled in a preliminary way, and in St. Petersburg, they even gave official consent to the exchange of the appropriate missions. In accordance with custom, the result of the development of trade relations between Russia and the United States was the recognition, in the fall of 1803, of L. Harris as American Consul in St. Petersburg. Some time later, during 1808-1809, official diplomatic relations between both countries were established.[3]

As the materials studied by us show, the events and ideas of the American Revolution of the 18th century were perceived very sympathetically by advanced circles of Russian society. The sharpest class contradictions within the Russian Empire, the most frightful yoke of serfdom, joined with the new bourgeois forms of exploitation in connection with the capitalistic accumulation which was beginning to arise in the vitals of feudalism, the mighty wave of the elemental peasant movement, which did not die down after the suppression of Yemlyan Pugachyov's uprising—all this created a favorable situation for the spreading of revolutionary, democratic, and liberating ideas in the country.

It was not possible, of course, in the conditions of the Tsarist Autocracy, to speak openly about the Russian people's right of revolution, about democratic freedoms, and about a change of the political structure of one's country, but by virtue of a number of favorable reasons, it turned out to be possible to write more or less objectively about the right to freedom and independence of the American people, and its experience of victorious revolutionary struggle against England. At the same time, the publication of a large quantity of factual material about the War of the American Revolution in serfdom-ridden Russia took on special meaning and significance through its objective content. A reading of the reports about the successful military operations of the rebelling colonist against the royal troops, the fact of the victorious conclusion of the revolutionary war for independence, and the confirmation in America of a republican state, forced the Russian reader to take a critical look at the accompanying activity, to compare republican America with serfdom-ridden Russia, and led to the idea of the possibility of a successful struggle with the Tsarist Autocracy. The enlightening activity of Nikolay Ivanovich Novikov, the extensive and varied material about America and the American Revolution of the 18th century published in the pages of the *Moscow News,* and also the journals and books brought out by him, had first rank significance in this connection. The Russian people may also rightfully take pride in the achievement of Aleksandr Nikolayevich Radishchev, who sang of the American Revolution in his undying ode "Freedom," and who gave a detailed and profound analysis of the situation in America in *Journey from Petersburg to Moscow.* Evaluating highly the revolutionary achievement of the American people, Radishchev and Novikov at the same time condemned angrily Negro slavery and the destruction of the Indians.

The same elements were characteristic also for advanced representatives of Russian society later. Pestel, Muravyov, Ryleyev, and later, Herzen, Chernyshevsky, and others, followed attentively the revolutionary movement in Western Europe and America, and in particular, rated highly the War of the American Revolution, the Constitution of 1787, and the activity of Washington, Franklin, and other outstanding American leaders. They were interested in events taking place in America, read various works of American authors (principally in translation into the French language), and also books about the history of the United States. But, it goes without saying, we must not think that all this was the basic source of the development of revolutionary attitudes, or that they absorbed uncritically what they read, and blindly copied West European or American experience. The Decembrist A.V. Poggio expressed himself on this score with exceptional precision and skill: "How could we by reading some Warden[4] borrow from him the determination to introduce into Russia too a Republic such as the one about which he speaks. While complexity serves the United States as a strength and a bulwark, we feared that our state might fall apart with the introduction of a federal administration—they have nine million inhabitants, we have forty million. They had colonists of England, we had Russians! There vengeance was directed against outside enemies, while we sought enemies in our midst. . . . Of course, all drew from books the laws, the jury courts, and the like, but the thoughts about rebellion, decisiveness, boldness cannpt be explained as having originated in books, but in our hearts, amidst all the passions which agitated them! Here are the nests where all conceptions roosted, from where they descended with consuming flame."[5]

Poggio's testimony seems to us extraordinarily important. The Americans fought above all with a foreign foe, they fought for independence, against the tyranny of the British Crown. Other tasks confronted Russia, Russian society. It was necessary to struggle, not for national independence, but for the destruction of serfdom, for a radical change of the existing order, and for the overthrow of the Tsarist Autocracy.

Serious attention is devoted in the work to the study of the question of the arrival in Russia of the first Americans, and also the journeys of Russian subjects in the United States in the 18th century. The archival and published materials about the American journey of Fyodor Vasilyevich Karzhavin and his socio-political views were subjected to detailed, multi-faceted analysis.

Steady attention was focused in Russia on the successes of the young republic, and the possibility of using American experience for the extension of national industry. For this purpose, in particular, the well known report of Alexander Hamilton on manufacturing was published in 1807, on the initiative of the Minister of Finances, D.A. Guryev. "The similarity of the American United Provinces and Russia," wrote in the foreword of the book its translator, the well known Russian man of the

Enlightenment, V. Malinovsky, "exists both in consideration of the disproportionate size of the population, and that youthfulness in which various generally useful habits are found; because of this, all the rules, remarks, and methods proposed here are very suitable for our fatherland also."6

In the literature they often cite the letter of Thomas Jefferson of July 20, 1807, in which the President of the United States wrote about Russia as the Power friendliest to the Americans, and about the correspondence of Russo-American interests with respect to neutral navigation, etc.7

In welcoming the arrival in America of the first Russian diplomatic representative, A. Ya. Dashkov, as the "precursor" of the friendly relations of Russia and the United States, the famous American political leader wrote: "Both countries, being by character and in practice exclusively peace loving, they have common interests in the preservation of the rights of peace loving nations."8

The mutually advantageous trade connections of both countries acquired ever greater significance. Halfway through 1827-1839, from America to Russia were being sent goods worth 20,447,000 rubles (in paper money), including 36,300 *puds* of sugar (16,695,700 rubles); 25,100 *puds* of raw cotton (698,800 rubles), etc. On the other hand, from Russia to the United States were sent during these years such important goods as 358,800 *puds* of iron (1,709,200 rubles); 96,000 pieces of linen and hempen cloth (341,200 rubles); 199,200 *puds* of hemp (1,531,500 rubles), etc.9

On December 6/18, 1832, the Russian Minister of Foreign Affairs, K.V. Nesselrode, and the American Minister in St. Petersburg, James Buchanan, signed a trade treaty, officially strengthening with respect to both countries the principle of most favored nation, and laying a basis for all the subsequent development of Russo-American trade connections in the 19th century and the beginning of the 20th century. Thanks to the "liberal terms" of this treaty, remarked President Andrew Jackson, a "flourishing and increasing" trade was developing between Russia and the United States, which, in its turn, "furnishes new motives for that mutual friendship which both countries have so far nourished with respect to each other."[10]

As a whole, the history of Russo-American relations in the 18th and 19th centuries shows that in the most difficult critical periods of the history of the United States—during the War of the Revolution, 1775-1783, the Anglo-American War of 1812, and finally, the Civil War of 1861-1865—the position of Russia, by virtue of a number of concrete reasons, turned out to be objectively benevolent. It goes without saying that this does not mean that we never had differences, contradictions, and even conflicts. Nevertheless our countries never fought each other (if the intervention of the United States in the period of the Civil War in Soviet Russia is not considered), and we were allies in two world wars. Both countries have accumulated a great and varied experience of fruitful scientific, cultural, social-political, and trade ties. The substantial turning point in the relations between the USSR and the United States which has taken place in recent years makes it possible to hope that these traditions will experience further development, to the benefit of our peoples and of all mankind.

Documents

FROM THE UNPUBLISHED REPORTS OF RUSSIAN DIPLOMATS ON THE AMERICAN REVOLUTION

Author's Note: The published documents, which were found in the Archive of the Foreign Policy of Russia, are related to 1774-1779. In connection with publication, passages which are not related to the theme have been omitted. N. N. Bashkina, V. I. Zhilenko, and the Deputy Chief of the Historical-Diplomatic Administration of the Ministry of Foreign Affairs of the USSR, V. M. Mazayev, furnished me gracious cooperation and assistance in connection with work in the Archive of the Foreign Policy of Russia.

#1.

A. S. Musin-Pushkin, the Minister in London, to N. I. Panin, Chairman of the College of Foreign Affairs, No. 68, October 31/November 11, 1774.

Most Serene Count, Most Gracious Sovereign! Letters received here yesterday from America emphasize in a most convincing way how firm, and so almost unanimous, is the intention of the local inhabitants not to obey any orders such as are inclined, however little, towards the confirmation of the right of legislating for them here; they are formally refusing General Gage not only all necessaries most needed for the troops under his command, but also the most unskilled laborers needed for the construction of barracks. It has already been decided by the general congress in Philadelphia not to export any American goods here, and not to receive there any from here. To supply sufficiently the city of Boston, blockaded on all sides, with all that is required. Beyond this, various cities and provinces are collecting voluntary contributions for the latter, and the sort of generous ones on which the inhabitants of the latter were able to subsist continuously, in a secure fashion, three years ago.

Such a situation justly alarms the administration here, and the more in that all the advantages which trade and factories

191

here receive, both from raw materials brought here from America, and from goods manufactured here and exported there, are well known to it. The local annual exports herefrom attain, in general, a value of no less than three million pounds sterling, while New York Province sends in six hundred thousand pounds sterling annually, and Philadelphia Province, often seven hundred thousand. Any shutting off of such exports, if it does not undermine all manufactures here completely, at least injures them very perceptibily.

(Rest of text of despatch in code.) An aroused France, and Spain, will not fail to intervene in the dispute between England and her colonists. Two frigates under the flag of the former have already appeared near Boston, loaded, as is heard, with various military supplies, while the latter has already despatched five warships from Ferrol, probably to America. Or at least, the Admiralty here has received a first-hand report about this in recent days from Gibraltar.

The Portuguese matter continues to arouse little interest here. Now, of course, there is no time to move into it with all the required force, and they are trying here to put off the carrying on of that negotiation. The Court of Lisbon was inclined to renew the latter again, when Spain cut short the latter with her improper invitation to the Bourbon Family Compact, instead of any answer to that Court to the memorial submitted by it to her.

With complete ....

Aleksey Musin-Pushkin.

Received November 23, 1774.

(AVPR, f. Snosheniya Rossii s Angliyey, 1774 g., d. 261, 11. 158-159. Original.)

#2.

A. S. Musin-Pushkin, the Minister in London, to N. I. Panin, Chairman of the College of Foreign Affairs, No. 8, February 3/14, 1775.

Most Serene Count, Most Gracious Sovereign! The merchants trading in the West Indies have presented their petitions for the greatest possible clarification of the consequences of American affairs to both Houses of Parliament, where they were equally rejected, because, in the opinion of the ministers, "all commercial considerations must already give way to the carrying out of those measures which have been occasioned now by the forthcoming conflicts between Great Britain and the colonies." As to what sort of protest was made on this to the Upper Chamber, a translation[1] of the latter is most respectfully attached hereto, and hopefully, the more opportunely, in that it explains to a considerable degree, in another form, a matter of such great importance as that of just how frightful is the declaration of the Americans as insurrectionists. The internecine war with them therefore seems the more unavoidable, in that they are pushed thereto by the extremity either of obeying all laws here, contrary to custom, or of fighting against that which is, so to speak, burdensome, and also restrictive of their natural and legal rights. Many wise and impartial people fear that the suppression of American trade, navigation, and fishing in Newfoundland, the changes in the charters granted them, and the reestablishment of a completely new form of administration, in the form of the destruction of their most treasured rights — *les Jurés, le Habeas Corpus & le Droit de se faire taxer par des Représentans*[2] — (which are considered unnecessary here), will not fail to force them, out of desperation, to choose the latter, but most dangerous, course of resistance. In case of the best successes there in the direction of the subjugation by force of those now disobedient, it will scarcely fail to be necessary already to rule them henceforth by force, and to entrust that solely to His Majesty. In case of this, not a little danger for freedom here is foreseen, and more still for the public credit. From the diminution of trade, the profits of all industries here are diminished, and finally the state revenues too, while expenses, on the other hand, are exceeding the latter most sensibly; in that, besides all other expenses, it has already been decided to add two thousand sailors and 490 marines to the existing number, at 52 pounds sterling per year per man; and in that the fleet here is therefore being put in such a condition that it would be sufficient, not only for the actual suppression of any American trade, but also for the protection of this island itself from any surprise attacks at some point. Already close to a hundred individual ships of the line are being armed in the ports here. Lord Sandwich, First Lord of the Admiralty, declared yesterday in Parliament that upon assuming his duties, he found the fleet in such a disorderly condition that in the last three years around 40 ships had been dismantled, while more already are not more useful than these. There was no timber reserve at individual docks, and he may now dispose of around 80 ships of the line for the entire service; but soon twenty more besides these can be outfitted; henceforth all timber construction is reserved for three years, along with everything that pertains to shipbuilding.

With the most complete. . . .

Aleksey Musin-Pushkin.

Received March 5, 1775.
(AVPR, f. Snosheniya Rossii s Angliyey, 1775 g., d. 266, 11. 18-20. Original.)

#3.

A. S. Musin-Pushkin, the Minister in London, to N. I. Panin, Chairman of the College of Foreign Affairs, No. 29, May 19/30, 1775.

Most Serene Count, Most Gracious Sovereign! When I had the honor to report to Your Excellency in the last post about the pliability of the Philadelphia Quakers to the well known peace proposal of Lord North, it was impossible to know in advance then that the royal troops had made an actual hostile attack on the provincial American militia around Boston. Their first volley brought around 50 men to the place, and produced such alarm in the province that the inhabitants who had hastened thither from various places with arms threw back the royal troops and pursued them as far as the warship itself, under the guns of which they could guarantee their safety from attack, with losses, however, of around 150 men. All this took place, Most Gracious Sovereign, on April 8/19, probably without any formal plan of internecine war. The Americans, considering this event the precise beginning thereof, besieged Boston with an impressive number of their militia, with the intention of taking possession of it. The ship which brought this very unpleasant news here yesterday left America in such a situation.

His Highness the Prince of Holstein-Gottorp arrived here three days ago. Tomorrow he will be presented by me to His Majesty the King, and day after tomorrow to Her Majesty the Queen.

The Spanish Ambassador Prince Masseran returned here again in great haste three days ago. Yesterday he was granted a private audience with His Majesty, and he has already been seen more than once with Lord Rochefort, for the sake, of course, of calming down any fear of the Court here of Spanish armaments.

In connection with the dissolution of Parliament, after adding up the account of my extraordinary expense here above the sum allotted to me by the Most All-Gracious One, I take the liberty of most humbly making an application, requesting Your Most Gracious Excellency that I be paid therefore two hundred and three pounds sterling and 20 shillings in paper money, which I am taking the liberty of transferring this day in Your Excellency's name to the Russian Consul here, Mr. Baxter.

As for the rest, I have the honor ....

Aleksey Musin-Pushkin.

Received June 10, 1775.

(AVPR, f. Snosheniya Rossii s Angliyey, 1775 g., d. 226, 11. 83-84. Original.)

#4.

A. S. Musin-Pushkin, the Minister in London, to N. I. Panin, Chairman of the College of Foreign Affairs, No. 32, June 1/12, 1775.

Most Serene Count, Most Gracious Sovereign! Her Imperial Majesty's warship *Saratov* has already actually arrived at Portsmouth Roads with the frigate named *Zapasny*, whither, of course, the two other remaining frigates of the squadron will not be slow in appearing. The appropriate representations have already been made for the permission to exit, and for the lifting

of quarantine for them, so that, after taking on board a sufficient amount of water, My Lord Rear Admiral Basbal will of
course not delay further in setting sail for the Baltic.

The ship recently expected here from Boston with despatches from General Gage arrived here three days ago, and
the news received by the Court about the skirmish which took
place between the royal troops and the provincial American
troops was printed this evening in the Court Circular, with all
the circumstances, which differed from the details broadcast
earlier only in this way, that the beginning of the military operations there is ascribed to the Americans, who, from their homes
and from hiding places, fired stealthily on the royal troops,
sent for the destruction of the military supplies stored by the
Americans. In the account of the Governor of Boston, the
malice and barbarism of the insurrectionists, who cut off the
ears of the prisoners who fell into their hands, and otherwise
mutilated them, is noted particularly. Among the dead are one
lieutenant and 62 privates; among the wounded are 15 officers
and 157 soldiers; and among the missing are one lieutenant
and 24 soldiers. The losses on the side of the insurrectionists
are unknown; however, they are considered to be very considerable.

Meanwhile, news came here yesterday from New York which
reveals that the inhabitants there, taking up arms, took possession of the fortress of the capital and the garrison, and the leaders of this uprising established a new administration, subject
only to the general American congress. However unpleasant
all such news received is in general, both for all the well intentioned ones, and also especially to the ministry, it is, nevertheless, still unknown what measures the latter will take for the
pacification of the internecine war which has begun there, and
for the punishment of the insurrectionists, but above all, we
must of course await the actions of the new troops sent thither,
which are arriving there, and the final decisions of the Philadelphia congress.

The French Ambassador, the Comte de Guines, returned

here last Sunday, and will be received in audience by His Britannic Majesty tomorrow.

With most complete ....

Aleksey Musin-Pushkin

Received July 4, 1775.

(AVPR, f. Snosheniya Rossii s Angliyey, 1775 g., d. 266, 11. 92-93. Original.)

#5.

V. G. Lizakevich, Counsellor of the Embassy in London, to N. I. Panin, Chairman of the College of Foreign Affairs, No. 38, December 8/19, 1775.

Most Serene Count, Most Gracious Sovereign! Last Sunday, the Court here broadcast news received from Canada, that the Governor there, General Carlton, deploying a considerable corps of troops in the neighborhood of Montreal, was preparing to go to the rescue of the fortress of St. John, formally besieged by the insurrectionists, and that he hoped soon, not only to force them to lift their siege, but also to expel them completely from the limits of the riverain province. The more this gave probability to the report about the speedy freeing of Canada from the enemy attempts which threaten it, the more the news which arrived here therefrom yesterday impressed everyone—that the provincial troops, driving away the corps under the command of General Carlton himself with losses, actually took possession on November 3 of the fortresses of Champlain and St. John, whose garrisons, consisting of 600 men, surrendered, with all the artillery and military ammunition. This unexpected news brings alarm to the ministry, the more in that the same fate must now be feared for Montreal and Quebec, upon the capture of which cities, all Canada may fall into enemy hands before they succeed in sending there a sufficient number of troops, about whose despatch it is already impossible to think prior to the forthcoming spring. The conquest by the Americans of such an extensive province gives them more resources, in that besides abundance in everything else, they will find there all materials needed for the construction and equipment of ships. In debates which took place yesterday in the Upper Chamber on the contents of the bill which forbids trade with the colonies, the Opposition was strengthened by these unpleasant reports for a delay of further discussion thereon until the forthcoming month, when the ministry, despite this, insisted on the necessity of the speediest passage of this ordinance, particularly now, when these details received from Canada show indisputably the decision already long since taken by the Americans to carry out hostile actions against the Government here, and to construct there a Power completely independent of Great Britain. On this occasion, the Opposition fiercely reviled that article of the bill being debated, which turns over all goods confiscated on ships to be divided up among the sailors, noting among other things that such an unbecoming incentive may inspire many to commit outrages and attacks on neutral ships, from which not only a formal complaint, but sometimes a war, may be produced. Despite everything, the majority of votes in favor of the Court overcame all these objections, and the bill was approved with some slight changes in favor of their islands of the West Indies, so that now there remains only His Majesty's approval for the final statute, which will be given hopefully within two days, and then the session of both Houses will be adjourned for three weeks.

His Excellency Prince Grigory Grigoryevich Orlov, with His Lordship General and Cavalier Bauer, departed three days ago for Holland, and the Privy Kammerherr of Her Imperial Majesty, Mr. Zinovyev, remained here for some weeks still to try the waters of Bath, the use of which was advised by a doctor here.

As for the rest, I have the honor ....

V. Lizakevich

Received January 2, 1776.

(AVPR, f. Snosheniya Rossii s Angliyey, 1775 g., d. 267, 11. 107-119. Original.)

#6.

V. G. Lizakevich, Counsellor of the Embassy in London, to N. I. Panin, Chairman of the College of Foreign Affairs, No. 42, December 29, 1775/January 9, 1776.

Most Serene Count, Most Gracious Sovereign! The administration here has already entered into negotiations with various German princes about the search for the required number of troops for their intended military operations in America. Although the terms offered each of them are still not known precisely, nevertheless there are reliable calculations about the supplying of the troops here, from which it appears that the Landgrave of Hesse-Cassel is obligated to give 12,000 men;
the ruling Prince of Brunswick. . . . . 4,000 men;
the Prince of Waldeck . . . . 500 " ;
the Hanau administration . . . . 500 " ;
adding to which three Scottish regiments, comprising in
all . . . . 3,000 " ;
and which they hope here to receive from Holland[3];
all these forces are to consist in all of . . . . 20,000 men —
foreign troops paid by Great Britain, not making mention even of the regiments levied by volunteers in Hanover and in other neighboring places, which are also carried in the total of this state. It cannot now be foreseen whether all this corps will be sent to America, judging by the rumored reluctance of these German princes to risk their troops in unknown regions and climes, so that probably they will be striving in every way to the end that at least the great part of the latter be used in Europe in place of regiments here sent out from Great Britain and Ireland. However this may be, they emphasize here with conviction that the entire army which it is intended to deploy in America next spring has up to 40 thousand men.

On the other hand, they are ordering there up to 30 various warships, which, joining the squadrons which are already in America, constitute a fleet sufficient for the total suppression, both of trade with other nations, and also mutual communications by sea between the colonies, and this method is considered the most reliable for leading the latter to the desired submission.

No reliable news has yet been received about the fate of Quebec, although in general everyone thinks that that city is hardly able to defend itself. Meanwhile, there is the report carried here by the royal frigate which arrived from Boston on the 21st that the Americans have again seized three English transports with troops and ammunition, and that with the heavy frosts which have begun there, the royal troops have already gone into winter quarters, and thus it does not remain to expect anything important from those regions until the beginning of spring.

As for the rest, I have the honor ...

V. Lizakevich

Received February 3, 1776.

(AVPR, f. Snosheniya Rossii s Angliyey, 1775 g., d. 267, 11. 121-122. Original.)

#7.

I. S. Baryatinsky, the Minister in Paris, to I. A. Osterman, Vice-Chancellor, No. 33, May 25/June 6, 1776.

Most Illustrious Count, Gracious Sovereign! [Text of the report is in code.] They are talking here more than ever about the affairs of England with her colonists, and they think that England is in extremely bad circumstances. The evacuation of the city of Boston produced, so they say, a great sensation among the royalists, and satisfaction on the part of the Americans. Among the public here, they are trying to verify whether they have the most accurate news that the English troops were expelled therefrom by force, but the Ministry here does not give out anything about this, and the English royalists who are here refute these rumors, and offer the assurance that General Howe left that place according to orders, in line with a plan offered to the Ministry by his brother. They are also saying here publicly that allegedly he, General Howe, at the time of the evacuation of Boston, weathered a storm of such magnitude that all his ships were so scattered that they do not know where a great part of them are. The last division of Hesse-Cassel and Brunswick troops has still not actually gone aboard ship. There is reliable news here to the effect that England so far is still not finding the money to engage transports for carrying these troops. The Duke of Richmond who, as Your Excellency knows, is a part of the Opposition to the present English ministry, said in confidence to some of his friends here that he thinks that the colonies will never agree to any peace proposals. On all occasions, the Court here continues to offer assurances to England as to the continuation of friendship and peace. A rumor recently came to me from a quite reliable source, it seems, that allegedly there is already an American emissary here with whom the Ministry here is having conversations. If this is really true, then this matter is moving forward very secretively, since they still do not leak out at all who such emissaries might be, and with which of the ministers they are having conversations. Commerce between the Americans and France is now in quite a state of activity. They say that, of the American ships in almost all the French ports, no small number came in under their own flags...

As for the rest....

Prince Ivan Baryatinsky

Received June 18, 1976.
(AVPR, f. Snosheniya Rossii s Frantsiyey, 1776 g., d. 312, 11. 120-121. Original.)

#8

V. G. Lizakevich, Counsellor of the Embassy in London, to N. I. Panin, Chairman of the College of Foreign Affairs, No. 45, August 9/20, 1776.

Most Illustrious Count, Most Gracious Sovereign! Since the time of my last, most humble report[4], the Court here has not received any news from America. On the side, letters which have arrived here are filled of course with exaggerated details about the measures taken by the inhabitants there for the enlargement of their forces on sea and land, the latter of which is now being allegedly extended to 75,000 men. However that may be, matters there have already proceeded of course to the most desperate situation, so that it will scarcely be possible to set them right save by the coercive force of arms, a decisive success of which will perhaps produce the pliability desired by the colonies towards an amicable settlement of the present disputes. And from this very thing, a conclusion may easily be reached about the concern of the administration, when the slightest failure there of the troops from here may involve the most ruinous consequences for the state here, through the irreversible loss of its extensive and populous settlements in the New World, for the preservation of which such enormous expenses have already been incurred, and for the bringing of which into a state of obedience, they will be forced to use and to risk all the power and resources of this kingdom.

In the Declaration of Independence published on July 4 by the general congress, all the earlier complaints of the colonies are repeated, concerning the rectification of which they addressed themselves in vain to the King, to the Parliament, and to the nation here; that not foreseeing now any hope for the rectification of the oppressions suffered by them, they found themselves compelled to make this solemn declaration, by which they declared the United Colonies a free and independent state, thus destroying henceforth all their former connection with Great Britain; and that as a consequence of this independence of theirs, the United Colonies have the right and power to declare war, make peace, make alliances, establish trade, etc., obligating themselves moreoever to sacrifice life, honor, and all their possessions for the preservation of all the above-mentioned advantages.

The publication of this document, and the promulgation of a formal declaration of war against Great Britain, offer evidence of all the courage of the leaders there. In such a desperate situation, they are awaiting with impatience here news of the junction of Lord Howe with the General, his brother, and about the operations which the full powers given to him for pacification are producing in America, cherishing moreover the hope that in case of the failure of the latter, they will succeed, by some sort of decisive blow against the enemy, in frightening the popular American leaders, and despite this, in winning over the well intentioned inhabitants there, and thus hastening the reconciliation with Great Britain generally desired.

As for the rest, I have the honor. . . .

V. Lizakevich

Received September 3, 1776.

(AVPR, f. Snosheniya Rossii s Angliyey, 1776 g., d. 274, 11. 152-153. Original.)

#9

V. G. Lizakevich, Counsellor of the Embassy in London, to N. I. Panin, Chairman of the College of Foreign Affairs, No. 51, September 16/27, 1776.

On American affairs, the administration has still not received so far any trustworthy indication, and now it is known only, and that informally, about the junction of Lord Howe and General Clinton with the Commander-in-Chief of the royal troops in America, General Howe. Meanwhile, American public reports which came here in the last few days, and private letters, revealed some quite important details about what transpired there; from them it appears that, upon the junction of Lord Howe with his brother, he sent by an officer a letter from himself to the American General Washington, which, however, the latter declined to receive, despite the strongest assurances that the content of the latter consisted solely of friendly good wishes and the usual civilities; that in the refusal of it, he insisted above all on this, that on the envelope of the letter he was designated simply as "*Mister Washington,*" not giving him the title of *General of the American Army;* that the general congress publicly approved this conduct of General Washington, thereby giving notice for the information of all its commanders that they are not to receive at all any letters or memoranda sent to them, in which their various ranks and commands were not precisely indicated; that Lord Howe sent some warships up the river, which occupied an advantageous position near the New York capital; that the aforesaid Lord, together with the General, his brother, as the two plenipotentiary commissioners from the King, published a manifesto in which, referring to the power given to them in accordance with the act recently passed by Parliament to receive obedience from the various American colonies, and to pardon all those who come to repentance, they promise a reward to all those who will cooperate in the desired cessation of the disputes and confusions which have arisen there, and hasten the reconciliation of the colonies with Great Britain, expressing moreover their readiness to receive their just complaints, and to strive in every way to rectify them, and to reestablish there the legal administration, and general peace, in accordance with the gracious intentions of His Majesty; that as a result of this the general congress formally issued a declaration, in which, while refuting all the contents of this manifesto, it noted that the sly exhortations and promises included in it are designed solely for the deception of, and the weakening of the firmness of, the defenders of American freedom, and that these false caresses must now push all the inhabitants into greater caution, and show them that the preservation of their fortunes depends, not on the justice of a monarch still, but on their own courage and unanimity; that the Declaration of Independence of the colonies had been announced to all the American standing army at New York, and was received with universal satisfaction and applause; moreover, the people there, in their rapture and passion, pulled down the statue of the King which had been erected in the aforesaid city, and showered on it various curses and rage.

All these details, about the accuracy of which there is already not the slighest doubt, clearly demonstrate the firmly held American intention, in everything and for all time, to throw off the yoke of dependence on Great Britain, and also that already, they are not keeping up the slightest appearances about their intentions. And these revelations must, it seems, bring about a universal change in the ideas of the nation here, when now already it has been clearly shown that now the main question is not the rectification of complaints, but the keeping, or the total loss, of America. It is still unknown what role the Opposition intends to play in the forthcoming sessions of Parliament, which will begin on October 31 next. It is confirmed only that, in pondering the crisis to which this important dispute with the colonies has now led, one already may not expect, beyond the present measures, any sort of action for the retention of their colonies in America except coercive deeds of bloodshed.

The boldness of the American privateers daily alarms the merchants here. In addition to the large number of ships intercepted by them in the Atlantic Ocean, they are already carrying out their searches near the Spanish and Portuguese coasts. The packet boat which returned this week from Lisbon brought here the news that one ship which departed from Falmouth, destined for the Mediterranean Sea, and whose cargo was valued at from 20 to 30 thousand pounds sterling, was seized by an American privateer at Cape St. Vincent, and that many of their privateers are cruising around the coasts here, and have captured seven other merchant ships, which have already been sent to American ports with their cargoes. This news brought not a little disquiet here, and raised very much the price of insurance on all ships departing for the Ocean and the Mediterranean Sea, so that the merchants here have already submitted a memorial to the ministry in favor of the establishment of convoys in all parts of the world, as a result of which it has been decided to arm four ships for the protection of trade here between the English Channel and the Straits of Gibraltar.

With the most complete....

V. Lizakevich

Received October 13, 1776.

(AVPR, f. Snosheniya Rossii s Angliyey, 1776 g., d. 274, 11. 167-170. Original.)

#10.

I. S. Baryatinsky, the Minister in Paris, to I. A. Osterman, the Vice Chancellor, No. 77, December 4/15, 1776.

Most Serene Count, Gracious Sovereign! [Text of the report

is in code.] Franklin arrived in Paris yesterday. The public is so taken with him that they no longer talk about anything else except the reasons for his arrival here, and there are such various reports that it is impossible to know on what they are really based.

I consider it my duty to report to Your Excellency about all the rumors in view of the sensation which he produced. Some say that he came here only to put his two grandchildren in schools here, and is himself proceeding to Switzerland, and is taking with him gold ingots to the amount of 600,000 livres of the currency here, with the intention of buying himself a castle there and quietly ending his days. Others say that he had only just arrived in Nantes when he wrote Comte de Vergennes, declaring to him that he had been sent by the American Independent United Provinces to negotiate with France, and wants to know how they will receive him here; his proposal consists allegedly of this, that the American United Provinces desire to conclude a treaty of lasting friendship with France, if, under present circumstances, she will give them aid against the English. If France turns them down, then they will be reconciled with England, and moreover they declare to France that in the reconciliation they will introduce such articles as will not be to the advantage of France. Still others say that Franklin was sent here as a plenipotentiary from the Congress, in order to deal with England about a reconciliation from here. About this last conjecture, some are arguing in today's political gatherings that although that conjecture seems somewhat far-fetched from one point of view, from another it is necessary not to leave it out of consideration now, in consideration of the fact that recently there has been no news from General Howe, since after the capture of [New] York, both armies were in proximity to each other, and if there had been a battle between them, there would already have been news of this; and therefore it is necessary to suppose that finally there will be some sort of parleys, and therefore this conjecture above all has a basis, that the most justified rumor is the one which there was here, that the Americans had sent deputies to General Howe in order to negotiate with him about a pacification, and that he did not enter into a negotiation with them because the deputies demanded that he recognize them as ambassadors from independent provinces, and that among these deputies was Franklin. In a word, according to the general opinion of our corps here, the arrival of the Franklins here is of course producing some sort of important *évenément.* Franklin allegedly offers the assurance, concerning American circumstances and forces, that the successes over the Americans proclaimed by the English were insignificant to no small degree, that General Howe captured only those individual places which were not necessary to the Americans, that the American army is great in numbers, is in very good condition, and is firmly resolved on defense, that the army of General Howe is also in good condition, but cannot winter at all in those places where it now finds itself, and that it is sure to be forced to go to Halifax. Deane, the American Commissioner here, about whom I have already reported to Your Excellency more than once, is doing much here to the advantage of the Americans. A few days ago, he sent out around thirty persons of the waiting officers on a French merchant ship, having armed it with twenty seven guns. The Ministry here is always trying to conceal the aid given to the Americans under the table, and therefore the passports of the officers sent out were issued to Saint-Domingue, allegedly for their private affairs.

Yesterday the order was given by the police to all coffee houses and taverns that there be no discussions of American affairs, and least of all especially of the connivance in the despatch there of French officers.

As for the rest, I remain....

Prince Ivan Baryatinsky

Received January 1, 1777.
(AVPR, f. Snosheniya Rossii s Frantsiyey, 1776 g., d. 312, 11. 245-248. Original.)

#11.

I. S. Baryatinsky, the Minister in Paris, to I. A. Osterman, the Vice Chancellor, No. 22, March 23/April 3, 1777.

… The English Ambassador is saying that they have news from America that discord among the Americans is increasing more by the hour by reason of the appointment of Washington as a dictator, that already a great part consider the power given to him contrary to a free government, and object that they find it more preferable to obey the authority of their former sovereign.

One fine young gentleman here by the name of the Marquis de Lafayette, a captain in the service here, son-in-law of the son of Field Marshal de Noailles, and relative by marriage to the Ambassador from here to London, in recent days requested permission to go to Italy, and went from there to Bordeaux, wherefrom the news has been received here that he arrived there with eight persons from the officers here, among which was one Brigadier, a person already fully mature, and that he engaged and armed a ship, paying five thousand livres for all this, and that he went to America with the intention of entering the service of the struggling colonies, that he, the Marquis, also changed his name and called himself Gilbert du Motier, native of the village of Cavaignac. Upon the receipt of this news the Government immediately sent a courier to stop him, but the courier arrived there too late; now a corvette has been sent after them with orders to arrest them where they overtake them, and to return them to France; the relatives of Lafayette are greatly outraged. His wife's first cousin, the Vicomte de Noailles, is now saying that Lafayette, before the day of his departure from Paris, invoking his honor, revealed his enterprise to him; that he formed this intention already more than six months ago; that in the last month he went to England solely with this view, that he take from partisans of the colonies there a complete report about all the circumstances of the Americans; and that after contacts with the latter he was so enthralled that, upon his return from England, he revealed his intention to Franklin and Deane, and asked their advice thereon; that they both praised his enterprise, but did not give him any advice, but on the contrary, said to him that they have need only of engineer and artillery officers, but that other officers were not necessary to them; however, such a dry answer could not deflect him. In departing herefrom, he, Lafayette, put his domestic affairs in good order, and took with him ready cash, more than a hundred and fifty thousand livres and a large quantity of muskets and ammunition. I am reporting to Your Excellency in such detail, for the reason that this produced a great sensation here among the public and at the Court. All are extremely impressed that such a young man, being in the very best circumstances here, took such a strange part, but along with this, they draw the conclusion that he is perhaps also clever in thinking out his whole conduct in this enterprise, and in the keeping of a secret. The King is very upset by this action, and I know that the Ministry is responding that if England takes them captive and deals with them with all severity, the Court here may not make any solicitations on their behalf.

As for the rest, with deepest....

Prince Ivan Baryatinsky

Received April 20, 1777.

(AVPR, f. Snosheniya Rossii s Frantsyey, 1777 g., d. 323, 11. 72-74. Original.)

#12.

A. S. Musin-Pushkin, the Minister in London, to N. I. Panin, the Chairman of the College of Foreign Affairs, No. 6, December 19/30, 1777.

... Some officers who were at the surrender of General Burgoyne,[5] have brought various despatches to the Court. The contents of the latter still remain up to now an impenetrable secret. Meanwhile it is known that the Americans did not fail to maintain with their prisoners not only all possible humanitarianism and indulgence, but also such courtesy that they cannot quite fail to marvel at it, nor to be extremely pleased with it here. This well-advised and perhaps calculated conduct earned them here a much better opinion than the former conduct, and therefore it already would serve to attract more sympathy to them.

The cities of Manchester and Liverpool have set various other cities the example of enlisting at their own expense soldiers for the service of His Majesty the King in America. However much the example of such patriotic devotion is pleasing in itself, it is doubtful nevertheless that it would produce the success desired, and on the contrary, it will scarcely fail to hinder it even. Good sense itself showed that from the beginning of the intentions here against America, the Americans were strengthened not otherwise than precisely to the degree of the premature preparations threatening them here. However much disposed the thirteen provinces were to differ among themselves and to be opposed to one another, nevertheless they were united by the danger from England, common and equal for all. Along with all this, the permanent local interests of these provinces left, moreover, in the northern ones a greater desire for independence than in the southern ones, which, because of remoteness still from danger, are now demonstrating their sympathies in this internecine war not otherwise than in a constrained fashion. The almost general subscription and collection here for the enlistment of one Manchester regiment, of one from Wales, of nine from Scotland, of 5,000 Irishmen and other Catholics here, and of ten battalions of Englishmen, makes the decision, of course, for an appropriate defense of all in America who have still remained in some wavering position; so that this new preparation here can henceforth be considered the knot of the general confederation there, and above all, the Americans, while transferring all trade to France, Spain, and Holland, will end all their accounts with Englishmen to their advantage, the more in that Englishmen do not owe them large sums, but they owe large sums here. This very consideration forced the merchants here not to sign their names, in order thereby not to bring down on themselves personal hatred.

The Ministry here has all this time been engaged especially both in drawing up a new plan of military operations, and at the same time, also peace proposals at times, if a suitable occasion should be discovered for this, and also with the compilation of those papers which it has been decided to lay before Parliament on February 2.

They are expecting General Burgoyne here with all his corps in a short time. The rumored defeat of General Washington did not have the slighest basis; on the contrary it is well known here unofficially that General Clinton, fearing to stay in the field any longer, led his corps to the city of [New] York, which he is fortifying with all speed and care ...

For the rest....

Aleksey Musin-Pushkin

Received January 13, 1778.
(AVPR, f. Snosheniya Rossii s Angliyey, 1777 g., d. 282, 11. 27-29. Original.)

#13.

A.S. Musin-Pushkin, the Minister in London, to N.I. Panin, Chairman of the College of Foreign Affairs, No. 2, January 9/20, 1778.

Most Serene Count, Most Gracious Sovereign! (The first paragraph of the report is in code.) From my earlier reports Your Excellency had already deigned to review sufficiently all the difficult position of the Court here, because of American affairs, and almost more even because of the French and Spanish hostile attitudes which have emerged at this time, and with such intentions for the future that it is necessary that this fear be as great; and how clear it is that the ministry is already thinking seriously about peace with its colonies, in order that thereby it may be more capable of thwarting the malevolent designs of the Courts of Versailles and Madrid. But just as various, still almost insuperable, difficulties now insist on this, so in recent days two of my recent acquaintences and very best ministerial friends of the Scotland Party showed, although separately, with equal passion (of course, not for themselves, but on the ins-truction of their protectors) every regret over the inexcusable omission to conclude a treaty of alliance with Russia, and the sincere desire to carry the latter now to completion, not only with the granting to Russia of all possible advantages, whatever happened to England, but asking my personal opinion, so to speak, as to how should be begun here now the important and inevitably necessary negotiation and what success I was able to expect therefrom. To avoid any direct answer, I moved away from this to the general political positions of one Court with respect to the other one, adding that the negotiation with the Porte was still not settled at all, and that all the necessary mea-sures with respect to it, and also with respect to other matters concerning the Court of the Most High, Her Imperial Majesty, have been agreed upon with the Vienna Court, and especially with the Berlin Court; something was said to me accordingly still yesterday, a second time, with the addition that England would with joy assume those subsidies which the Prussian King pays Russia, and if necessary, greater ones. Although surprise was expressed to my reply as to lack of knowledge, it was, however, without any foundation, since it is scarcely possible to have exhortation to such a negotiation, of which it is impos-sible to foresee the temporary or the general circumstances, or the most remote one in which it has been put by England herself.

General Lord Cornwallis arrived here three days ago from America with news of the end of the campaign and of the entry of both armies into winter quarters, the royal one in the city of Philadelphia and its surroundings, and the American one fifty versts away in Reading and around it. The numerical size of the latter did not exceed 16,000 men, and after the junction there-with of the corps of Gates.

It was proposed three days ago to the magistracy of this capital that it hold a subscription for the enlistment of soldiers and sailors against the rebelling Americans, but upon consid-eration being taken, it was decided by a majority of votes that any assistance to such an obviously and painfully reprehensible war as the present one, ruinous to trade here, would be inhumane, and the more in that at the present time no just representations towards a pacification have yet been made to America, concerning which it was then decided expressly to to address a special petition to His Majesty the King, for the drawing up of which the City Council is to meet tomorrow.

Today the session of Parliament was resumed. Lord George Germaine, the Secretary of State for American Affairs, who has recently become a widower, has asked for his discharge. But it is doubtful that it will be granted to him, both because of the difficulty of finding at the present time another capable person for such a now important place, and also for the sake of other reasons of a parliamentary nature.

As for the rest. . . .

Aleksey Musin-Pushkin

Received February 3, 1778.
(AVPR, f. Snosheniya Rossii s Angliyey, 1778 g., d. 288, 11. 5-8. Original.)

#14.

I.S. Baryatinsky, the Minister in Paris, to I.A. Osterman, the Vice-Chancellor, No. 17, February 26/March 8, 1778.

. . . [Text in code] I had the honor to report to Your Excellency in No. 1,[6] that Lamode Picquette had gone to sea with his squadron; he did originally sail out at that time. Then we learned that he went into the bay called Quiberon, lying below the city of L'Orient. It was then divulged here that he himself was sick, but that it must be expected hourly that he would proceed with the assigned cruise. All of us here have remained of the opinion that already recently it had been gotten underway. Now, Gracious Sovereign, it is known unofficially that Lamode Picquette waited in Quiberon Bay in order to convoy all the ships with military supplies which are to proceed from L'Orient and Nantes and go on to America, in which number there are also some American ships. They are acting in such an obvious way, as they give assurance, as a result of a treaty concluded with the Americans,[7] which allegedly has already been really signed and delivered. Serving as evidence of this is the fact that already, upon the conclusion of the treaty, there followed the speech of General Washington, delivered by him to the American troops at the time of the entry into winter quarters, that France would soon announce openly the aid being given to America. That speech was published in a newspaper with the title of *Courier de l'Europe,* in No. 16 of December 17, from General Headquarters at Schylkill. This speech is a real one of General Washington, since before the newspaper, I saw it in the hands of one of the friends of Franklin, who had it from the latter himself. The main articles of the aforementioned treaty are allegedly substantially the following: first, that France recognizes the Americans as independent; second, to have mutual trade; third, the Americans remain neutral if war breaks out between England and the Bourbon Courts, and that they will continue war against England only on their own behalf. Moreover, allegedly the Americans included precisely that if there should be war in the future between England and the House of Bourbon, they will never fight against England. In connection with conversation on this matter they have made the judgment that France made a mistake in waiting a long time to do this, since she could have had more advantageous terms with the Americans if she had made up her mind on this in the month of July last; then the Americans would have protected themselves with ties to France, and they would perforce have owed their independence to her assistance. Now, however, the Americans feel that they are winning freedom with their own resources, and they conclude, moreover, that France decided to move towards them only when she was accurately advised about the adventure of General Burgoyne. As to the factor of time, they think that the treaty mentioned must be announced in the month of next April; moreover, they say too that already the plan of war with England has been made here. The Spaniards will operate in the Mediterranean Sea, and France, on the Ocean.

Privy Counselor Mr. Fonvizin arrived here a few days ago. As for the rest....

Prince Ivan Baryatinsky

(AVPR, f. Snosheniya Rossii s Frantsiyey, 1778 g., d. 333, 11. 74-77. Original.)

NOTES

INTRODUCTION

[1]Karl Marx and Friedrich Engels, *Sochineniya,* XVI, 17.

[2]V. I. Lenin, *Polnoye sobraniya sochinenii,* XXXVII, 48.

[3]For a critical survey of the historiography of the War of the American Revolution, see N. N. Bolkhovitinov, "Voyna SShA za nezavisimost, i sovremennaya amerikanskaya istoriografiya," *Voprosy istorii,* 1969, No. 12; the same, "Nekotoryye problemy istoriografii Amerikanskoy revolyutsii XVIII v.," *Novaya i novyeyshaya istoriya,* 1973, No. 6; P. B. Umansky, "Problemy pervoy amerikanskoy revolyutsii," in *Osnovnyye problemy istorii SShA v amerikanskoy istoriografii.* Moscow: 1971; and others.

[4]Richard B. Morris, *The Peacemakers. The Great Powers and American Independence,* 147-190. Harper & Row. New York: 1965.

[5]*Istoriya diplomatii,* I, 382-403. 2nd Ed. Moscow: 1959; A. V. Yefimov, *Ocherki istorii SShA. Ot otkrytiya Ameriki do okonchaniya grazhdanskoy voyny,* 106-136. 2nd Ed. Moscow: 1969.

[6]"Politicheskaya perepiska imp. Yekateriny II, vols. 1-9, 1762-1777," *Sb. RIO,* vols. 48, 51, 57, 67, 87, 97, 118, 135, 145, and vols. 8 and 9 under the title "Diplomaticheskaya perepiska ..." St. Petersburg:1885-1914.

[7]"O vooruzhennom morskom neytralitetye. Sostavleno ... po dokumentam Moskovskogo glavnogo arkhiva ministerstva inostrannykh del." St. Petersburg: 1859. [Henceforth: "O vooruzhennom morskom neytralitetye."]

[8]Francis P. Renault, *Les relations diplomatiques entre la Russie et les Etats-Unis (1776-1825).* Editions de Granouli. Paris: 1923; William P. Cresson, *Francis Dana, A Puritan Diplomat at the Court of Catherine the Great.* L. McVeagh, The Dial Press. New York: 1930.

[9]See bibliography at the end of the book.

[10]N. N. Bolkhovitinov, *Stanovleniye russko-amrikanskikh otnosheny, 1775-1815,* 45-164. Moscow: 1966. English Translation: Nikolai N. Bolkhovitinov, *The Beginnings of Russian-American Relations, 1775-1815.* Translated by Elena Levin, with an Introduction by Lyman H. Butterfield. Harvard University Press. Cambridge: 1975. (In press).

CHAPTER 1.

[1]Merrill Jensen, *The Founding of a Nation: A History of the American Revolution, 1763-1776,* 593. Oxford University Press. New York: 1968; *idem.,* "The American People and the American Revolution," *The Journal of American History,* vol. LVII, June, 1970, pp. 22-23.

[2]"Proclamation of Rebellion," August 23, 1775, in Henry S. Commager, ed., *Documents of American History,* 95-96. 8th Edition. Appleton-Century-Crofts. New York: 1968.

[3]Thomas Paine, *Izbrannyye proizvedeniya,* 31, 56. Moscow: 1959; Bernard Bailyn, ed., "Common Sense," in *Fundamental Testaments of the American Revolution,* 7-22. Washington: 1973.

[4]Commager, *Documents of American History,* I, 100-101. Given all the progressive and revolutionary significance of the Declaration of Independence, we must keep in

mind that this document carried the imprint of bourgeois restrictedness, since it applied only to the propertied, only to whites, and only to males. Its framers—the American men of the Enlightenment and revolutionaries of the 18th century—did not note, or did not want to note, that 600,000 Negro slaves, many tens of thousands of indentured servants, the entire female population of the new state, and also the aboriginal inhabitants of the country, the Indians, were left beyond the pale of the Declaration. It is true that initially in the draft of the declaration, Negro slavery and the slave trade were viewed as "a pitiless war against human nature itself," but subsequently, on the insistence of the slaveholders of South Carolina and Georgia, supported by the Northern merchants and shipowners who were interested in the trade in Negroes, a whole paragraph on the condemnation of slavery was expunged. Andrew A. Lipscomb and Albert E. Bergh, eds., *The Writings of Thomas Jefferson,* I, 28, 34-35. 20 vols. U.S. Government Printing Office. Washington: 1905.

⁵"Proyekt instruktsii I. G. Chernyshevu." AVPR, f. Snosheniya Rossii s Angliyey, 1768 g., op. 36/6, d. 202, 1. 3. On the significance of the instruction, see V. N. Aleksandrenko, *Russkiye diplomaticheskiye agenty v Londonye v XVIII v.,* I, 38. 2 vols. Warsaw; 1897. On N. I. Panin's "Northern System" see also D. M. Griffiths, "The Rise and Fall of the Northern System: Court Politics and Foreign Policy in the First Half of Catherine II's Reign," *Canadian Slavic-Studies,* vol. IV, No. 3, pp. 547-569, Fall, 1970.

⁶*Sb. RIO,* XII, 16ff.

⁷F. Martens, *Sobraniye traktatov* .... IX/X, 242-259. St. Petersburg: 1892.

⁸For more details see I. Yu. Rodzinskaya, "Russko-angliskiye otnosheniya v shestidesyatykh godakh XVIII v.," *Trudy Moskovskogo gosudarstvennogo istoriko-arkhivnogo instituta,* vol. 23, pp. 139-190, Moscow, 1967.

⁹Martens, *Sobraniye traktatov,* IX, 259-287; I. Yu. Rodzinskaya, "Angliya i russko-turetskaya voyna (1768-1774)," *Trudy Moskovskogo gosudarstvennogo istoriko-arkhivnogo instituta,* vol. 23, pp. 139-190, Moscow, 1967.

¹⁰George III to Catherine II, October 1, 1775. *Sb RIO,* XIX, 478-479. An autograph copy in the French language is preserved in AVPR, f. Snosheniya Rossii s Angliyey, 1775 g., d. 36, 1. 2.

¹¹Suffolk to Gunning, September 1, 1775. *Sb. RIO,* XIX, 476-478. For the treaty project see *Ibid,* 483-487. According to a cynical remark of Suffolk in a letter to a member of the English Parliament, William Eden, the Russian soldiers would be "charming guests" in New York, and would civilize this part of America in a "splendid way." See M. Haiman, *Poland and the American Revolutionary War,* 3. Chicago: 1932.

¹²*Recueil des instructions données aux ambassadeurs et ministres de France. Russie (1749-1789),* II, 329-330. Paris: 1890.

¹³I. S. Baryatinsky to I. A. Osterman, September 27/October 8, 1774. AVPR, f. Snosheniya Rossii s Frantsiyey, 1775 g., op. 93/6, d. 303, 11. 100-103.

¹⁴A. S. Musin-Pushkin to N. I. Panin, October 31/November 11, 1774. AVPR, f. Snosheniya Rossii s Angliyey, 1774 g., d. 261, 1. 158.

¹⁵*Ibid,* 1. 159.

¹⁶About this, see A. S. Musin-Pushkin to N. I. Panin, February 3/14, 1775. AVPR, f. Snosheniya Rossii s Angliyey, 1775 g., d. 266, 1. 18 ff.

¹⁷*Ibid.*

¹⁸A. S. Musin-Pushkin to N. I. Panin, February 10/21, 1775. AVPR, f. Snosheniya Rossii s Angliyey, 1775 g., op. 35/6, d 266, 1. 28.

¹⁹Same to Same, May 19/30, 1775. *Ibid.,* II. 83-84.

[20]Same to Same, June 1/12, 1775. *Ibid.*, 11. 92-93.

[21]Catherine II to Madame Bjelke, June 11/30, 1775. *Sb. RIO*, XXVII, 44. Translation from the French made more precise.

[22]*Sb. RIO*, XXVII, 44. Catherine preserved subsequently her conviction of the unavoidability of the loss by England of her colonies in America: "What say you about these colonies which are bidding farewell to England forever?" she asked her correspondent a year later. Catherine II to Madame Bjelke, September 5/16, 1776. *Ibid.*, 119. And still later, on June 7/18, 1778, returning to an evaluation of George III, the Tsaritsa wrote: "Everything in the wrong hands goes wrong. Franklin and Deane do not at all deserve to be hanged because when they were in England, they represented things just as they were: they should have listened to them, and acted like Englishmen; it did not follow to irritate the Americans, and then put the burden on the King ..." Draft of a letter of Catherine II to an unknown lady, June 7/18, 1776. *Ibid.*, 154.

[23]Catherine II to George III, September 23/October 4, 1775. *Sb. RIO*, XIX, 500-501; AVPR, f. Snosheniya Rossii s Angliyey, 1775 g., op. 35/6, d. 37, 11. 4-5.

[24]Reports of Gunning to Suffolk of September 20/October 1, 1775, No. 60, and of September 26/October 7, 1775, Nos. 62, 64. *Sb. RIO*, XIX, 489-499, 503-505.

[25]Letters of Vergennes to Guines, the French Ambassador in London, of September 25 and November 9, 1775. Henri Doniol, *Historie de la participation de la France à l'établissment des États-Unis d'Amerique. Correspondence diplomatique et documents*, I, 178-179, 219. 5 vols. Imprimerie nationale. Paris: 1886-1892; A. I. Startsev, "Amerikansky vopros i russkaya diplomatiya v gody voyny SShA za nezavisimost," in *Mezhdunarodnyye svyazi Rossii v XVII-XVIII vv.*, 452-453. Moscow: 1966.

[26]V. G. Lisakevich, the Counsellor of the Russian Embassy in London, furnished detailed information about this in a report to N. I. Panin of December 29, 1775/January 7, 1776. AVPR, f. Snosheniya Rossii s Angliyey, 1775 g., d. 267, 11. 121-122.

[27]I. S. Baryatinsky to I. A. Osterman, May 25/June 6, 1776. AVPR, f. Snosheniya Rossii s Frantsiyey, 1776 g., op. 93/6, d. 312, 11. 120-121.

[28]V. G. Lizakevich to N. I. Panin, August 9/20, 1776. AVPR, f. Snosheniya Rossii s Angliyey, 1776 g., d. 274, 11. 152-153.

[29]N. I. Panin to Catherine II, October 10/21, 1776. *Sb. RIO*, CXLV, 243-244. 30.

[30]I. S. Baryatinsky to I. A. Osterman, December 4/15, 1776 g., No. 77. AVPR, f. Snosheniya Rossii s Frantsiyey, 1776 g., d. 312, 11. 245-248.

[31]Same to Same, March 23/April 3, 1777. *Ibid.*, 1777 g., op. 93/6, d. 323, 11. 72-74.

[32]A. S. Musin-Pushkin to N. I. Panin, December 19/30, 1777. AVPR, Snosheniya Rossii s Angliyey, 1777 g., d. 282, 1. 27 ff.

[33]Commager, *Documents of American History*, I, 105-107.

[34]I. S. Baryatinsky to I. A. Osterman, February 26/March 9, 1778. AVPR, f. Snosheniya Rossii s Frantsiyey, 1778 g., d. 333, 11. 76-77.

[35]About the cooperation of D. I.Fonvizin with N. I. Panin in the "Plot" of 1773-1774 for the purpose of the overthrow of Catherine II, and the preparation of a constitutional project limiting the Autocracy, see the details in N. Ya. Eydelman, *Gertsen protiv samodershaviya, Sekretnaya politicheskaya istoriya XVIII-XIX vekov i volnaya pechat*, 113-120. Moscow: 1973; G. P. Makogonenko, *Denis Fonvizin. Tvorchesky put*, 153-163. Moscow-Leningrad: 1961; and others.

[36]D. I. Fonvizin to his sister, F. I. Argamakovaya, December 31, 1777/January 11,

Notes 219

1778. *D. I. Fonvizin, Sochineniya, pisma i izbrannyye perevody,* 428. St. Petersburg: 1866.

[37]D. I. Fonvizin to P. I. Panin, March 20/31, 1778, *Ibid.,* 331-332.

[38]D. I. Fonvizin to his sister, F. I. Argamakovaya, August, 1778, *Ibid.,* 445.

[39]P. V. Vyazemsky, *Polnoye sobraniye sochinenii,* V, 91. 10 vols. St. Petersburg: 1880.

[40]N. I. Panin to I. S. Baryatinsky, October 11/22, 1779. AVPR, f. Snosheniya Rossii s Frantsiyey, 1779 g, d. 345, 11. 91-92.

[41]There exist quite a significant number of monographs about the events of 1771 in Bolsheretsk and their consequences, among which may be named the article of V. N. Berkh, "Pobeg grafa Benyevskogo iz Kamchatki vo Frantsiyu," *Syn otechestva,* Nos. 27 and 28, 1821: "Zapiski kantselyarista Ryumina o priklyucheniyakh ego s Benio-vskim," *Severnyy arkhiv,* No. 507, 1822; and also "Zapiski o buntye, proizvedennom Beniovskim v Bolsheretskom ostrogye i posledstviyakh onogo," *Russky arkhiv,* No. 4, pp. 417-438, 1865. One must distinguish especially also the work of A. S. Sgibnev, based on the materials of the secret file on "the Benyowski uprising" in the papers of the Irkutsk archives: "Bunt Benyevskogo v Kamchatkye v 1771 g., *Russkaya starina,* vol. 15, pp. 526-547, 756-769, 1876. Widely known also are the memoirs of Benyow-ski himself, published in Paris in 1791 in two parts, and then translated into all the basic European languages: *Voyages et mémoires de Maurice Auguste comte de Ben-yowski.* Paris: 1791.

[42]For more details see Eufrosina Dvoichenko-Markov, "Benjamin Franklin and Count M. Benyowski," *Proceedings* of the American Philosophical Society, vol. 99, No. 6, pp. 405-417, December, 1955.

[43]I. S. Baryatinsky to N. I. Panin, December 15/26, 1779. AVPR, f. Snosheniya Rossii s Frantsiyey, 1779 g., d. 344, 1. 173 ff.

[44]See Eufrosina Dvoichenko-Markov, "Shturman Gerasim Izmaylov," *Morskiye. zapiski,* vol. 13, No. 4, New York, 1955; James Cook, *Voyage to the Pacific Ocean....* II, 497-500. London: 1785; *Poslednyeye puteshestviye okolo sveta kapitana Kuka,* 85-87. St. Petersburg: 1788; James Cook, *Tretye plavaniye Dzhemsa Kuka,* 390-392, 395-396. Translated from the English by Ya. M. Svet, with a commentary. Moscow: 1971.

[45]"From the journeys of Vancouver and Puget and the maps attached hereto," it was later pointed out in a secret "instruction" to the Main Administrator of the Russian colonies in America, A. A. Baranov, "you will see that they themselves pointed out there those places as occupied by our industrial artels, calling them Russian fac-tories. Vancouver describes the manner of the Russians towards the Americans with the highest praise, saying that they have acquired mastery over the wild peoples not by victories, but by finding a way to their hearts. Noting from volume II of Vancouver's travels, that some of your industrialists gave the English charts of your voyages, the Main Administration assumes the duty of making you aware of this." M. M. Buldakov, Ye. I. Delarov, and I. Shelikhov to A. A. Baranov, April 18/30, 1802. U.S. National Archives, Records of the Russian-American Company, 1802-1867, vol. I, pp. 3-4.

[46]*Russkaya starina,*1876, vol. 15, pp. 765-766; *Poslednyeye puteshestviye okolo sveta kapitana Kuka,* 124; *The Voyages of Captain James Cook Round the World,* 377. London: 1949.

[47]*Russkaya starina,* 1876, vol. 15, p. 67.

[48]*Ibid.*

[49]V. I. Lenin, *Polnoye sobraniye sochinenii*, XXXVII, 56.

[50]On James Harris's mission, see the monograph: Isabel de Madariaga, *Britain, Russia, and the Armed Neutrality of 1780. Sir James Harris's Mission to St. Petersburg during the American Revolution.* Yale University Press. New Haven: 1962. A detailed analysis of this book was given by us in the journal *Istoriya SSSR*, 1964, No. 1, pp. 206-209. For the documentary materials on the negotiations of Harris see also: James Howard Harris, 3rd Earl of Malmesbury, ed., *Diaries and Correspondence of the First Earl of Malmesbury*, vol. I. 4 vols. R. Bentley. London: 1844.

[51]James Harris to N. I. Panin, April, 1778. AVPR, f. Snosheniya Rossii s Angliyey, 1778 g., d. 596, 11. 21-24.

[52]N. I. Panin to James Harris, May 6/17, 1778. AVPR. *ibid.*, d. 595, 11. 3-8.

[53]James Harris to N. I. Panin, November 26, 1779. AVPR. f. Snosheniya Rossii s Angliyey, 1779 g., d. 600, 11. 11a-13.

[54]N. I. Panin to James Harris, December 5/16-7/18, 1779. *Ibid.*, d. 599, 11. 15-16: *Mezhdunarodnaya zhizn*, 1974, No. 7, p. 159.

[55]Catherine II to I. M. Simolin, July 15/26, 1779. V. N. Aleksandrenko, *op. cit.*, II, 195-199.

[56]George Washington to Marquis de Lafayette, March 8/10, 1779. John C. Fitzpatrick, ed., *The Writings of George Washington. From the Original Manuscript Sources, 1745-1799.* XIV, 226. 40 vols. U. S. Government Printing Office. Washington: 1931-1944.

[57]George Washington to Henry Clinton, March 6, 1779. *Ibid.*, XIV, 196.

[58]Secret Report of the College of Foreign Affairs to Catherine II of July 31/August 11, 1779. The original is preserved in AVPR, f. Sekretnyye mneniya, 1725-1798 gg., d. 597, 11. 110-114. A copy was published in the book: *Arkhiv kn. Vorontsova*, Book 34, pp. 388-405.

CHAPTER 2.

[1]D. M. Griffiths, "An American Contribution to the Armed Neutrality of 1780," *Russian Review*, vol. 30, No. 2, pp. 166-167, 169, n. 17, April, 1971. (This researcher makes the special qualification that his goal is "more to broaden than to change" [*Ibid.*, 164] the most extended earlier interpretation of Isabel de Madariaga, but reference to the appropriate pages of her monograph shows that she presents the matter in question more accurately, although with less details). See Madariaga, *Britain, Russia and the Armed Neutrality of 1780,* 72 ff.

[2]"Most Humble Presentation" of N. I. Panin of December 20/31, 1778. TsGADA, f. 1274, OP. 1 (Panins), d. 131, 11. 245-251: "O vooruzhennom morskom neytralitetye," 24-27. St. Petersburg: 1859.

[3]TsGADA, f. 1274, op. 1, d. 128, 11. 252-254.

[4]"O vooruzhennom morskom neytralitetye," 29 ff.

[5]See, for example, A. S. Musin-Pushkin to N. I. Panin, November 28/December 8, 1778. AVPR, f. Snosheniya Rossii s Angliyey, 1778 g., d. 288, 1. 241.

[6]Catherine II to I. M. Simolin, November 8/19, 1779. AVPR, f. Londonskaya missiya 1779-1781 gg., op. 36, d. 345, 11. 62 and 66. Published in part in V. N. Aleksandrenko, *op. cit.*, II, 200-202. According to the calculations of Isabel de Madariaga,

during the war England seized 17 Russian ships. Madariaga, *Britain, Russia and the Armed Neutrality of 1780*, 374.

[7]Catherine II to I. M. Simolin, February 27/March 9, 1780. AVPR, f. Londonskaya missiya 1779-1781 gg., d. 345, 11. 2-6.

[8]Later it was reported that the fleet fitted out in Kronshtadt, divided into three squadrons, was sent for the defense of neutral navigation in the Mediterranean Sea, to the "heights of Lisbon," and to the North Sea. Catherine II to I. M. Simolin, June 7/18, 1780. AVPR. f. Londonskaya missiya, 1779-1781 gg., d. 345, 11. 10-11.

[9]For the text of the declaration of February 27/March 9, 1780, see "O vooruzhennom morskom neytralitetye," 64-66, and F. Martens, *Sobraniye traktatov*, vol. IX/X, pp. 307-310.

[10]Karl Marx and Friedrich Engels, *Sochineniya*, XXII, 25.

[11]Christian Wilhelm von Dohm, *Denkwürdigkeiten meiner Zeit*, II, 100-150, 5 vols. Helwing. Hannover: 1814-1819: Comte de Goertz, *Mémoire ou precis historique sur la neutralité armée et son origine, suivi de pieces justificatives*. Basel: 1801.

[12]Among the proponents of this viewpoint were such competent persons as Georg Martens, Guillaume de Garden, and also Bergbohm. Carl Bergbohm, *Die bewaffnete Neutralität, 1780-1783*, 239-247. Püttkamer & Mühlbrecht. Berlin: 1884.

[13]V. Leshkov, *Istoricheskoye issledovaniye nachal neytraliteta otnositelno morskoy torgovli*, 105-107. Moscow: 1841; V. Danevsky, *Istorichesky ocherk neytraliteta*, 69-77. Moscow: 1879.

[14]*Ocherki istorii SSSR. Period feodalizma. Rossiya vo vtoroy polovinye XVIII veka*, 128 and *passim*. Moscow: 1956.

[15]Samuel F. Bemis, *The Diplomacy of the American Revolution: The Foundations of American Diplomacy, 1775-1823*, 151. D. Appleton Century Co. New York and London: 1935; O. Feldback, *Dansk neutralitetspolitik under krigen 1778-1783*, 39, 77, and *passim*. Copenhagen: 1971.

[16]Herbert Aptheker, *Amerikanskaya revolyutsiya 1763-1783*, 229-230, 235, 243. Moscow: 1962.

[17]James Madison to Ingersoll, July 28, 1814. Gaillard Hunt, ed., *The Writings of James Madison*, VIII, 282-286. 9 vols. G. P. Putnam's Sons. New York and London: 1900-1910.

[18]George III to Catherine II, November 5, 1779. Harris, ed., *Diaries and Correspondence of the First Earl of Malmesbury*, I, 265; *Istoriya diplomatii*, I, 394. 2nd Ed. Moscow: 1959.

[19]James Harris to Stormont, December 13/24, 1780. Memorandum of a Conversation of December 7/18. Harris, ed., *Diaries and Correspondence of the First Earl of Malmesbury*, I, 355.

[20]F. Martens, *Sobraniye traktatov*. IX/X, 297. On the whole Martens, although he also gives an interesting, documented presentation of the history of the proclamation of armed neutrality, nevertheless is inclined to evaluate excessively the personal role of Catherine, to whom he in essence fully ascribes the main, if not the exclusive, authorship. Isabel de Madariaga is also partially inclined towards exaggeration of the role of the Empress. See Madariaga, *Britain, Russia and the Armed Neutrality of 1780*, 173 ff.

[21]See "Dnevnik A. V. Khrapovitskogo" in *Arkhiv kn. Vorontsova*, Book 9, 133, 485. Moscow: 1901; and also *Russky arkhiv*, 1875, Book 2, 123-124.

[22]This refers even to such an informed researcher as Francis Renault, who mis-

takenly thought that Russian policy with respect to Holland was passive. Francis P. Renault, *Les Provinces-Unies et la Guerre d'Amerique (1775-1784)*. 3 vols. Éditions du Graouli. Paris: 1924.

[23]The author considers it his duty to note that the deceased Yu. Ya. Moshkovskaya first invited his attention to the role of D. A. Golitsyn. The activity of D. A. Golitsyn is also illuminated in the work of Isabel de Madariaga, although not fully, and with account taken only of the Dutch sources. Madariaga, *Britain, Russia and the Armed Neutrality of 1780*, 151-154, 160, 168-169.

[24]On the views of D. A. Golitsyn on the peasant question, see V. I. Semevsky, *Krestyansky vopros v Rossii*, vol. I. St. Petersburg: 1888; and I. S. Bak, "Dmitry Alekseyevich Golitsyn: filosofskiye, obshchestvennopoliticheskiye i ekonomicheskiye vozzreniya," *Istoricheskiye zapiski*, vol. 26, pp. 258-272, Moscow, 1948.

[25]A. A. Bezborodko to I. A. Osterman, May 21/June 1, 1782. AVPR, f. Vysochayshye aprobovannyye doklady po snosheniyam s inostrannymi derzhavami, 1782 g., d. 8, l. 185. "The St. Petersburg Court went so far in its inflexibility," an unknown author of a survey of the policy of Catherine with respect to the United States, from the ranks of the lesser officials of the Russian Foreign Ministry, wrote justly later, "that Prince Golitsyn received a very sharp reprimand because he received and forwarded a package received from America, addressed to Mr. Dana, who was in St. Petersburg in the capacity of a traveller with full powers for his recognition as Minister of the United States of America." TsGADA, f. 15, d. 214, 1. 1 ff.

[26]I. A. Osterman wrote on this subject on May 6/17, 1782: "At the present time, when the Estates General of Holland has officially recognized Mr. Adams in the capacity of Plenipotentiary Minister of the United States of America, it is necessary that I advise Your Excellency that Her Imperial Majesty does not desire that you express in any way whatsoever her approval of this démarche. In this connection, Prince, you must refrain from receiving or visiting both Mr. Adams and any other person accredited by the colonies which have broken away from Great Britain." AVPR, f. Snosheniya Rossii s Gollandiyey, 1782 g., d. 28, l. 10.

[27]D. A. Golitsyn to N. I. Panin, February 7/18, 1780. AVPR, f. Snosheniya Rossii s Gollandiyey, 1780 g., d. 207, 11. 35-39. Simultaneously this report was also sent to I. A. Osterman. *Ibid.*, 11. 41-46.

[28]D. A. Golitsyn to N. I. Panin, March 3/14, 1780. AVPR, f. Snosheniya Rossii s Gollandiyey, 1780 g., d. 206, 11. 3-6.

[29]Benjamin Franklin to Charles W. F. Dumas, June 5, 1780. Albert H. Smyth, ed., *The Writings of Benjamin Franklin*. VIII, 82. 10 vols. The Macmillan Company. New York: 1907. A copy of Franklin's letter was apparently handed to D. A. Golitsyn by Charles Dumas and attached to the report of June 27/July 8, 1780. AVPR, f. Snosheniya Rossii s Gollandiyey, 1780 g., d. 208, 1. 36.

[30]George Washington. *Writings*. XX, 122.

[31]John Adams to the President of the Continental Congress, April 26, 1780. F. Wharton, ed., *The Revolutionary Diplomatic Correspondence of the United States*. III, 632-633. 6 vols. 50th Congress, 1st Session. House of Representatives Misc. Doc. 603. Government Printing Office. Washington: 1889.

[32]United States. Library of Congress. *Journals of the Continental Congress. 1774-1789*. XVIII, 866. 34 vols. Government Printing Office. Washington: 1904-1937.

[33]These instructions were given on November 27, 1780. See E. Albrecht, "Die Stel-

lung der Vereinigten Staaten von Amerika zur bewaffneten Neutralität von 1780," *Zeitschrift für Völkerrecht und Bundesstaatsrecht,* Band VI, Heft 5 and 6, 443, 1913.

[34]Resolution of the Continental Congress, October 5, 1780. *Journals of the Continental Congress,* XVII, 905-906. It was reported in the Russian press about the approval by the United States of Russia's Declaration of Armed Neutrality. *S. -Peterburgskiye vedomosti,* No. 17, 1781.

[35]*Istoriya diplomatii,* 396; A. V. Yefimov, *SShA. Puti razvitiya kapitalizma,* 400. Moscow: 1969.

[36]Copie d'une lettre du President du Congres au Chargé des Affaires de Sa Majesté, Philadelphie, octobre 7, 1780. AVPR. f. Snosheniya Rossii s Frantsiyey, d. 611 (1781), 11. 1-2.

[37]John Adams to D. A. Golitsyn, March 8, 1781. AVPR, f. Snosheniya Rossii s Gollandiyey, 1781 g., d. 218, 1. 24, 26. Still earlier, this resolution, along with the debates in the Continental Congress which preceded it, was transmitted to D. A. Golitsyn by Charles Dumas, about which a confirming signature on the document despatched testifies: "C.W.F. Dumas, Agent of the United States." From the protocols of the Continental Congress for September 1-October 5, 1780. *Ibid.*

CHAPTER 3.

[1]Secret Report of the College of Foreign Affairs to Catherine II, July 31/August 11, 1779. AVPR, f. Sekretnyye mneniya, 1725-1798 gg., d. 597, 1. 114.

[2]Protocol on the Matter of the Armed Neutrality of March 5, 1780, Written in the Hand of A. A. Bezborodko. "O vooruzhennom morskom neytralitetye," 89.

[3]D. A. Golitsyn to N. I. Panin, February 7/18, 1780. AVPR, f. Snosheniya Rossii s Gollandiyey, 1780 g., d. 207, 11. 35-39; A. A. Bezborodko to P. A. Rumyantsev, February 26/March 8, 1780. *Pisma A. A. Bezborodko k grafu P. A. Rumyantsevu, 1775-1793 gg.,* 62. St. Petersburg: 1900.

[4]Bemis, *Diplomacy of the American Revolution,* 181-182, 187; Morris, *The Peacemakers,* 173-190.

[5]The existence of the proposals of N. I. Panin is presented in reports of Vérac to Vergennes of September 1 and October 11, 1780. See Madariaga, *Britain, Russia and the Armed Neutrality of 1780,* 245-246: Morris, *The Peacemakers,* 169-170; and especially D. M. Griffiths, "Nikita Panin, Russian Diplomacy, and the American Revolution," *Slavic Review,* vol. 28, No. 1, March, 1969, pp. 13-15. Investigations carried out by us in the memoranda of the conversations of N. I. Panin with the French Minister, both in the archives of the College of Foreign Affairs (AVPR, f. Vnutrenniye kollezhskiye dela, "konferentsialnyye zapiski"), and also in the personal papers of N. I. Panin in TsGADA (f. 1274) and manuscripts in the Lenin State Library (f. 222) did not yield positive results.

[6]Marie Daniel Bourrée, Baron de Corberon, *Un diplomat francais à la cour de Catherine II, 1775-1780: Journal intime du Chevalier de Corberon, Chargé d'Affaires de France en Russie,* II, 322-323. 2 vols. Plon. Nourrit et Cie. Paris: 1901.

[7]Alfred, Ritter von Arneth, ed., *Maria Theresa und Joseph II: Ihre Correspondenz sammt Briefen Joseph's an seinen Bruder Leopold, III,* 252. 3 vols. C. Gerold's Sohn. Vienna: 1867-1868.

[8]James Harris to Lord Stormont, December 13/24, 1780. Harris, ed., *Diaries and*

Correspondence of the First Earl of Malmesbury, I, 357. *Russkaya starina,* September, 1908, pp. 457-458.

[9]*American Military History,* 87-88. Washington: 1969; J. Shy, "The American Revolution. The Military Conflict Considered as a Revolutionary War," in S. G. Kurtz and J. H. Hutson, eds., *Essays on the American Revolution,* 141. University of North Carolina Press. Chapel Hill: 1973; Don Higginbotham, *The War of American Independence.* New York: 1971.

[10]Doniol, *Histoire de la participation de la France,* III, 617-625; Samuel F. Bemis, *The Hussey-Cumberland Mission and American Independence.* Princeton University Press. Princeton: 1931.

[11]Doniol, *Histoire de la participation de la France,* III, 593-603, 626-638. Referring later to the various means of ending the military conflict, the Spanish Minister of Foreign Affairs, Conde Floridablanca, in a conversation with the Russian Minister in Madrid, S. S. Zinovyev, insisted especially on the advantages of the conclusion of an armistice. "With such a move," England "will not strengthen herself in the slightest, and will not show scorn, because already recently, she herself has been dealing formally with the colonies about peace," reported the Russian diplomat to N. I. Panin on December 16/27, 1780. See AVPR, f. Snosheniya Rossii s Ispaniyey, op. 58, d. 388, 11. 318-321.

[12]Griffiths, "Nikita Panin, Russian Diplomacy, and the American Revolution," 15-18.

[13]Vergennes to Vérac, October 12, 1780. RO GBL, f. 222 (Panins), karton IV, yed. khr. 1, 1. 348.

[14]United States. The President of the United States. *Secret Journals of the Acts and Proceedings of Congress From the First Meeting Thereof to the Dissolution of the Confederation, By the Adoption of the Constitution of the United States,* II, 412-423, 434. 4 vols. Thomas B. Wait. Boston: 1820-1821.

[15]For the full text of the instructions of Vergennes of October 12, 1780, see RO GBL, f. 222, karton IV, yed. khr. 1, 11. 348-354.

[16]Vérac to N. I. Panin, October 24, 1780 (O.S.?). RO GBL, f. 222, karton IV, yed. khr. 1, 1. 347.

[17]Harris to Stormont, October 16/27, 1780. Harris, ed., *Diaries and Correspondence of the First Earl of Malmesbury,* I, 338-339.

[18]Harris to Stormont, September 29/October 10, 1780. *Ibid.,* 336.

[19]Harris to Stormont, October 23/November 3, 1780. *Ibid.,* 339-341.

[20]Catherine II to I. M. Simolin, October 27/November 7, 1780. AVPR, f. Londonskaya missiya, 1779-1781 gg., op. 36, d. 345, 11. 15-17, and f. Snosheniya Rossii s Angliyey, op. 35/6, d. 68, 11. 7-11; *Mezhdunarodnaya zhizn,* 1974, No. 7, p. 157.

[21]I. M. Simolin to Catherine II, December 15/26, 1780, and the reply of Stormont to Simolin's note of December 16, 1780. AVPR, f. Snosheniya Rossii s Angliyey, op. 35/6, d. 310, 11. 24-29, and f. Snosheniya Rossii s Avstriyey, d. 632, 11. 5-7. As for the French Government, although in general it took a quite benevolent attitude towards the peace initiative of N. I. Panin, it promised to give its final answer only after consultation with the United States, since the King "does not have from the Congress any authority to proceed into any sort of bargain relating to it." See N. K. Khotinsky to N. I. Panin, December 4/15, 1780. No. 36. AVPR, Snosheniya Rossii s Frantsyey, d. 355, 11. 200-210.

[22]AVPR, Snosheniya Rossii s Avstriyey, 1781 g., d. 632, 11. 24-33. The full text of

this memorandum and a number of other documents were published by us in *Amerikansky yezhyegodnik 1975 g.,* Moscow, 1975, pp. 231-245.

²³For the rescript of February 4/15, 1781 and the full powers to D. M. Golitsyn of February 6/17, 1781, see AVPR, f. Snosheniya Rossii s Avstriyey, 1781 g., d. 632, 11. 1-4, 36-37.

²⁴*Ibid.,* 11. 5-6, 13-23, 44-49, and others.

²⁵Rescripts to I. M. Simolin, N. K. Khotinsky, and S. S. Zinovyev of February 4/15, 1781. AVPR, f. Snosheniya Rossii s Angliyey, op. 35/6, d. 318, 11. 80-83; f. Snosheniya Rossii s Frantsiyey, op. 93/6, d. 365, 11. 6-9, and others.

²⁶AVPR, f. Snosheniya Rossii s Avstriyey, 1781 g., d. 632, 1. 33.

²⁸Catherine II to I. M. Simolin, January 30/February 10, 1781. AVPR, f. Londonskaya missiya, 1779-1781 gg., d. 345, 11. 90-92.

²⁸I. M. Simolin to N. I. Panin, March 2/13, 1781. AVPR, f. Snosheniya Rossii s Angliyey, d. 320, 1. 125.

²⁹See Secret Report of the College of Foreign Affairs to Catherine II, April 9/20, 1781. AVPR, f. Sekretnyye mneniya, d. 593, 1742-1799 gg.; 11. 163-176 and 177-186.

³⁰Articles pour servir de base à la négociation du rétablissement de la paix générale, 21 mars 1781. AVPR, f. Snosheniya Rossii s Avstriyey, op. 32/6, d. 638, 11. 36-37.

³¹D. M. Golitsyn to Catherine II, May 11/22, 1781, No. 37. *Ibid.,* 1. 31.

³²Morris, *The Peacemakers,* 183.

³³*Ibid.,* 192.

³⁴John Adams to the President of the Continental Congress, July 11, 1781. *Revolutionary Diplomatic Correspondence,* IV, 560.

³⁵John Adams to Vergennes, July 13, 1781. *Ibid.,* 571-573.

³⁶See letters of John Adams to the President of the Continental Congress of July 15 and to Comte de Vergennes of July 16, 1781. *Ibid.,* IV, 575-577.

³⁷John Adams to Vergennes, July 21, 1781. *Ibid.,* IV, 595-596. Two days earlier, John Adams invited attention to the irregularity of the term "American colonies," which implied the existence of "a mother country," a "supreme political governor," i.e., to all that which had always been rejected by the United States. The "American colonies" were not fighting "with Great Britain." The country which was in a state of war was the "United States of America." See John Adams to Vergennes, July 19, 1781. *Ibid.,* IV, 592.

³⁸Morris, *The Peacemakers,* 210.

³⁹See also Lyman H. Butterfield, ed., *Diary and Autobiography of John Adams,* II, 458, and IV, 263-264. 4 vols. Belknap Press of Harvard University Press. Cambridge: 1961; Bemis, *The Diplomacy of the American Revolution,* 184, 186-187; Richard B. Morris, "The Treaty of Paris of 1783," in *Fundamental Testaments of the American Revolution,* 91-92. Washington: 1973.

⁴⁰I. M. Simolin to N. I. Panin, March 12/23, 1781. AVPR, f. Snosheniya Rossii s Angliyey, d. 320, 11. 157-158.

⁴¹I. M. Simolin to N. K. Khotinsky, June 19/30, 1781. AVPR, f. Parizhskaya missiya, 1781 g., d. 4, 11. 30-32.

⁴²I. M. Simolin to I. A. Osterman, November 5/16, 1781. AVPR, f. Snosheniya Rossii s Angliyey, 1781 g., d. 323, 11. 60-61.

⁴³Cited in Morris, *The Peacemakers,* 185.

[44]D. A. Golitsyn to N. I. Panin, January 29/February 9, 1781. AVPR, f. Snosheniya Rossii s Gollandiyey, d. 223, 11. 7-8.

[45]Secret Report of the College of Foreign Affairs to Catherine II, April 9/20, 1781. AVPR, f. Sekretnaya missiya, d. 593, 11. 177-186.

[46]Harris, ed., *Diaries and Correspondence of the First Earl of Malmesbury*, I, 450.

[47]*Ibid*, 415.

[48]The project of a treaty of alliance between Russia and Austria was transmitted to the Austrian Minister in St. Petersburg on January 19/30, 1781. AVPR, f. Snosheniya Rossii s Avstriyey, d. 1016, 1. 2 ff.

CHAPTER 4.

1. *Journals of the Continental Congress*, XVIII, 1155-1156; Edmund C. Burnett, ed., *Letters of Members of the Continental Congress*, V, 496. 8 vols. The Carnegie Institution of Washington. Washington: 1921-1936.

2. *Journals of the Continental Congress*, XVIII, 1166.

3. *Ibid.*, 1166-1173.

4. *Ibid.*, XVIII, 1168-1169; *Revolutionary Diplomatic Correspondence*, IV, 201.

5. Robert Livingstone to Francis Dana, October 22, 1781. *Revolutionary Diplomatic Correspondence*, IV, 802-805.

6. Francis Dana to Vergennes, March 31, 1781, and Francis Dana to the President of the Congress, April 4, 1781. *Ibid.*, IV, 343-344, 349-351.

7. Benjamin Franklin to Francis Dana, April 7, 1781. *Ibid.*, 353-354.

8. John Adams to Francis Dana, April 18, 1781. *Ibid.*, 368-369.

9. Journal from Amsterdam to St. Petersburg in the Months of July and August, 1781. Massachusetts Historical Society, Boston, Mass. Francis Dana Papers. Letters of Francis Dana to the President of the Congress, Samuel Huntington, from Berlin on July 28, and from St. Petersburg on September 15, 1781. *Revolutionary Diplomatic Correspondence*, IV, 610-613, 710-714.

10. John Quincy Adams Diary, roll 7, p. 162, and roll 8, pp. 87-88. The Adams Papers. Massachusetts Historical Society. John Quincy Adams also talked, in his letters to his father John Adams and his mother Abigail Adams, about his trip to Russia and impressions upon arrival in St. Petersburg, sometimes in a childishly naive way, and sometimes in a serious way beyond his years. Russia seemed to the young diplomat a mysterious country of "Princes and Slaves." Delighting in the splendor and luxury of the Courts of the capital, at the same time he criticized sharply the order reigning in the country. "A people who are in personal bondage cannot be happy," wrote the young John Quincy in a slight work composed by him upon his return from Russia, based on personal observations and literary data. "I met a man who paid a landlord 45,000 rubles for his freedom and the freedom of his children," wrote John Quincy Adams, and correctly saw in this fact evidence of how highly the Russian people valued personal freedom. Worthington C. Ford, ed., *Writings of John Quincy Adams*, I, 4-14. 7 vols. The Macmillan Company. New York: 1913-1917; *John Quincy Adams and Russia*, 6. Quincy, Mass.: 1965. In connection with the necessity of continuing his education, John Quincy Adams left St. Petersburg on October 30, 1782. Possessing the most promising abilities, the young Adams, according to the testimony of Francis

Dana, produced everywhere "the most favorable impression." Francis Dana Papers. Letterbook K, p. 188. Massachusetts Historical Society.

11. Francis Dana to Vérac, August 21/September 1, 1781, and Vérac to Dana, August 22/September 2, 1781. *Revolutionary Diplomatic Correspondence, IV*, 683-685; U.S. National Archives. Papers of the Continental Congress, 1774-1789, roll 117, pp. 562-563, 594-596 (Original in French).

12. Francis Dana to Verac, August 23/September 3, 1781, and Verac to Dana, September 12, 1781. *Revolutionary Diplomatic Correspondence, IV*, 695-699, 705-707; U.S. National Archives. Papers of the Continental Congress, roll 117, pp. 570-576, 590-592 (Original in French).

13. Francis Dana to Samuel Huntington, September 15, 1781, No. 14. *Revolutionary Diplomatic Correspondence, IV*, 710-714; U.S. National Archives. Papers of the Continental Congress, roll 117, pp. 582-589 (Original in French).

14. I. M. Simolin to N. I. Panin, March 26/April 6, 1781. AVPR, f. Snosheniya Rossii s Angliyey, 1781, g., d. 220, 11. 188-189.

15. James Harris to Lord Grantham, March 11, 1783. Harris, *Diaries and Correspondence of the First Earl of Malmesbury*, II, 36-38.

16. Francis Dana Papers. Journals, February 19, 21, 22 (O.S.). 1783. Massachusetts Historical Society; Francis Dana to I. A. Osterman, February 24/March 7, 1783, and April 10/21, 1783. *Revolutionary Diplomatic Correspondence, VI*, 275-390.

17. Francis Dana Papers. Journals, March 2, 20 (O.S.). 1783. Massachusetts Historical Society; Catherine II to I.S. Baryatinsky and A. I. Morkov, March 15/26, 1783. AVPR, f. Snosheniya Rossii s Frantsiyey, op. 93/6, d. 401, 11. 407; Memorandum of Conversation of Francis Dana with I. A. Osterman, April 12/23, 1783. AVPR, f. Snosheniya Rossii s SShA, 1783 g., d. 1, 11. 1-4. In reporting about the position of the Tsarist Government in the question of the recognition of the American Government, A. A. Bezborodko wrote: "Already recently there has been found here the Minister of the American independent states, Mr. Dana, who has already formally made his presence known. His recognition and audience have been held up pending the conclusion of the definitive treaty, and then a Minister will be sent herefrom to America." A. A. Bezborodko to P. A. Rumyantsev, February 28/March 11, 1783. *Pisma A. A. Bezborodko k grafu P. A. Rumyantsevu, 1773-1793.* 103-104. St. Petersburg: 1900.

18. Francis Dana to I. A. Osterman, April 27/May 8, 1783. *Revolutionary Diplomatic Correspondence, VI*, 411-415.

19. I. A. Osterman to Francis Dana, June 3/14, 1783. AVPR, f. Snosheniya Rossii s SShA, 1783 g., d. 3, 11. 1-2. The "Project of a Verbal Answer to the American Dana with regard to Recognition of him here in a Public Character from the American United States" was presented by A. A. Bezborodko to Catherine II, and received the approval of the Empress on May 29/June 9, 1783. AVPR, f. Vysochayshye aprobovannyye doklady po snosheniyam s inostrannymi derzhavami, 1783 g., d. 9, 1. 91. The "verbal note" of I. A. Osterman has been published in English translation. *Revolutionary Diplomatic Correspondence, VI*, 494-495.

20. Memorandum of a Conversation of I. A. Osterman with Francis Dana, June 3/14, 1783. AVPR, f. Snosheniya Rossii s SShA, 1783 g., d. 1, 11. 5-6.

21. Francis Dana to I. A. Osterman, June 5/16, 1783. *Revolutionary Diplomatic Correspondence, VI*, 495.

22. Robert Livingstone to the President of the Congress, February 26, 1783. *Ibid.,* VI, 264-265.

23. John C. Hildt, *Early Diplomatic Negotiations of the United States with Russia,* 26. The Johns Hopkins Press. Baltimore: 1906. In informing Congress of this decision, Robert Livingstone remarked that only the conduct of negotiations about a trade treaty, but not its signing, formed part of Francis Dana's full powers. See Robert Livingstone to Francis Dana, May 1, 1783. *Revolutionary Diplomatic Correspondence,* VI, 403-404. We must take into account that Robert Livingstone became Secretary for Foreign Affairs by defeating Arthur Lee in the election with the support of the French Minister. With unconcealed irritation, the latter [Arthur Lee] wrote Francis Dana: "The present Secretary for Foreign Affairs (R. A. Livingstone) is a decided supporter of Doctor Franklin and an enemy of Mister Adams . . . Everything that you learn or receive from him you may consider dictated by the French Minister." *Letters of Members of the Continental Congress,* VI, 379. For more details about the struggle of the Lee-Adams group with the supporters of the French orientation, see D. M. Griffiths, "American Commercial Diplomacy in Russia, 1780 to 1785," *William and Mary Quarterly,* vol. XXVII, No. 3, July, 1970, pp. 403ff.

24. *Revolutionary Diplomatic Correspondence,* VI, 482. About the attitude of the United States towards the armed neutrality, see also E. Albrecht, "Die Stellung der Vereinigten Staaten von Amerika zur bewaffneten Neutralität von 1780," pp. 436-449; and W. S. Carpenter, "The United States and the League of Neutrals of 1780," *American Journal of International Law,* vol. XV, 1921, pp. 511-522.

25. Francis Dana to I. A. Osterman, August 3/14, 1783. *Revolutionary Diplomatic Correspondence,* VI, 656.

25a. Francis Dana to E. Dana, September 30, 1783. Francis Dana Papers. Letterbook k, p. 229. Massachusetts Historical Society.

26. Catherine II to I. S. Baryatinsky and A. I. Morkov, June 11/22, 1783. AVPR, f. Snosheniya Rossii s Frantsiyey, op. 93/6, d. 401, 1. 56.

27. Instructions of Samuel Huntington to Francis Dana of December 19, 1780. *Journals of the Continental Congress,* XVII, 1168-1169; *Revolutionary Diplomatic Correspondence,* IV, 201.

27a. Commenting on the reply of the Tsarist Government, Francis Dana wrote Charles Dumas on June 9/20, 1783 that the ports of the Russian Empire were "opened for the citizens of the United States and their independence has received complete recognition, but as a result of the mediation, it was considered expedient to delay his audience until the conclusion of the final treaty." Francis Dana Papers. Letterbook K, p. 200. Massachusetts Historical Society.

28. I. S. Baryatinsky to Catherine II, June 29/July 10, 1783. AVPR. f. Snosheniya Rossii s Frantsiyey, 1783 g., d. 393, 1. 204. At first glance, our conclusion about the *de facto* recognition of the United States by the government of Catherine II may show a certain "modernization", but we must also invite attention to a short survey of the policy of Catherine II with respect to the United States which was drawn up on the basis of the materials of the College of Foreign Affairs by a lesser official thereof around 160 years ago, in which the author came essentially to an analogous conclusion. See Survey of the Relations of Russia with the United States during the Reign of Catherine II. Undated. No earlier than 1796 and no later than the first years of the 19th century (established by the text of the survey). TsGADA, f. 15, d. 214, 11. 1-18.

29. A. A. Bezborodko to I. A. Osterman, February 14/25, 1782. AVPR, f. Vysochayshiye aprobovannyye doklady po snosheniyam s inostrannymi derzhavami, 1782 g., d. 8, 11. 43-44. The Vice Chancellor, understandably, carried out this arrangement, and appropriate instructions were given to Morkov. I. A. Osterman to A. I. Morkov, February 21/March 4, 1782. AVPR, f. Snosheniya Rossii s Gollandiyey, 1782 g., d. 236, 11. 1-2.

30. I. M. Simolin to I. A. Osterman, June 7/18, 1782. AVPR, f. Snosheniya Rossii s Angliyey, 1782 g., d. 332, 11. 7-10.

31. John Adams to Robert Livingstone, June 9, 12, and 16, 1783. *Revolutionary Diplomatic Correspondence*, VI, 529, 539, 551-552.

32. I. S. Baryatinsky to I. A. Osterman, August 13/24, 1783. AVPR, f. Snosheniya Rossii s Frantsiyey, 1783 g., d. 397, 11. 43-44.

33. John Adams to President of the Congress, September 5, 1783. *Revolutionary Diplomatic Correspondence*, VI, 674-676.

34. AVPR, f. Snosheniya Rossii s Frantsiyey, op. 93/6, d. 403, 11. 62-84, 90-115, 116-126, 127-144.

35. *Ibid.,* 11. 58-60, 11. 145-156.

36. I. S. Baryatinsky to Catherine II, August 30/September 10, 1783. AVPR, f. Snosheniya Rossii s Frantsiyey, op. 96/6, d. 394, 1. 10.

37. S. A. Kilychev to I. A. Osterman, June 7/18, 1784. AVPR, f. Snosheniya Rossii s Gollandiyey, 1784 g., d. 271, 11. 9-10.

38. I. A.Osterman to S. A. Kilychev, August 23/September 3, 1784. AVPR, f. Snosheniya Rossii s Gollandiyey, 1784 g., d. 268, 1. 7; *Mezhdunerodnaya zhizn*, 1974, No. 7, p. 160.

CHAPTER 5.

1. J. M. Frederickson, "American Shipping in the Trade with Northern Europe, 1783-1880," *Scandinavian Economic History Review*, vol. IV, No. 2, 1956, p. 119; V. D. Harrington, *The New York Merchant on the Eve of the Revolution*, 198. Gloucester, Mass.: 1964; Alfred W. Crosby, *America, Russia, Hemp, and Napoleon: American Trade with Russia and the Baltic, 1783-1812,* 7. Ohio State University Press. Columbus: 1965.

2. N. S. Saul, "The Beginnings of American-Russian Trade, 1763-1766," *William and Mary Quarterly,* vol. XXVI, No. 4, October, 1969, pp. 596-600.

3. See D. M. Griffiths, "American Commercial Diplomacy in Russia, 1780 to 1783."

4. Walther Kirchner, "Ukrainian Tobacco for France," *Jahrbücher für Geschichte Osteuropas,* Band 10, Heft 4, December, 1962, p. 507. Taking into account the growing significance of this trade, the French Minister in St. Petersburg, Marquis de Vérac, sent the Tsarist Government in May, 1781 a special note on the subject of the "excessive export duty" which was being collected "on Russian tobacco exported to France." Catherine II gave this note the attention deserved, and appropriate instructions were sent to the Russian representative in Copenhagen. AVPR, f. Vnutrenniye kollezhskiye dela, d. 828, Report to Catherine of May 22/June 2, 1781, p. 4; f. Snosheniya Rossii s Frantsiyey op. 93/6, d. 91, 1.1.

5. Jacob M. Price, *The Tobacco Adventure to Russia: Enterprise, Politics, and Di-*

plomacy in the Quest for a Northern Market for English Colonial Tobacco, 95. American Philosophical Society. Philadelphia: 1961.

6. TsGADA, f. 276, op. 1, d. 668, 1. 1, 2-3.

7. Ibid., 1. 4. The document cited, signed on September 5/16, 1778, offers interest not only by virtue of its intrinsic contents. It takes on additional significance in connection with the fact that among the persons who signed it we encounter a name unceasingly dear to each Russian person: Alexander Radishchev. Owing to the nature of his mundane activity, the author of Journey from Petersburg to Moscow was involved with questions of the establishment of the trade contacts of Russia with the new republic and beyond. On July 1/12, 1785, in a letter to the then President of the College of Commerce, A. R. Vorontsov, A. N. Radishchev remarked: "There have been very few American ships this year. Up to now, only one, which arrived from London. It is desirable that they not tire of coming to us. But their correspondent here is not a very reliable man. Mr. Cramp thinks much of the wenches of the theater, and while playing cards, he reckons, by the thousands." A. N. Radishchev, Polnoye sobraniye sochinenii, III, 316. Moscow: 1952.

8. A. Wittfooth to the College of Foreign Affairs, December 26, 1778. AVPR, f. Snosheniya Rossii s Frantsiyey, d. 684, 11. 20-22, 23-24.

9. Same to Same, August 1 (?), 1780. Ibid, d. 688, 11. 3-6, 7-16.

10. Reports of A. Wittfooth to the College of Foreign Affairs of December 16, 1780 and January 9, 1781. Ibid, d. 688, 11. 19-20, 21-22, d. 692. 11. 1-2, 3-5.

11. A. Wittfooth to the College of Foreign Affairs, January 29, 1782. Ibid., d. 696, 11. 1-2.

12. Wittfooth to College of Commerce, July 30, 1782. Arkhiv LOII, f. Vorontsovykh (36), op. 1, d. 544, 1. 84.

13. Among the little known facts, still in need of additional confirmation, about indirect Russo-American connections in the period of the War of the American Revolution is the curious episode of the construction by one A. Bell (to all appearances, this was the customary pseudonym of the American Samuel Sayre who was in Russia) "of a ship for the colonies of Great Britain which have revolted" in Archangel in 1781. Learning about this development from a letter of A. Bell to Franklin, Catherine II ordered the Governor-General of Archangel, A. P. Melgunov, "to investigate" this matter in detail, and in any "decent way to obstruct the construction of ships for the Americans, not allowing it to take place except by well known and reliable people." The aforementioned ship was built and "allowed to go to sea," wherewith Melgunov requested that he be advised "whether there is not something doubtful in this departure of the ship." A. A. Bezborodko informed the Governor-General on July 3/14, 1781 that Catherine II "deigned to respond that Your Excellency acted very well in permitting the ship to depart . . . and henceforth obstacles must not be put to their departure, unless obvious signs should appear that the Americans are building the latter on their account, in which case, Your Excellency should report to Her Majesty." Russky arkhiv, 1893, Book 1, No. 3, p. 314. For details about Samuel Sayre's activity in Russia, see D. M. Griffiths, "American Commercial Diplomacy in Russia, 1780 to 1783."

14. "Circular Letter Issued by the British Foreign Office, 1777. The London Chronicle, June 17-19, 1777," Pennsylvania Magazine of History and Biography, vol. XVI., 1892, pp. 463-464.

15. I. M. Simolin to I. A. Osterman, December 7/18, 1781. AVPR, f. Snosheniya Rossii s Angliyey, op. 35/6, d. 323, 11. 116-118.

16. I. M. Simolin to I. A. Osterman, April 18/29, 1783. *Ibid.*, d. 341, 1. 18.

17. TsGADA, f. 19, d. 360, 1. 7.

18. *Arkhiv kn. Vorontsova*, Book 34, pp. 388-405; AVPR, f. Sekretnyye mneniya, 1725-1798, kn. 597, pp. 100-114.

19. Francis Dana to J. Jackson, February 17/28, 1782, and to John Adams, April 12/23, 1782. Francis Dana Papers. Letterbook K, pp. 13-14, 26-29; Letterbook H (Official Letters), pp. 94-114. Massachusetts Historical Society.

20. D. M. Ladygin, *Izvestiye v Amerikye o seleniyakh anglitskikh, v tom chislye nynye pod nazvaniyem Soyedinyonnykh Provintsiy, vybrano perechnem iz novyeyshikh o tom prostranno sochinitelyey,* 58-59. St. Petersburg: January, 1783.

21. *Yezhyenedelnyye izvestiya volnogo ekonomicheskogo obshchestva 1788 goda,* vol. 1, pp. 164-165.

22. *Von den Handlungsvortheilen, welche aus der Unabhängigkeit der Vereinigten Staaten von Nord-Amerika für das russische Reich entspringen,* 5. Ein Versuch von M. Karl Philip Michael Snell, Rektor der Domschule zu Riga, bey Johan Friedrich Hartknoch, 1783.

23. *Ibid.,* 3-6.

24. *Ibid.,* 9, 29.

25. *Ibid.,* 43-44.

26. Francis Dana to D. MacNeill, June 27, 1783. Francis Dana Papers. Letterbook K, p. 208. Massachusetts Historical Society.

27. *Revolutionary Diplomatic Correspondence,* VI, 502-503; 739; Crosby, *America, Russia, Hemp, and Napoleon,* 40-44. Francis Dana returned to Boston in December, 1783 on the ship *Kingston,* after a 95-day trip. See letters of Francis Dana to E. Dana, September 30, 1783, and to the President of the Congress, December 17, 1783. Francis Dana Papers. Letterbook K, p. 229, Massachusetts Historical Society. *Revolutionary Diplomatic Correspondence,* VI, 739.

28. *Neues St. Petersburgisches Journal vom Jahre 1784,* 372; J. D. Phillips, "Salem Opens American Trade with Russia," *The New England Quarterly,* vol. XIV, No. 4, December, 1941, pp. 685-689; Samuel E. Morison, *The Maritime History of Massachusetts, 1783-1860.* 154. Houghton, Mifflin Co. Boston: 1941.

29. United States. Secretary of State. *Diplomatic Correspondence of the United States of America from the Signing of the Definitive Treaty of Peace, 10th September, 1783 to the Adoption of the Constitution, March 4, 1789,* I, 110-116. 7 vols. Printed by Francis Preston Blair. Washington: 1833-1834.

30. John Adams, Benjamin Franklin, and Thomas Jefferson to I. S. Baryatinsky, September 22, 1784. AVPR, f. Snosheniya Rossii s Frantsiyey, 1784 g., op. 93/6, d. 411. 1. 201.

31. Humphrey to I. S. Baryatinsky, September 22, 1784, *Ibid.,* 1. 198.

32. I. S. Baryatinsky to Catherine II, September 15/26, 1784. *Ibid.,* 11. 196-197.

33. Quoted in Hildt, *Early Diplomatic Negotiations.* 30, n91.

34. J. D. Phillips, "Salem Opens American Trade with Russia."

35. TsGADA, f. 19, op. 1, d. 262. "On the Arrival of Foreign Ships in the Port of Kronshtadt." 1743-1810, 14 parts.

36. TsGADA, f. 19, op. 1, d. 262, ch. XI. Kronshtadt Reports, 1781-1784.

37. TsGADA, f. 19, op. 1, 1. 262, ch. XII, 1. 93.

38. *Ibid.*, 1. 94.

39. *Ocherki istorii SSSR,* 128.

40. TsGADA, f. 19, op. 1, d. 433 (from the papers of A. K. Razumovsky), 1. 83.

41. *Politichesky zhurnal,* Pt. V, 1791, pp. 183-184.

42. TsGADA, f. 168, d. 166, 1. 3.

43. John J. Oddy, *European Commerce . . .,* 126. London, W. J. & J. Richardson, 1805; Wilhelm Christian Friebe, *Ueber Russlands Handel, landwirthschaftliche Kultur, Industrie und Produkte.* Gerstenberg und Dittmar. Gotha: 1796-1798; TsGADA, f. 19, op. 1, d. 262, ch. XIII, 1. 139.

44. See "Vzglyad na torgovyye snosheniya mezhdu Rossiyskoyu imperiyeyu i Amerikanskimi Soyedinyonnymi Shtatami," June 9/21, 1808. TsGAOR, f. 907 (A. Ya. Dashkov), op. 1, d. 107, 11. 55-100.

45. Timothy A. Pitkin, *Statistical View of the Commerce of the United States of America,* 230, 257. New Haven, Durrie & Peck, 1835.

46. A. Rasch, "American Trade in the Baltic, 1783-1807," *Scandinavian Economic History Review,* vol XIII, No. 1, p. 24, 1965.

CHAPTER 6.

1. As is well known, A. N. Radishchev had already first developed the theme of Benjamin Franklin and M. V. Lomonosov in his undying *Journey from St. Petersburg to Moscow* (1790). Comparatively recently a series of special works was published in which the history of Russo-American scientific and cultural ties in the 18th century received, finally, more or less complete illumination: Eufrosina Dvoichenko-Marcoff, "Benjamin Franklin, the American Philosophical Society, and the Russian Academy of Sciences," *Proceedings* of the American Philosophical Society, August. 1947, vol. 91, No. 3; *idem.,* "The American Philosophical Society and Early Russian-American Relations," *ibid.,* 1950, vol. 94, No. 6; *idem.,* "K istorii russko-amerikan-skikh nauchnykh svyazyey vtoroy poloviny XVIII v.," *Sovetskoye slavyanovedeniye,* 1966, No. 2; M. I. Radovsky, *Venyamin Franklin i yego svyazi s Rossiyey.* Moscow-Leningrad: 1958; G. M. Lester, "Znakomstvo uchyonykh Severnoy Ameriki kolonial-nogo perioda s rabotami M. V. Lomonosova i Peterburgskoy akademii nauk," *Voprosy istorii yestyestvoznaniya i tekhniki,* No. 12, Moscow, 1962; N. N. Bolkhovitinov, "Stanov-leniye nauchnykh i kulturnykh svyazyey mezhdu Amerikoy i Rossiyey," *Istoriya SSSR,* 1965, No. 5; *idem.,* "B. Franklin i M. V. Lomonosov: iz istorii pervykh nauchnykh svyazyey mezhdu Rossiyey i Amerikoy," *Novaya i novyeyshaya istoriya,* 1973, No. 3.

2. A. N. Radischev, *Polnoye sobraniye sochineniy,* I, 391. Moscow-Leningrad: 1938.

3. *Experiments and Observations on Electricity made at Philadelphia in America by Mr. Benjamin Franklin and Communicated in Several Letters to Mr. P. Collinson, of London, F.R.S.* London: 1751. A much later edition of *Experiments* was sent by Benjamin Franklin to Russia with the author's signature: "From the Author." *Experiments and Observations. . .* 2 vols. London: 1769. See also Benjamin Franklin, *Opyty i nablyudeniya nad elektrichestvom.* Moscow-Leningrad: 1956.

4. The scientific work of Benjamin Franklin was described in a masterly way by

Pyotr Leonidovich Kapitsa in a report of January 17, 1956 in connection with the 250th anniversary of the birthday of the great American: *Vestnik AN SSSR*, 1956, No. 2, pp. 65-75. P. L. Kapitsa, *Zhizn dlya nauki. Lomonosov, Franklin, Rezerford, Lanzheven*, 21-35. Moscow: 1965. Recently, interesting works about Benjamin Franklin, Franz Aepinus, and G. Cavendish have been published by Professor R. W. Home of Melbourne University: R. W. Home, "Franklin's Electrical Atmospheres," *The British Journal for the History of Science* 1972, vol. 6, No. 22, pp. 131-151, *passim*.

5. P. L. Kapitsa, "Nauchnaya deyatelnost B. Franklina," *Vestnik AN SSSR*, 1956, No. 2, p. 72.

6. *S.-Peterburskiye vedomosti*, June 12/23, 1752, No. 47, pp. 371-372.

7. M. V. Lomonosov to P. P. Shuvalov, July 26/August 6, 1753. G.-V. Rikhman, *Trudy po fizikye*, 545. Moscow: 1956. On the significance of the works of G.-V. Rikhman see also: T. P. Kravets and M. I. Radovsky, "K 200-lyetiyu so dnya smerti akademika G.-V. Rikhmana," *Uspekhi fizicheskikh nauk*, vol. II, No. 2, 1953.

8. See for example the works of G.-V. Rikhman first published in 1956: *Razbor soobshcheniy po nedavno izobretennom sposobeye otvrashchat molniyu ot zdaniy; Razmyshleniya, utverzhdennyye na opyte, o skhodstvye iskusstvennogo elektrichestva s elektrichestvom yestyestvennym, porozhdennym, molniyey, i o sposobye otvrashchat molniyu; Izvestiye o nablyudeniyakh, imyeyushchikh byt proizvedennym nad grozovym elektrichestvom..; Franklinovy opyty;* and many others. See G.-V. Rikhman, *Trudy po fizikye.*

9. M. V. Lomonosov, *Polnoye sobraniye sochineniy*, III, 15-99. Moscow-Leningrad, 1952.

10. *Ibid.*, 121-123, and also 147-149.

11. *Ibid.*, 103.

12. *Ibid.*, 105.

13. For details about the life and activity of Aepinus see R. W. Home, "Science as a Career in Eighteenth Century Russia: The Case of F.U.T. Aepinus," *The Slavonic and East European Review*, vol. 41, 1973, pp. 75-94.

14. F. U. T. Aepinus, *Teoriya elektrichestva i magnetizma*, 10-11. Leningrad: 1951. (For numerous references to Benjamin Franklin, see, for example, p. 561).

15. M. I. Radovsky, *Venyamin Franklin i yego svyazi s Rossiyey*, 8.

16. See R. W. Home, "Aepinus and the British Electricians: The Dissemination of a Scientific Theory," *Isis*, vol. 63, No. 217, 1972, pp. 190-204.

17. James Bowdoin to Benjamin Franklin, November 12, 1753, and Franklin to Bowdoin, December 13, 1753. Leonard W. Labaree, ed., *The Papers of Benjamin Franklin*, V, 112, 154-155. 17 vols. Yale University Press. New Haven: 1959-1973.

18. *Papers of Benjamin Franklin*, V, 219-220. There is also reason to think that known to Benjamin Franklin was the work of Georg Wilhelm Rikhman, published in the notes of the Petersburg Academy of Sciences (vol. XIV). *Ibid.*, VII, 332; G. W. Richmann, "De electricitate in corporibus producenda nova tentamina," *Commentarii Academiae Scientiarum Imperialis Petropolitanae*, vol XIV (1744-1746). (*Commentarii*, 1751). pp. 299-324.

19. Benjamin Franklin to Ezra Stiles, May 29, 1763. *Papers of Benjamin Franklin*, X, 265. Franklin gave a high evaluation to the works of F. U. T. Aepinus earlier, in particular in letters to W. Heberden of June 7, 1759 and to C. Colden of February 26, 1763, *Ibid.*, VIII, 395, and X, 204.

20. For more details see G. M. Lester, "Znakomstvo uchyonykh Severnoy Ameriki . . .", 134.

21. Letters of Benjamin Franklin to C. Colden of February 26, 1763, and to Ezra Stiles of May 29, 1763. Papers of Benjamin Franklin, X, 202, 265-266.

22. Papers of Ezra Stiles. Temometrical Register, vol. I. An Extract from W. Watson's account read to the Royal Society May 1761, of artificial cold produced at Petersburg by J. Brown, by which mercury was frozen: an account whereof in Latin being first laid before the Royal Academy at Petersburg by Professor Braunius and then sent to the Royal Society in London, who appointed W. Watson to give a summary account of it (4 p.). Yale University, Beineke Rare Book and Manuscript Library, New Haven, Conn. Xerox copies of the documents mentioned here were received by us during a stay at Yale University in September, 1975, thanks to the gracious cooperation of Professor E. Morgan and Professor G. Selesky. Eufrosina M. Dvoichenko-Markoff first discovered the copies with the letter of Stiles to Braun and Lomonosov in 1954. Sovetskoye slavyanovedeniye, 1966, No. 2, p. 44.

23. Ezra Stiles to I. A. Braun, May 15, 1765. Papers of Ezra Stiles. Yale University. Only many years later, in February, 1786, success was finally achieved in repeating, in Salem, the experiments of Braun on the freezing of mercury. Ibid. Ezra Stiles, Literary Diary, vol. 12, February 3, 1786.

24. Ezra Stiles to M. V. Lomonosov, February 20, 1765. G. M. Lester,."Znakomstvo uchyonykh Severnoy Ameriki . . . ," 45-47, and Papers of Dr. Franklin, vol. 49, p. 19. The American Philosophical Society, Philadelphia, Pa. A Xerox copy of the letter of Ezra Stiles to M. V. Lomonosov in the Latin language on four pages was received by us during a research trip in the United States in 1968.

25. The viewpoint that allegedly a sea free of ice spread out at the pole was widespread from the 16th century, and was preserved right up to the beginning of the 20th century. Only the drift of the Fram (1895-1896) and the reaching of the North Pole by Perry in 1909 definitely showed the mistaken nature of this view. For the details, see L. S. Berg, "Lomonosov i pervoye russkoye plavaniye dlya otyskaniya severo-vostochnogo prokhoda," Izvestiya Geograficheskogo obshchestva, 1940, No. 6.

26. Ezra Stiles to Benjamin Franklin, February 20, 1765. Papers of Benjamin Franklin, XII, 71-77.

27. Sovetskoye slavyanovedeniye, 1966, No. 2, p. 44.

28. Benjamin Franklin to Ezra Stiles, July 5, 1765. Papers of Benjamin Franklin, XII, 194-196. Concerning Franklin's interest in Russian geographical discoveries and his familiarity with the works of G. F. Miller, G. V. Steller, S. P. Krasheninnikov, and Ya. Ya. Stählin, see Papers of Benjamin Franklin, X, 90-92, 94, 268. See also Sovetskoye slavyanovedeniye, 1966, No. 4, p. 46.

29. Papers of Benjamin Franklin, XII, 71-72, n8.

30. Benjamin Franklin to F. U. T. Aepinus, London, June 6, 1766. The original in the English language is preserved in: Lewis-Neilson Papers. W. D. Lewis. Miscellaneous Letters and Documents. The Historical Society of Pennsylvania, Philadelphia, Pa. The letter was published by us for the first time in Amerikansky yezhyegodnik. 1971. Moscow, 1971, pp. 330-331. The ties between the two scholars continued to be preserved subsequently, about which the letter of Aepinus to Franklin of February 1/12, 1783, preserved in this same archive, in particular, offers evidence.

31. Benjamin Franklin to B. Dubourg, March 10, 1773. *Writings of Benjamin Franklin,* VI, 23-26.

32. *Acta Academiae Scientiarum Imperialis Petropolitanae pro anno MDCCLXXII,* 26. St. Petersburg: 1780.

33. D. A. Golitsyn to Benjamin Franklin, January 28, 1777. Eufrosina Dvoichenko-Marcoff, "Benjamin Franklin . . . ," *Proceedings* of the American Philosophical Society, August, 1947, vol. 91, No. 3, p. 252.

34. Essentially, it would be more correct to translate the name "philosophical" as "scientific," since in contemporary usage, the word "philosophical" does not reflect its earlier meaning. The American Philosophical Society was founded by Benjamin Franklin "for promoting Useful Knowledge" and for a long time embodied in Europe all American science as a whole.

35. *Transactions of the American Philosophical Society, held at Philadelphia, for promoting Useful Knowledge,* vol. I. From January lst, 1769 To January lst, 1771. Philadelphia: 1771.

36. Eufrosina Dvoichenko-Markoff, "Benjamin Franklin, the American Philosophical Society and the Russian Academy of Sciences," *Proceedings* of the American Philosophical Society, vol. 94, No. 6, December, 1950, p. 549.

37. *Protokoly zasedaniy konerentsii imperatorskoy Akademii nauk s 1725 po 1803 g.,* III (1771-1785), 144. St. Petersburg: 1900. In the note it was remarked that the volume was presented from the American Philosophical Society through "the famous Mr. Franklin" and that the Secretary was instructed to thank the Society for this gift.

38. Eufrosina Dvoichenko-Markoff, "Benjamin Franklin, the American Philosophical Society and the Russian Academy of Sciences," p. 552.

39. *Akademicheskiye izvestiya,* pt. II, 1779, pp. 193, 205, and others.

40. Lafayette to Franklin, February 10, 1786. Jared Sparks, ed., *The Works of Benjamin Franklin,* X, 248. 10 vols. Hilliard, Gray, & Co. Boston: 1836-1840.

41. Besides Harmer and Butler mentioned above, the Agent of the United States for the affairs of the Southern Indians and then member of Congress from North Carolina, Hawkins, the geographer Hutchins, and others were here. See in particular: George Washington to T. Hutchins, August 20, 1786. *Writings of George Washington,* XXVIII, 525. George Washington to B. Butler, November 27, 1786. *Ibid.,* XXIX, 88-90 ff.

42. Benjamin Franklin to Lafayette, April 17, 1787. *Works of Benjamin Franklin,* X, 299.

43. George Washington to Lafayette, January 10, 1788. *Writings of George Washington,* XXIX, 374.

44. Same to Same, January 10, 1788. *Writings of George Washington,* XXIX, 373-375.

45. *Ibid.,* 375.

46. *Sravnitelnyy slovar vsyekh yazykov i narechiy po azbuchnomu poryadku raspolozhennyy.* 4 vols. St. Petersburg: 1790-1791. In the summer of 1812, this publication was presented by the Russian Minister in the United States, A. Ya. Dashkov, to the American Philosophical Society. Later, on a special request from America, F. Adelung sent the Society the first edition of the dictionary, put together by P. S. Pallas in 1787-1789; *Linguarum totius orbis vocabularia comparativa: augustissimae cura*

collecta. St. Petersburg: 1787-1789. *Proceedings* of the American Philosophical Society, vol. 94, No. 6, pp. 563, 583, 588. We note also that the first American Minister in St. Petersburg, John Quincy Adams, who conversed on this subject with a member of the Petersburg Academy, Tilezus, in April, 1810, was interested in the dictionary of Pallas. Charles Francis Adams, ed., *Memoirs of John Quincy Adams,* II, 115. 12 vols. Philadelphia: 1874-1877.

47. P. S. du Ponceau to F. P. Adelung, May 13, 1819. LO Arkhiva AN SSSR, f. 89, op. 2, d. 43, 1. 4; *Proceedings* of the American Philosophical Society, vol. 94, No. 6, p. 562; *Memoirs of the American Academy of Arts and Sciences,* IV, 321. Cambridge: 1818.

48. See Eufrosina Dvoichenko-Markoff, "Benjamin Franklin . . . ," *Proceedings* of the American Philosophical Society, August, 1947, vol. 91, No. 3, p. 254; *Writings of Benjamin Franklin,* X, 346.

49. *Proceedings* of the American Philosophical Society, August, 1950, vol. 94, No. 6, p. 555. In 1792, an excerpt from these *Works,* under the title of "Izvestiya o Severnoy Amerikye" was published in Russian translation: *Novyye yezhyemesyachnyye sochineniya,* 1792, vol. 67, pp. 10-24, and vol. 68, pp. 16-28.

50. Arkhiv AN SSSR, f. 1, op. 2, 1791, d. 6, 1, 8.

51. *Protokoly zasedaniy . . . ,* vol. IV (1786-1803), pp. 269-270.

52. "Bumagi knyagini Ye. R. Dashkovoy (urozhdennoy grafini Vorontsovoy)," *Arkhiv kn. Vorontsova,* Book 21, p. 286. It is necessary to say that communication with America at that time was no easy matter. One of the packages addressed to Ye. R. Dashkova, with a letter of Benjamin Franklin, turned out to be captured during the war with Sweden (1788-1790), and fell into the hands of the Duke of Sudermania, brother of the Swedish King, who transmitted it with an accompanying letter to Admiral Greig. The Admiral immediately sent the package directly to the State Court, and already therefrom, on the orders of Catherine II, the package, unopened and undamaged, was sent by courier to Ye. R. Dashkova in the country. The "postal service" of the Princess operated, as we see, irreproachably, and was not subjected to any censorship, either abroad or in Russia. Ye. R. Dashkova herself rated highly Benjamin Franklin, and considered him "a superior man, who combined enormous erudition with simplicity in manners and outward appearance, along with a natural modesty and great indulgence towards others." *Ibid.,* 285-286.

53. T. Bond, "Anniversary Oration. Delivered May 21st, before the American Philosophical Society. Held in Philadelphia, for the Promotion of Useful Knowledge, for the Year 1782," 31-32. Printed by John Dunlap. Philadelphia: 1782.

54. American Academy of Arts and Sciences. Records, I, 51. Boston Athenaeum. Boston, Mass.; *Protokoly zasedaniy . . . ,* III, 577.

55. *Rukopisnyye materialy Leonarda Eylera v arkhivye AN SSSR,* I, 226. Moscow: 1962.

56. Eufrosina Dvoichenko-Markov, "The Russian Members of the American Academy of Arts and Sciences," *Proceedings* of the American Philosophical Society, February, 1965, vol. 109, No. 1, p. 53.

57. American Academy of Arts and Sciences. Catalogue. Boston Athenaeum.

58. *Memoirs of the American Academy of Arts and Sciences to the End of the Year 1783, Volume I.* Boston: 1785.

59. *Nova Acta Academiae Scientiarum Imperialis Petropolitanae,* 1788, p. 10, and 1792, p. 16.

60. *Protokoly zasedaniy* . . . , IV, 204. Concerning Franklin's election, see also: *Nova Acta Academiae Scientiarum Imperialis Petropolitanae*, 1789, p. 8.

61. *Works of Benjamin Franklin*, X, 405-406.

62. Johan Albrecht Euler to Benjamin Franklin, November, 1789. LO Arkhiva AN SSSR, f. 1, op. 3, d. 83, 1. 2.

63. About this, see also: A. I. Startsev, "Venyamin Franklin i russkoye obshchestvo XVIII v.," *Internatsionalnaya literatura*, 1940, Books 3-4.

64. *Ucheniye dobrodushnogo Rikharda.* St. Petersburg: 1784. Somewhat earlier, on June 4/15, 1778, there appeared in *S. -Peterburgskikh yezhyenedelnykh sochineniyakh* an excerpt in translation from the French edition, *La Science du Bonhomme Richard.* Other excerpts from the works of Benjamin Franklin appeared from time to time in the periodical press. Extracts from Franklin's compilation about the lightning rod were translated by Aepinus and published in *Trudy volnogo ekonomicheskogo obshchestva* already in 1770. In February, 1778, in *S. -Peterburgsky vestnik*, the journal of G. L. Branko which was beginning to appear, there was published a selection of excerpts from Benjamin Franklin's letters to Miss Stevenson, under the title, "O tsvetakh platya (iz pisma gospodina Franklina)," and in June, 1780, there appeared in this same journal an epitaph composed by Benjamin Franklin (see *S. -Peterburgsky vestnik*, Pt. VI, 1780, p. 38). Finally, it is desired to invite attention that in March, 1776, there was published *Vypiska iz pisem nekotorogo filadelfiyskogo zhitelya k svoemy priyatelyu Barbe di Burg v Parizhye*, in which the civil administration in America, where everything went on "according to the laws of Nature" was praised. According to the words of the author, in the "laws and rules" of Pennsylvania, "a simplicity, of which there has not yet been in history an example," ruled, etc. (see *Sobraniye raznykh sochineniy i novostyey*, March, 1776, pp. 14-15).

It is scarcely appropriate to doubt that "*nekotorogo filadelfiyskogo zhitelya (some inhabitant of Philadelphia)*" was, to all appearances, Benjamin Franklin: the French scholar Barbier Dubourg was a great friend and translator of the great American, while the contents of the "*vypiska (extract)*" corresponds fully with the views of Franklin.

65. Benjamin Franklin, *Izbrannyye proizvedeniya*, 493. Moscow: 1956.

66. *Kak blagopoluchno vek prozhit, nauka dobrogo cheloveka Rikharda.* Moscow: 1791.

67. *Memoires de la vie privée de Benjamin Franklin, écrit par lui-meme, et adresses à son fils.* Paris: 1791.

68. *Moskovsky zhurnal*, Pt. IV, 1791, p. 355. N. M. Karamzin continued to be interested in the compilations of Benjamin Franklin subsequently. In 1798, in the *Penteonye inostrannoy slovesnosti* published by him, Book III, pp. 221-235, he put in some moral-philosophical sayings of Franklin (see also: N. M. Karamzin, *Perevody*, VIII, 143, 145, 148. St. Petersburg: 1835).

69. "Otryvok iz zapisok Franklina, pisannykh im samim," *Priyatnoye i poleznoye preprovozhdaniye vremeni*, Pt. XX, Moscow, 1798, pp. 3-23.

70. See also "Otryvok iz Franklinovykh zapisok," *Sobraniye raznykh sochineniy Venyamina Franklina*, 165-191. Moscow: 1803.

71. L. Feuchtwanger, "Prebyvaniye B. Franklina v Parizhye," in *Lisy v vinogradnikye.* Moscow: 1959.

72. Benjamin Franklin, *Izbrannyye proizvedeniya*, 418.

73. See Eufrosina Dvoichenko-Markov, "Benjamin Franklin and Leo Tolstoy," *Proceedings* of the American Philosophical Society, vol. 96, No. 2, April, 1952, pp. 119-128.

74. *Irtysh prevrashchayushchiysya v Ipokrenu,* February, 1790, pp. 56-57.
75. *Moskovsky zhurnal,* Pt. II, 1791, p. 218.

CHAPTER 7.

1. Karl Marx and Friedrich Engels, *Sochineniya,* XXIII, 9.
2. *Ibid.,* XVI, 17.
3. On the attitude of Russian society towards the events of the French Revolution, see M. M. Shtrange, *Russkoye obshchestvo i frantsuzskaya revolyutsiya, 1789-1794 gg.* Moscow: 1956.
4. "Pisma imp. Yekateriy II baronu Melkhioru Grimmu," *Sb. RIO,* vol. XXIII. St. Petersburg: 1878; "Pisma barona Melkhiorye Grimma k imp. Yekaterinye II," *Sb. RIO,* vol. XXXIII. St. Petersburg: 1881.
5. N. D. Chechulin, ed., *Zapiski knyagini Dashkovoy,* 137. St. Petersburg: 1907.
5a. Many years later, in 1858, the compilation of M. M. Shcherbatov, *O povrezhdenii pravov v Rossii,* was published at the Free Press of A. I. Herzen in London. "The angry exposure of the life of the Court, made by the pen of a historian of the Opposition . . . appeared very essential in the conditions of the revolutionary situation of the end of the 1850's." (for details see N. G. Eidelmann, *Gertsen protiv samoderzhaviya,* 104-109).
6. Baron de Corberon, *Un diplomat francais à la cour de Catherine II,* 49.
7. A. S. Pushkin, *Polnoye sobraniye sochineniy.* VIII, 125. Moscow-Leningrad: 1949.
8. M. V. Nechkina, "Volter i russkoye obshchestvo," in V. P. Volgin, *Volter. Stati i materialy.* 69. Moscow: 1948.
9. *Trudolyubivaya pchela.* November, 1759, p. 704 (see also N. I. Novikov, ed., *A. N. Sumarokov. Polnoye sobraniye sochineniy.* IX, 156-157. Moscow: 1787.
10. "Dissertatsiya o veroyatnyeyshem sposobye, kakim obrazom v Severnoy Amerikye pervyye zhiteli poyavilis. S latinskogo na rossiysky yazyk perevedennaya grafom Artemiyem Vorontsovym," *Sobraniye luchshikh sochineniy.* Pt. IV, 173. 1762.
11. *Opisaniye zemel Severnoy Ameriki i tamoshnikh prirodnykh zhitelyey.* Translated from the German by A. Rasumovich. St. Petersburg: 1765. *Svodnyy katalog russkoy knigi XVIII veka. 1725-1800.* II, No. 4938, p. 355. 5 vols. Moscow: 1963-1967.
12. *Akademicheskiye izvestiya.* Pt. III, 1779, pp. 267, 391, and Pt. IV, pp. 19, 185.
13. *Akademicheskiye izvestiya.* Pt. III, 1779, p. 267.
14. William Robertson. *Izvestiya o Amerikye.* William Robertson, preeminent Professor at Edinburgh University, and Royal Historiographer for Scotland. Translation from the English (A. I. Lulkov), Pts. I-II. St. Petersburg: 1784. In the introduction to this work, William Robertson reported about his successful trip to Russia, where he collected material about the geographic discoveries in Northwest America which permitted him to offer a "circumstantial description of the successes and the extensive nature of the Russian discoveries." pp. vii-ix.
15. D. M. Ladygin. *Izvestiye v Amerika o selyeniyakh aglitskikh, vo tom chislye nynye pod nazvaniyem Soyedinyonnykh Provintsiy, vybrano perechnem iz novyeyshikh o tom prostrannykh sochinitelyey.* St. Petersburg: 1783. It is characteristic that already in the very title of the book, the author emphasized the new name of the state arising in place of the old English colonies in North America: "the United Provinces."

We must also give him credit for propagating the idea of the expediency of the establishment and development of trade relations between Russia and the new state: pp. 58-59.

16. E. B. Bossieu, *Novyye puteshestviya v Zapadnuyu Indiyu* . . . Translated from the French. Moscow: 1783.

17. F. V. Taube, *Istoriya o aglinskoy torgovlye, manufakturakh, seleniyakh i moreplavanii v drevniye, sredniye i novyeyshiye vremena do 1776 goda; s dostovernym pokazaniyem spravedlivykh prichin nyneshnyey voyny v Severnoy Amerikye i prochikh tomu podobnykh veshchey do 1776 g.* Translated from the German. Moscow: 1783.

18. *Ibid.,* 121 (note).

19. Guillaume T. F. Raynal, *Histoire philosophique et politique des établissement et du commerce des Européens dans les deux Indes.* 10 vols. Chez J. -L. Pellet. Geneva: 1780-1781. The chapters devoted to the American Revolution came out in a separate publication: *idem., Revolution de l' Amerique.* London, L. Davis, and sold at the Hague at P. F. Gosse, 1781.

20. For details about Guillaume Raynal's work and its spreading in Russia, see Lekhtblau, "Iz istorii prosvetitelnoy literatury v Rossii," *Istorik marksist,* 1939, No. 1 (71), pp. 197-202.

21. Catherine II to Grimm, July 24/August 4, 1780. *Sb. RIO,* XXIII, 183. (The original: "la pancarte américaine rempli de declarations de peu de sagesse et de beaucoup de hardiesse déplacée.").

22. Catherine II to Grimm, April 1/12-4/15, 1782. *Ibid.,* 231, 235. Incidentally, Catherine II was acquainted with an earlier variant of Raynal's work, and already at the end of 1774, ordered Count Münnich to read the section on Russia and make his comments. See Catherine II to Grimm, December 21, 1774/January 1, 1775. *Ibid.,* 13.

23. P. I. Bogdanovich, "O Amerikye," *Akademicheskiye izvestiya,* Pt. VII, 1781, pp. 671-672.

24. *Moskovskiye vedomosti,* July 24/August 4, 1787, No. 59, p. 551; *Svodnyy katalog . . .,* III, 24. Only many years later, at the beginning of the 19th century, taking into consideration the undiminished interest of Russian society in the compilation of Raynal, a prepared "translation" of this work was finally published "by the will of the Most High": *Filosoficheskaya i politicheskaya istoriya o zavedeniyakh i kommertsii yevropeytsev v obyeikh Indiyakh, sochinennaya abbatom Reynalyem.* Translated from the French (Grigoriy Gorodchaninov). 6 vols. St. Petersburg: 1805-1811.

25. *S. -Peterburgskiye vedomosti,* June 22/July 3, 1781, No. 50.

26. *Moskovskiye vedomosti,* November 13/24, 1781, No. 91.

27. *S. -Peterburgskiye vedomosti,* October 26/November 6, 1781, No. 50.

28. M. V. Muratov and N. N. Nakoryakov, eds., *Knizhnaya torgovlya,* 98. Moscow-Leningrad: 1925. The extensive development of the book business began especially to worry the Tsarist authorities in the 1790's, after the beginning of the revolution in France. Prince A. A. Prozorovsky, not without reason, complained to Catherine II in a letter of May 20/31, 1792 "that all books which are only printed in France may be bought here secretly," and requested that "an end be put to the sale of foreign books." By her last official decree of September 16/27, 1796, Catherine II established a stringent inspection of literature from abroad, and at the end of the reign of Paul I, in April, 1800, there followed a complete prohibition of the importation of foreign books into

the Russian Empire. V. V. Sipovsky, "Iz proshlogo russkoy tsenzury," *Russkaya starina*, vol. 98, 1899, pp. 164-165, 451.

29. A more or less systematic account of the war of the English colonies in North America for independence appeared in Russian translation only in 1790 in the form of an appendix to the book of Cooper on the history of England: *Sokrashchennaya aglinskaya istoriya s drevnyeyshikh do nynyeshnikh vremen, sochinennaya G. Kuperom, po rasporyazheniye grafa Chesterfilda, s prisovokupleniyem v dopolneniye iz drugogo avtora opisaniya voyny Anglii s Soyedinyonnymi Amerikanskimi Oblastyami,* 171-238. Translated from the English. St. Petersburg: 1790. As is apparent from the dedication to Ye. R. Dashkova, the author of the translation was Ivan Livotov.

30. For a detailed description of the journals above-mentioned, see the book: P. N. Berkov, *Istoriya russkoy zhurnalistiki XVIII vekye,* 320, 326, 348, 413. Moscow-Leningrad: 1952.

31. *Sobraniye raznykh sochineniy i novostyey,* St. Petersburg, September, 1775, pp. 103-104.

32. See in particular "Vypisku iz pisem nekotorogo filadelfiyskogo zhitelya k svoemy priyatelyu Barbe di Burg v Parizhye.," in *Ibid.*, March, 1776, pp. 14-15.

33. *Akademicheskiye izvestiya,* Pt. VII, 1781, pp. 244-254.

34. P. Bogdanovich, "O Amerikye," *Ibid.*, pp. 225, 363, 528, and Pt. VIII, 1781, pp. 646, 784, 934. This work was devoted basically to the Spanish possessions in America, and only at the very end (Pt. VIII, p. 934 ff.) did P. Bogdanovich turn to the situation in the "English settlements." It is important to note, however, that the author condemned "ruinous despotism" and remarked the spread of precious freedom in the English colonies "in the region of the New World."

35. See in particular *S. -Peterburgsky vestnik*, 1779, Pt. III, March, p. 250; Pt. IV, July, pp. 78-79, etc.

36. M. N. Shprygova, "Osveshcheniye v *Sankt-Peterburgskikh vedomostyakh* voyny Severnoy Ameriki za nezavisimost," *Ucheniye zapiski MGPI i. V. I. Lenina*, No. 286, Moscow, 1967, pp. 5-21; *idem.,* "Voyna Ameriki za nezavisimost v osveshchenii *Moskovskikh vedomostey* N. I. Novikova," *Nauchnyye doklady vysshey shkoly istoricheskoy nauki,* 1961, No. 3, pp. 74-89; A. Startsev, *Amerika i russkoye obshchestvo.* Moscow: 1942; *idem.,* "Amerikanskaya voyna za nezavisimost v russkoy pechati kontsa XVIII v. Obzor redkikh izdaniy," *Istoricheskaya literatura,* 1940, No. 5-6, and other works. Some supplementary information is contained also in the dissertation of M. N. Nikolskaya (Shprygova), "Russkaya pechat o voynye Severnoy Ameriki za nezavisimost v XVIII b." MGPI im. V. I. Lenina, 1968.

37. On I. F. Bogdanovich, see *Russky arkhiv,* 1911, No. 9, pp. 108-116.

38. *St. -Peterburgskiye vedomosti,* February 13/24, 1775, No. 13; *Moskovskiye vedomosti,* February 24/March 7, 1775, No. 16.

39. Thus at that time did they call the Governor of Massachusetts, General Gage.

40. *S. -Peterburgskiye vedomosti,* June 16/27, 1775, No. 48; *Moskovskiye vedomosti,* June 30/July 11, 1775, No. 52.

41. *S. -Peterburgskiye vedomosti,* June 19/30, 1775, No. 49: *Moskovskiye vedomosti,* July 3/14, 1775, No. 53.

42. *S. -Peterburgskiye vedomosti,* June 30/July 11, 1775. It is interesting, incidentally, to compare this report, which is absent in *Moskovskiye vedomosti*, with the report of the Russian Minister in London, A. S. Musin-Pushkin to N. I. Panin of June 1/12,

1775. In presenting the most official English materials, the Russian Minister in London wrote in somewhat subdued expressions about the collision between the "royal troops and the American provincial ones." A. S. Musin-Pushkin noted that contrary to the "earlier broadcast details" in the Court Circular, the beginning of military operations "is ascribed to the Americans, who, from their homes and from hiding places, fired stealthily on the royal troops, sent for the destruction of the military supplies stored by the Americans." A. S. Musin-Pushkin to N. I. Panin, June 1/12, 1775. AVPR, f. Snosheniya Rossii s Angliyey, 1775 g., d. 266, 11. 92-93.

43. See *S. -Peterburgskiye vedomosti*, June 10/21, August 23/September 3, 1776, March 15/26, 1777, and also M. N. Shprygova, "Osveshcheniye v *Sankt-Peterburgskikh vedomostyakh* voyny Severnoy Ameriki za nezavisimost," *Uchenyye zapiski MGLI im. V. I. Lenina*, No. 286, Moscow, 1967, p. 9.

44. *S. -Peterburgskiye vedomosti*, October 14/25, 1776, No. 83.

45. *Moskovskiye vedomosti*, July 14/25, 1775, No. 56.

46. *S. -Peterburgskiye vedomosti*, July 7/18, 1775, No. 54; *Moskovskiye vedomosti*, July 17/28, 1775, No. 57.

47. *S. -Peterburgskiye vedomosti*, July 15/25, 1775, No. 56; *Moskovskiye vedomosti*, July 28/August 8, 1775, No. 60.

48. On the reporting of Franklin's mission to Paris in the Russian press, see A. Startsev, "Venyamin Franklin i russkoye obshchestvo XVIII veka," *Internatsionalnaya literatura*, 1940, No. 3-4, p. 213 ff. M. I. Radovsky, *Venyamin Franklin . . .* , pp. 24-33.

49. *S. -Peterburgskiye vedomosti*, December 29, 1777/January 9, 1778, No. 104.

50. For details about N. I. Novikov, see G. Makogonenko, *Nikolay Novikov i russkoye prosveshcheniye XVIII veka.* Moscow-Leningrad: 1951.

51. *Moskovsky telegraf*, 1830, Pt. 31, p. 206; Vl. Orlov, *Russkiye prosvetiteli 1790-1800-kh godov*, 35. Moscow: 1953.

52. N. M. Karamzin, "O knizhnoy torgovlye i lyubovi k chteniyu v Rossii," in *N. I. Novikov i yego sovremenniki*, 415. Moscow: 1961.

53. A. N. Neustroyev, *Istoricheskoye rozyskaniye o russkikh povremennykh izdaniyakh i sbornikakh za 1703-1802*, 69. St. Petersburg: 1874; *Svodnyy katalog knig*, IV, 15.

54. *Moskovskiye vedomosti*, November 3/14, 1781, No. 88; N. I. Novikov, *Izbrannyye sochineniya*, 565. Moscow-Leningrad: 1954.

55. Such an authoritative bibliographer as A. N. Neustroyev (*op. cit.*, 69) mentions this number for the period prior to 1779.

56. N. M. Karamzin, "O knizhnoy torgovlye i lubvi k chteniyu v Rossii," in *N. I. Novikov i yego sovremenniki*, 415.

57. *Moskovskiye vedomosti*, January 8/19, 1780, No. 3.

58. For details see M. N. Shprygova, "Voyna Ameriki za nezavisimost," *Nauchnyye doklady vysshyey shkoly. Ist. nauki*, 1961, No. 3, pp. 77-80. In these years there began to come forward in favor of the liquidation of the ruinous American war even persons who earlier had defended it "with great passion." *Moskovskiye vedomosti*, May 16/27, 1780, No. 10.

59. *Moskovskiye vedomosti*, January 1/12, 1780, No. 41.

60. *S. -Peterburgskiye vedomosti*, May 22/June 2, 1780, No. 41.

61. *Ibid.*, August 25/September 5, 1780, No. 68.

62. *Moskovskiye vedomosti*, March 25/April 5, 1780, No. 25.

63. "Perechen odnogo pisma iz Filadelfii," *Ibid.*, April 22/May 3, 1780, No. 33.

64. *Ibid.*, October 23/November 3, 1781, No. 85.

65. *Ibid.*, 1782, Nos. 102, 103; 1783, Nos. 2, 3, 4, and many others.

66. *Ibid.*, September 10/21, 1782, No. 73.

67. An explanation of the published material, and the introduction of special "notes" was one of the characteristic peculiarities of the Russian press of that time. As a rule, these "notes" offer the opportunity to draw a conclusion about the attitude of the publisher or translator to the material published, and in some cases also take on a definite independent significance. Yakov Kozelsky first used this method in the 1760's, and somewhat later, A. N. Radishchev, who published in 1773 at the press of N. I. Novikov a translation of Mably's work *Reflections sur l'histoire grecque,* with his own commentaries, among which was a notable note "on autocracy." G. P. Makogonenko, *Nikolay Novikov . . .* , 396-397.

68. *Moskovskiye vedomosti,* September 2/13, 1783, No. 71.

69. *Moskovskoye yezhemesyachnoye izdaniye,* Pt. II, 1781, pp. 189-190, 193.

70. *S. -Peterburgskiye vedomosti,* February 17/28, 1783, No. 14; *Moskovskiye vedomosti,* March 1/12, 1783, No. 17, pp. 129-130; March 4/15, 1783, No. 18, pp. 138-140; March 8/19, 1783, No. 19, pp. 146-149; March 11/22, 1783, No. 20, pp. 154-155.

71. *S. -Peterburgskiye vedomosti,* September 22/October 3, 1783, No. 76; *Moskovskiye vedomosti,* September 27/October 8, 1783, No. 77, pp. 611-612; September 30/October 11, 1783, No. 78, p. 619.

72. N. I. Novikov, *Izbrannyye proizvedeniye,* 568.

73. *Ibid.*, 507-561. This tract was printed in the *Supplements* to *Moskovskiye vedomosti* without a signature, in the name of the editor. G. P. Makogonenko thinks the author of the tract was N. I. Novikov himself. Some investigators (L. Lechtblau, "Iz istorii prosvetitelnoy literatury v Rossii," *Istorik-marksist,* 1939, No. 1 (71), p. 202) mistakenly ascribe authorship to Raynal.

74. N. I. Novikov, *Izbrannyye proizvedeniya,* 529.

75. *Ibid.*, 538.

76. *Ibid.*, 534.

77. "Kratkoye opisaniye zhizni i kharaktera gen. 'Vasgintona'," *Supplement* to *Moskovskiye vedomosti,* 1784, pp. 362, 369, Nos. 46, 47.

78. N. I. Novikov, *Izbrannyye proizvedeniya,* 577. Precisely at this time was begun a systematic investigation of N. I. Novikov and the restriction of his enlightening activity, which found its culmination in the arrest of N. I. Novikov in 1792, and the total destruction of his publishing business. Materials on the investigation of Novikov, his arrest and prosecution, *Ibid.*, 577-672.

79. Among them may be mentioned: "O vliyanii nezavisimosti Soyedinyonnykh Oblastyey Severoamerikanskikh v politicheskoye sostoyaniye Yevropy," *Supplement* to *Moskovskiye vedomosti,* 1784, pp. 306, 313, 321, 329, 337; "Razmyshleniya o predpriyatiyakh, kasayushchikhsya do torgovli s Severnoy Amerikoy," *Ibid.*, 1783, pp. 302, 305, 309, 311; "Obraz pravleniya i grazhdanskiye ustanovleniya v Amerike," *Ibid.*, 1783, p. 516; "Vsyoobshchyeye opisaniye amerikanskikh nravov," *Ibid.*, 1784, pp. 489, 497, 505, 513, 521; "Izvestiye o Pensilvanii," *Ibid.*, 1784, No. 18, p. 137; "Torgovlya yevropeytsyev v Amerikye," *Ibid.*, 1783, p. 265, and others.

80. *Supplement* to *Moskovskiye vedomosti,* 1784, pp. 521-564, Nos. 72, 73, 74.

Some authors, in particular V. I. Rabinovich, attribute this article and some other works on American themes, without sufficient reasons, to F. V. Karzhavin. V. I. Rabinovich, *Revolyutsionnyy prosvetitel F. V. Karzhavin,* 44. Moscow: 1966; *idem., S gishpantsami v Novyy York i Gavanu,* 42, 68-69. Moscow: 1967. It is obvious that neither Karzhavin, nor even more Raynal (a convinced opponent of slavery and tyranny) could be the author of this article.

81. N. I. Novikov, *Izbrannyye proizvedeniya,* 562.

82. *Moskovskiye vedomosti,* April 24/May 5, 1787, No. 33. (On the uprising, see also *Moskovskiye vedomosti* of February 3/14, 1787, and others). Despite the malevolent tone of the reports about the uprising of Daniel Shays, the attentive reader could draw his own conclusions about the events which had transpired, when he learned, for example that the leader of the "rebels", "Sher" (like "Shair" too, this, of course, is the same as Shays) "served in the late war with the American troops, and fully demonstrated his fearlessness. All who are complaining under the burden of taxation seem inclined to serve under his leadership." *S. -Peterburgskiye vedomosti,* April 2/13, 1787, No. 27.

83. Avrahm Yarmolinsky, *Russian Americana. Sixteenth to Eighteenth Centuries. A Bibliographical and Historical Study,* 36-37, 43. New York Public Library. New York: 1943.

CHAPTER 8

1. A. N. Radishchev, *Polnoye sobraniye sochineniy,* I, 14. 3 vols. Moscow-Leningrad: 1938-1952.

2. For details about A. N. Radishchev and his views see A. I. Startsev, *Radishchev v gody Putechestviya.* Moscow: 1960; G. Shtorm, *Potayennyy Radishchev.* 3rd Ed. Moscow: 1974; D. S. Babkin, *A. N. Radishchev. Literaturno-obshchestvennaya deyatelnost.* Moscow-Leningrad: 1966; Yu. F. Karyakin, Ye. G. Plimak, *Zapretnaya mysl obretayet svobodu. 175 let borby vokrug ideynogo naslediya Radishcheva.* Moscow: 1966; and others.

In our treatment, it is a question only of A. N. Radishchev's attitude towards America and the American Revolution.

3. V. P. Semennikov, *Radishchev. Ocherki i issledovaniya.* Moscow-Petrograd: 1923; A. I. Sartsev, "O zapadnykh svyazyakh Radishcheva," *Internatsionalnaya literatura,* 1940, No. 7/8, pp. 256-265; Yu. F. Koryakin and Ye. G. Plimak, *op. cit.,* pp. 77-126 and others.

4. V. I. Semevsky in particular wrote about this (*Byloye,* 1906, No. 1, p. 26). See also V. N. Bochkarev, "Russkoye obshchestvo Yekaterininskoy epokhi i frantsuzskaya revolyutsiya," *Otechestvennaya voyna i russkoye obshchestvo,* I, 61. Moscow: 1911; D. S. Babkin, *op. cit.,* 288.

5. Both on this and on another occasion the method itself is similar: the salutation on the part of Radishchev to the "reknowned land," and on the part of Raynal to the "heroic land." And although, on the part of A. N. Radishchev, the basic content of the 46th strophe is completely different — it is, by the way, deeper and more extensive than the corresponding paragraph in Raynal — the ending of the text discloses a significant correspondence. Raynal expressed regret that the free and holy land would not cover his remains: Radishchev dreamed of this, that the "shore" of this land would "hide"

his "ashes." V. N. Semennikov, *op. cit.*, pp. 5-6, with the reference to *"Revolution de l'Amérique*, par l'Abbé Raynal. À Londres, 1781, p. 87." A. I. Startsev justly verifies that it would be more correct to refer to Raynal's *Philosophical History*, since the *Revolution in America* is only an abstract from a new revised version of the *Philosophical History* of 1780 (the last 15 chapters of the eighteenth book). See A. I. Startsev, "O zapadnykh svyazyakh Radishcheva," *Internatsionalnaya literatura*, 1940, No. 7/8, p. 260.

6. Recently, D. Land in England, K. Bittner in the Federal Republic of Germany, and R. Taylor in the United States, and others, have occupied themselves energetically with searches for the "western sources" of A. N. Radishchev. For a detailed critical analysis of these works, see Ye. G. Plimak, "Zloklyucheniya burzhuaznoy komparativistiki (k voprosu o kharaktera politicheskikh kontseptsiy A. N. Radishchev i G. Reynalya)," *Istoriya SSSR*, 1963, No. 3, pp. 183-213; Yu F. Karyakin and Ye. G. Plimak, "Zapretnaya mysl obretayet svobodu."

While emphasizing the revolutionary content of the ode "Freedom" and of the *History of the Two Indies*, Yu. F. Karyakin and Ye. G. Plimak remark that both A. N. Radishchev and Guillaume Raynal valued highly and propagated the ideas of the famous pamphlet of Thomas Paine, *Common Sense:* "Our rights were written on the bloody fields of Lexington. England herself crossed out with her own hand the ties binding us from that moment when she fired the first shot against us; Nature itself proclaimed us free and independent." Cited in Yu. F. Karyakin and Ye. G. Plimak, *op. cit.*, 91.

7. For details see N. N. Bolkhovitinov, "Dekabristy i Amerika," *Voprosy istorii*, 1974, No. 4, pp. 91-104.

8. A. N. Radishchev, *Polnoye sobraniye sochineniy*, I, 15.

9. V. P. Semennikov, *op. cit.*, 7. The viewpoint of V. P. Semennikov has received the widest recognition of the specialists, and as to publication, the ode "Freedom" is usually dated 1781-1783. A. N. Radishchev, *Polnoye sobraniye sochineniy*, I, 444; *Volnaya russkaya poeziya vtoroy poloviny—XVIII—pervoy poloviny XIX veka*, 120. Leningrad: 1970. Comparatively recently the writer G. Shtorm advanced the hypothesis that four strophes of the ode (including the 46th and 47th strophes cited above) were written by A. N. Radishchev significantly later, already in his declining years, most probably in 1799. G. Shtorm, "Potayennyy Radishchev," *Novyy mir*, 1964, No. 11, pp. 144-148, 156. In the opinion of D. S. Babkin, they were created in three stages (prior to the transmission of the manuscript of the *Journey* to the censorship, during the publication of the book, and finally, already after the publication of the *Journey* and the return of A. N. Radishchev from exile, when there was written, in particular, the 46th strophe). D.S. Babkin, *op. cit.*, 100-102. For a criticism of the views of G. P. Shtorm and D. S. Babkin, see, Yu. F. Karyakin and Ye. G. Plimak, *op. cit.*, 220-266.

10. M. N. Nikolskaya (Shprygova), "Russkaya pechat o voynye Severnoy Ameriki za nezavisimost v XVIII vekye." MGPI im. V. I. Lenina. Moscow: 1968. (Dissertation, p. 200).

11. D. S. Babkin, *op. cit.*, 98.

12. A. N. Radishchev, *Polnoye sobraniye sochineniy*, I, 16-17.

13. The *Journey* was first printed by A. N. Radishchev himself at his "Free Press" in 1790. For more than 100 years, this work was under the ban of the Tsarist authorities, despite the frequent attempts to publish it in a legal way. Only in 1905 did there

come out the first scientific and complete edition of the *Journey* under the editorship of N. P. Pavlov-Silvansky: A. N. Radishchev, *Polnoye sobraniye sochineniy*, vol. I, *Primechaniya*, 470 ff. Relatively recently, in 1958, the *Journey* was published in the United States: Leo Weiner, ed., P. Thaler, trans., *A. N. Radishchev, A Journey from St. Petersburg to Moscow.* Harvard University Press. Cambridge: 1958. If the translation of the book, carried out by the late Leo Weiner, deserves on the whole a positive evaluation, the commentaries of R. Thaler have an obviously tendentious character. Despite the text of the book, the commentator tries with all his efforts to present A. N. Radishchev, not a revolutionary, but as a reformer and liberal. (On this see Ye. G. Plimak, "Pravda knigi i lozh kommentariya," *Kritika burzhuaznykh kontseptsiy istorii Rossii perioda feodalizma*, 352-411. Moscow: 1962).

14. A. N. Radishchev, *Polnoye sobraniye sochineniy*, I, 346-347. Chapter "Torzhok" in *Kratkoye povestvoaniye o proiskhozhdenii tsensury.* See also Max M. Laserson, *The American Impact on Russia, Diplomatic and Ideological, 1784-1917*, 66-67. New York: 1950. As A. I. Startsev convincingly showed in his dissertation, A. N. Radishchev was acquainted with the American constitutional materials in a rare French translation: *Recueil des loix constitutive dès colonies angloises confédérées sous la denomination d'États-Unis de l'Amérique Septentrionale—auquel on a joint les Actes d'Independance, ade Confédération et autres Actes du Congrès général, traduit de l'anglis.* Dedié à M. le Docteur Franklin. À Philadelphie et se vend à Paris, 1778. See A. I. Startsev-Kunin, "Amerikanskaya revolyutsiya, Radishchev i russkoye obshchestvo XVIII veka (Doctoral dissertation)," Moscow, 1946, pp. 226, 299-303. See L. N. Beck, "Pennsylvania and Early Russian Radicals," *Pennsylvania Magazine of History and Biography*, vol. 75, April, 1951, pp. 194-195.

15. A. N. Radishchev, *Polnoye sobraniye sochineniy*, I, 334.

16. *Ibid.*, I, 316-317.

17. A. I. Startsev, "O zapadnykh svyazyakh Radishcheva," *Internatsionalnaya literatura*, 1940, No. 7/8, p. 262.

18. A. N. Radishchev, *Polnoye sobraniye sochineniy*, I, 324.

19. A. V. Khrapovitsky, *Pamyatnyye zapiski*, 340. St. Petersburg: 1874.

CHAPTER 9.

1. P. N. Durov, "Fyodor Vasilyevich Karzhavin," *Russkaya starina*, vol XII, 1875, pp. 272-297.

2. See M. P. Alekseyev, "Filologicheskiye nablyudeniya F. V. Karzhavina (Iz istorii russkoy filologii v XVIII v.)," *Romanskaya filologiya*, Leningrad, 1961, pp. 8-36; A. I. Startsev, "F. V. Karzhavin i yego amerikanskoye puteshestviye," *Istoriya SSSR*, 1960, No. 3, pp. 132-139. Eufrosina Dvoichenko-Markov, "A Russian Traveller to Eighteenth-Century America," *Proceedings* of the American Philosophical Society, vol. 97, No. 4, September, 1953, pp. 350-355.

3. V. I. Rabinovich, *S gishpantsami v Novyy York i Gavanu*, 3-4. Moscow: 1967. For a critique of the views of V. I. Rabinovich, see Yu. Ya. Gerchuk, "Etnograficheskiye nablyudeniya russkogo puteshestvennika F. V. Karzhavina v Amerikye (konets XVIII v.)," *Sovetskaya etnografiya*, 1972, No. 1; A. I. Startsev, "Byl li Karzhavin drugom Radishcheva?," *Voprosy literatury*, 1971, No. 4.

4. F. V. Karzhavin to V. N. Karzhavin and A. I. Karzhavina, September 1, 1785.

Arkhiv LOII, f. 238, I (Collection of P. N. Likhachev), karton 146 (F. V. Karzhavin), d. 3, 1. 17.

5. F. V. Karzhavin to V. N. Karzhavin, September, 1773. *Ibid.*, 1. 1; Reply of "a former father" to an "accursed" and "ingrate" son, "Fedka" of November 12/23, 1773. *Ibid.*, 11. 3-5.

6. "Skazka, pokazuyushchaya v kratse, v kokoye vremya i v kakikh mestakh ya na-khodilsya." (1788). ROIRL, Materialy F. V. Karzhavina iz sobraniya P. Ya. Durova, f. 93, op. 2, d. 100, 11. 7-10. One of the versions of the "Skazka" was published by P. N. Durov in *Russkaya starina*, vol XII, 1875, pp. 273-278.

7. F. V. Karzhavin to V. N. Karzhavin, May 19, 1775. Arkhiv LOII, f. 238, k. 146, d. 3, 1. 8.

8. V. I. Rabinovich called our attention to these last words. *S gishpantsami v Novyy York i Gavanu*, 19.

9. ROIRL, f. 93, op. 2, d. 100, correspondingly 11. 273, 274, 276, 11. The last date—April 15, 1787—makes it possible to define the time of the departure of F. V. Karzhavin from Virginia for the island of Martinique, and then to Russia (no earlier than mid-April, 1787).

10. Eufrosina Dvoichenko-Markov, "A Russian Traveller to Eighteenth-Century America," p. 330.

11. A. I. Startsev, "F. V. Karzhavin i yego amerikanskoye puteshestviye, 137.

12. "Semya volnodumtsev," *Niva*, 1872, Nos. 1-19. A novel of the Catherinian period.

13. *Arkhiv kn. Vorontsova*. Book II, p. 308 ff.

14. After the return from America, he published at N. I. Novikov's University Press *Sokrashchennyy Vitruviy, ili Sovershennyy arkhitektor. Perevod arkhitektury pomoshchnika Fyodora Karzhavina.* Moscow: 1789.

15. Arkhiv LOIII, f. 238, k. 146, d. 20, 1. 1.

16. F. V. Karzhavin, *Vozhak. pokazyvayushchiy put k luchshemu vygovory buku i recheniy frantsuzskikh. Le guide francais par Theodore Karjavine*, 198-199, 211. Moscow: 1794.

17. *Arkhiv kn. Vorontsova*. Book III, 312-322.

18. ROIRL, f. 93, op.2d. 100, 1.7; *Russkaya starina*, vol XII, 1875, pp. 274-275.

19. *Ibid.* The text of the "Skazka" of F. V. Karzhavin which is kept in the Institute of Russian Literature (Pushkin House) differs somewhat from the version published in *Russkaya starina*.

20. Eufrosina Dvoichenko-Markov, "A Russian Traveller to Eighteenth-Century America," p. 351.

21. *Ibid.*, pp. 351-352.

22. ROIRL, f. 93, op. 2, d. 100, 1. 7. Concerning the first journey to the United States, F. V. Karzhavin related his fresh impressions in detail in a letter from St. -Pierre (island of Martinique) to Barr of April 15, 1780. *Ibid.*, 1. 201 ff.

23. *Russkaya starina*. vol. XII, 1875, p. 289.

24. ROIRL, f. 93, op. 2, d. 100, 1. 8.

25. F. V. Karzhavin to V. N. Karzhavin and A. I. Karzhavina, September 1, 1785. Arkhiv LOII, f. 238, k. 146, d. 3, 1. 160b.

26. *Russkaya starina*. vol XII, 1875, p. 276. The accuracy of the information provided by F. V. Karzhavin agrees fully with other sources: the Marquis de Vaudreuil was

captain of the ship *Le Fendant,* which was in the harbor of York from November 20, 1779 to January 25, 1780. *Papers of Thomas Jefferson,* III, 210-211, 247-248.

27. A. I. Startsev, "F. V. Karzhavin i yego amerikanskoye puteshestviye," p. 139. It goes without saying that all this continues to remain only a hypothesis which we have not succeeded in verifying with any sort of documentary evidence. Nor did a search of the appropriate papers of Thomas Jefferson for the appropriate period yield positive result. See *Papers of Thomas Jefferson,* III.

28. Ye. I. Karzhavin (and F. V. Karzhavin), *Remarques sur la langue russienne et sur son alphabet. Publ., corr., et augm. par Theodore Karjavine.* St. Petersburg: 1791.

29. Fyodor Karzhavin, *Description du peu, vu au microscope. En francais et en russe.* Carouge: 1789; Eufrosina Dvoichenko-Markov, "A Russian Traveller to Eighteenth-Century America," pp. 153-154.

30. F. V. Karzhavin to K. P. Karzhavina, April 27, 1797. ROIRL, f. 93, op. 2, d. 100, 1. 87.

31. Carlo Bellini to F. V. Karzhavin, March 1, 1788 (in the Italian language), *Ibid.,* 1. 236. This friendly message of Bellini, sent on July 9, served as a reply to F. V. Karzhavin's letter of November 6, 1787. A. I. Startsev first invited attention to this letter, as well as to a number of other hitherto unknown documents of F. V. Karzhavin (see *Istoriya SSSR,* 1960, No. 3, p. 138). Among the papers of F. V. Karzhavin has also been preserved a letter from his other American correspondent, Louis Bernard, of May 1, 1789, in which it was pointed out in particular: "After Your departure for Russia, I did not have, Gracious Sir and dear friend, news of You; only through Mr. Bellini, to whom You wrote from Paris, I learned about your felicitous sojourn in this capital." Thus it is obvious that, having arrived in Paris at the beginning of 1788, F. V. Karzhavin wrote Carlo Bellini a letter, which was punctually received by the latter. Louis Bernard to F. V. Karzhavin, May 1, 1789, Port-au-Prince, received February 1/11, 1790. ROIRL, f. 93, op. 2, d. 100, 11. 213-214.

32. F. V. Karzhavin to N. K. Khotinsky, November 25, 1786. *Ibid.,* 11. 261-263, 265.

33. F. V. Karzhavin, *Frantsuzskiye, rossiyskiye i nemetskiye razgovory v polzu nachinatelyey . . . ,* 64. St. Petersburg: 1803. On another occasion, F. V. Karzhavin reported that he "was in Petersburg, Virginia, and saw Philadelphia and Boston . . . then he was made prisoner by the English . . . he travelled with the Spanish by sea to New York, to Cap Francais, and to Havana on the island of Cuba . . ." Ye. N. Karzhavin and F. V. Karzhavin, *Remarques sur la langue russienne et sur son alphabet.* A short bibliography of the works of F. V. Karzhavin, with interesting explanations, was first compiled by P. N. Durov. *Russkaya starina,* vol. XII, 1875, pp. 291-294.

34. F. V. Karzhavin, *Novoyavlennyy vedun, poveduyushchiy gadaniye dukhov . . . ,* 4. St. Petersburg: 1795.

35. *Ibid.,* 65.

36. *Ibid.,* 71.

37. F. V. Karzhavin, *Kratkoye izvestiye o dostopamyatnykh priklyucheniyakh kapitana D'Sivilya . . . Perevod Fyodora Karzhavina,* 26-27. Moscow: 1791.

38. ROIRL, f. 93, op. 2, d. 100, 1. 12.

39. M. P. Alekseyev, "Filologicheskiye nablyudeniya F. V. Karzhavina," 36.

40. Louis Adamic, *A Nation of Nations,* 147. New York and London: 1945. The visit to the Pennsylvania botanist John Bartram in 1769 of "a native from the shores

248   RUSSIA AND THE AMERICAN REVOLUTION

of Lake Ladoga," one Ivan Alekseyevich (Iwan Alexiewitz) is known from the book: H.S.J. Crevecoeur, *Letters from an American Farmer*, 154, 174. London: 1782. The reliability of this fact is very doubtful, and many investigators have not without reason expressed the opinion that this "Russian traveller," to all appearances, was the author of the book himself. *Proceedings* of the American Philosophical Society, vol. 94, No. 6, p. 550.

41. *Nyeschastnyye priklyucheniya Vasiliya Baranshchikova, meshchanina Nizhnego Novgoroda, v tryokh chastyakh sveta: v Amerikye, Azii i Yevropye s 1780 po 1787 gg.* St. Petersburg: 1787, 1788, 1793.

42. See "Nachrichten über die Familie Wetter nob. von Rosenthal in Ehstland." Central State Historical Archive of the Estonian SSR, f. 854 (Chancellery of the Estonian Nobility), op. 2, d. SP, 128, 11. 1, 15, d. SIU 54, 11. 1, 20, and others.

43. M. M. Boatner III, *Encyclopedia of the American Revolution*, 946-947. New York: 1966; F. B. Heitman, *Historical Register of Officers of the Continental Army*. Washington: 1914; *Ohio Archaeological and Historical Society Publications*, vol. VI, 1898, pp. 1-34 (J. H. Anderson).

44. M. M. Boatner, *Encyclopedia of the American Revolution,* 946.

45. Arkhiv LOII, f. 238, k. 146, d. 9, 1. 4.

46. Thomas Heyden, *Der Missioner Fürst Augustin Galitzin.* Hamburg: 1859; Sarah M. Brownson, *Life of Demetrius Augustine Gallitzin, Prince and Priest.* New York and Cincinnati, F. Pustet & Co., 1873. Paris, Didier, 1880. (The French translation of the book was used by us). And others. The Russian Consul General in Philadelphia, A. Ya. Dashkov, reported in the fall of 1809 a number of details about the life of Dmitry Golitsyn, his poverty-stricken material condition, and his encounter with him. TsGAOR, f. 907, op. 1, d. 57, 1. 13.

CONCLUSION

1. S. S. Jados, ed., *Documents on Russian-American Relations,* 14-15. Washington: 1955.

2. See also N. N. Bolkhovitinov, "B. Franklin i M. V. Lomonosov," *Novaya i noveyshaya istoriya,* 1973, No. 3; *idem.,* "Iz istorii russko-amerikanskikh nauchnykh svyazyey v XVIII-XIX vekakh," *SShA — ekonomika, politika, ideologiya,* 1974, No. 5.

3. For details see N. N. Bolkhovitinov, *Stanovleniye russko-amerikanskikh otnosheniy,* 1775-1815, 199-207, 346-381.

4. It is a question of the book: D. B. Warden, *Description statistique, historique et politique des États-Unis de l'Amérique Septentrionale* . . . 5 vols. Paris: 1820. This work was well known to many members of society; it was pointed out in the catalogue of the library of F. P. Shakhovsky; N. I. Turgenev, and many others, were acquainted with it.

5. *Vosstaniye dekabristov. Materialy. Dokumenty. Sledstvennyye dela,* XI, 43. 11 vols. Moscow: 1925-1969.

6. Alexander Hamilton, *Otchyot general-kaznacheya A. Gamiltona, uchinennyy Amerikanskim Shtatam 1791 g. o polzye manufaktur v otnoshenii onykh k torgovlye i zemledeliyu,* 1. St. Petersburg: 1807.

7. Thomas Jefferson to William Duane, July 20, 1807. *Writings of Thomas Jefferson,* XI, 290-292.

8. Thomas Jefferson to A. Ya. Dashkov, August 12, 1809. *Ibid.*, XII, 303-304.

9. *Materialy k peresmotru russko-amerikanskogo torgovogo dogovora*, Pt. II, 4, 6, 8. St. Petersburg: 1912.

10. *A Compilation of the Messages and Papers of the Presidents*, III, 22. Washington: 1903. For details about the extent and the significance of the trade ties of Russia and the United States in the first third of the 19th century, see N. N. Bolkhovitinov, *Russko-amerikanskiye otnosheniya, 1815-1832*, 358-450, 582-592. Moscow: 1975.

DOCUMENTS

1. The group of members of the House of Lords published a protest against the declaration of the American colonists as rebels, and the decision of Parliament to begin military operations against them; in the protest, the policy of the English authorities in the North American colonies and the refusal of Parliament to review the complaints of merchants trading in America and the West Indies, were condemned. AVPR, f. Snosheniya Rossii s Angliyey, 1775 g., d. 266, 1. 21-24.

2. *I. e.*, trial by jury and the right to levy taxes through their representatives. The Habeas Corpus Act was passed in 1679. The act defined the procedure of an arrest, obligated the court, upon the complaint of a person considering the arrest illegal, to require the appearance of the arrested one in court for verification of the legality of the deprivation of freedom; it foresaw the release of the imprisoned one on bail, on the condition of the delivery of an appropriate monetary guarantee, etc.

3. There had been maintained in Holland since the time of the war with Spain a Scottish brigade, created in 1572. The hopes of the British cabinet of the receipt of the Scottish soldiers from Holland were not justified. The Government of Holland did not agree to this, and sent the brigade to the Rhine and the Moselle. After the rupture with England, the Scottish brigade was disbanded and the 55 officers went to England.

4. He has in mind V. G. Lizakevich's report of August 2/13, 1776. AVPR, f. Snosheniya Rossii s Angliyey, 1776 g., d. 279, 11. 149-151.

5. The surrender of the English troops under the command of General Burgoyne took place at Saratoga on October 17, 1777. This victory brought the Americans rich military trophies and more than six thousand prisoners.

6. He has in mind a report to Vice Chancellor I. A. Osterman of January 4/15, 1778, in which I. S. Baryatinsky reported that an order had been given concerning the departure from Brest of a French squadron composed of three ships and four frigates. AVPR, f. Snosheniya Rossii s Frantsiyey, 1778 g., d. 333, 11. 1-2.

7. The Franco-American treaty of alliance was concluded on February 6, 1778. At the same time, a "treaty of friendship and trade" and a secret protocol, which foresaw the possibility of the adherence of Spain to the Franco-American alliance, were signed.

BIBLIOGRAPHY

TRANSLATOR'S NOTE: In the bibliography of the original Russian typescript of this book, the author used a rather elaborate system of classification of his materials. He also intermingled his American and West European sources with his Russian sources according to that system, using a method of citing the former likely to be unfamiliar to those readers of this book who do not read Russian. To enhance its usefulness to those in that category, the bibliography has been reorganized and revised in this translation. The Russian bibliography (including both the transliterations and the titles in languages other than Russian which were published in Russia) has been separated from the American-West European bibliography. The Russian bibliography is presented in accordance with the author's classification system, but the titles in each category are listed in the order of the Latin alphabet into which they have been transliterated. A simplified system of classification has been devised for the American-West European bibliography, and citations of titles listed therein, in the order of the Latin alphabet, are made in accordance with standard American practice.

A. RUSSIAN BIBLIOGRAPHY

Karl Marx and Friedrich Engels, *Sochineniya.*
    Volume XV:
        Karl Marx, "Amerikansky vopros v Anglii."
        ——————, "Grazhdanskaya voyna v Severnoy Amerikye."
        —————— , "Grazhdanskaya voyna v Soyedinyonnykh Shtatakh."
        —————— , "Obshchestvennoye mneniye Anglii."
    Volume XVI:
        Karl Marx, "Prezidentu Soyedinnyonykh Shtatov Ameriki Avraamu Linkolnu."
    Volume XXII:
        Friedrich Engels, "Vneshnyaya politika russkogo tsarizma."
    Volume XXIII:
        Karl Marx, "Kapital, Volume I."
    Volume XXVI:
        Karl Marx, "Teorii pribavochnoy stoimosti, Volume IV of *Kapital,* Second Part.

Arkhiv K. Marksa i F. Engelsa. Volume IV. Moscow, 1948.
   Friedrich Engels, "Konspekt knigi Glyukha 'Istoricheskoye opi-
   saniye torgovli, promyshlennosti i zemledeliya'."
Vladimir I. Lenin, *Polnoye sobraniye sochenenii.*
   Volume III:
   "Razvitiye kapitalizma v Rossii."
   Volume V:
   "Goniteli zemstva i Annibaly liberalizma."
   Volume XXVII:
   "Novyye dannyye o zakonakh razvitiya kapitalizma v zemledelii.
   Vypusk I. Kapitalizm i zemledeliye v Soyedinyonnykh Shta-
   takh Ameriki."
   Volume XXX:
   "O broshyurye Yuniusa."
   Volume XXXIV:
   "Grozyashchaya katastrofa i kak s ney borotsya."
   Volume XXXVII:
   "Pismo k amerikanskim rabochim."
   Volume XXXVIII:
   "Rech ob obmene naroda lozungami svobody i ravonstva 19
   maya 1919 g."

I. ARCHIVAL MATERIALS

Archive of the Academy of Sciences of the USSR, Leningrad Divi-
sion, cited as LO Arkh. An SSSR (Arkhiv Akademii Nauk SSSR,
Leningradskoye otdeleniye). f. 1, op. 3, 1789; f. 83, f. 1, op. 2,
1791; d. 6, f. 216, op. 3, d. 1731; f. 89, op. 1, d. 180; f. 129, op. 1,
d. 332-334, R. Sh., op. 1, d. 170; f. 1, op. 1, d. 33.
Archive of the Foreign Policy of Russia, cited as AVPR (Arkhiv
vneshney politiki Rossii), Moscow.
Materials on the Sojourn of Francis Dana in St. Petersburg (f.
   Snosheniya Rossii s SShA, 1783 g., dd. 1-3).
Vienna: f. Snosheniya Rossii s Avstriyey, op. 32/6 (perepiska za
   1781-1783 gg.), d. 632, 633, 637-642, 644, 650, 656, 657,
   666, 668, 1012, 1015-1017, 1022, 1023, 1025, 1032.
London: f. Snosheniya Rossii s Angliyey, op. 35/6, 1774 g., d.
   261; 1775 g., d. 266-267, 36-37; 1776 g., d. 274, 177, 282;
   1778 g., d. 288, 595-596, 295, 298; 1779 g., d. 599-600; 1780
   g., d. 310, 312; 1781 g., d. 318, 320, 604, 319, 323; 1782 g., d.
   331-333, 73; 1783 g., d. 341; f. Londonskaya Missiya, op. 36,

1779-1781 gg., d. 345; 1781 g., d. 357. Paris—f. Snosheniya Rossii s Frantsiyey, op. 93/6, 1775 g., d. 303; 1776 g., d. 312; 1777 g., d. 323; 1778 g., d. 333; 1779 g., d. 343-345; 1780 g., d. 354, 356; 1781 g., d. 365, 367-370; 1782 g., d. 381-383, 385-387; 1783 g., d. 392-398, 401-403, 406-408; 1780 g., d. 605; 1781 g., d. 611, 91; 1782 g., d. 93; 1784 g., d. 411; f. Parizhskaya Missiya, op. 941, 1781 g., d. 4; 1782 g., d. 1, ch. 1; 1783 g., d. 1.

Consulate in Bordeaux: f. Snosheniya Rossii s Frantsiyey, d. 684-697 (1778-1782 gg.) and others.

The Hague: f. Snosheniya Rossii s Gollandiyey, 1780 g., d. 207-208; 1781 g., d. 218, 223; 1782 g., d. 236-237, 28; 1784 g., d. 268, 271. Madrid: f. Snosheniya Rossii s Ispaniyey, op. 58/1, 1780-1781 g.), d. 388-396.

Materials of the So-Called Internal Correspondence, of the File of Secret Opinions, and of others: f. Sekretnyye Mneniya, 1725-1798 gg., d. 597; 1779-1783 gg., d. 593; 1742-1799, d. 593; f. Vysochayshye aprobovannyye doklady po snosheniyam s inostrannymi derzhavami, 1782 g., d. 8; 1783 g., d. 9; f. Vnutrenniye kollezhskiye dela, op. 2/6, d. 881, 883, 885, 828-833, 5629, 5630, 5644, 3769, 7244/27, and others.

Archive of the Leningrad Division of the Institute of History of the Academy of Sciences of the USSR, cited as Arkhiv LOII (Arkhiv Leningradskogo otdeleniya Instituta istorii AN USSR), Leningrad. f. 238, 1 (Collection of N. M. Likhachev), k. 146 (F. V. Karzhavin), d. 1-26; f. 36 (Vorontsovs), torgovlya Rossii XVIII—nach. XIX v., t. 1-7, op. 1, d. 543/520, 544/190, 545/191, 546/623, 547/418, 548/439, dela Komissii o kommertsii v 20-kh tomakh, d. 550/196, 551/1033, torgovlya salom, myasom, potashom i penkoy XVIII v., d. 563/840, 564-570, istoricheskoye opisaniye torgovli St. -Peterburga i Kronshtadta, de. 578/342, delo o navigatsii, 1780 g., d. 586/83.

Central State Archive of Ancient Formal Acts, cited as TsGADA (Tsentralny gosudarstvenny arkhiv drevnikh aktov), Moscow. Gosarkhiv. Razryad XV, d. 457, (about maritime neutrality), 448, 1092; f. 1274, op. 1 (Panins), d. 131, 128; f. 168, d. 166 (correspondence of Paul Jones); f. 15, d. 214 (Survey of Relations with the United States), 457, 668; f. 19, op. 1; Kronshtadtskiye raporty, d. 262 (14 chastey), ch. 11, 12, 13, d. 332, 360, 379b;

f. 13, d. 433; f. 246, op. 1, d. 668; f. 19, d. 264; Gos. arkhiv,
f. XXIV, op. 1, d. 62, ch. 2 i ch. 3 (John Ledyard); f. 1261 (Vorontsovs) op. 1, d. 608, 833, 874, 987; f. 796 (collection of G. V.
Yudin), d. 163, 182, 298.

Central State Archive of the Navy of the USSR, cited as TsGAVMF
(Tsentralny Gosudarstvenny arkhiv voyenno-morskogo
flota SSSR), Leningrad.

Materials on the Sojourn of Paul Jones in Russia—f. 172, op. 1,
d. 99, 349; f. 197, op. 1, d. 52, 67, 77; f. 223, op. 1, d. 63; f.
227, op. 1, d. 51, 53; f. 245, op. 1, d. 16, 17, 22.

Central State Archive of the October Revolution of the Highest
Organs of State Power and of the State Administration of the
USSR, cited as TsGAOR (Tsentralny gosudarstvenny arkhiv Okt-
yabrskoy revolyutsii vysshikh organov gosudarstvennoy vlasti i
gosudarstvennogo upravleniya SSSR), Moscow. f. 907 (A. Ya.
Dashkov); f. 728, op. 1, ch. 1, d. 174, d. 284; f. 109, op. 214, d.
168.

Central State Historical Archive of the Estonian SSSR, cited as
TsGIA Est. SSR (Tsentralny gosudarstvenny istorichesky arkhiv
Estonskoy SSR), Tartu.

Materialy ob uchastii v voyne SShA za nezavisimost G. Kh. Vetter-
Rozentalya, f. Kantselyariya estlyandskogo dvoryantsva (f. 854),
op. 2, d. SP 128, SIU 54.

Manuscript Division of the Institute of Russian Literature (Pushkin
House) of the Academy of Sciences of the USSR, cited as RO IRLI
(Rukopisny otdel Instituta russoky literatury (Pushkinsky dom)
AN USSR), Leningrad.

Materialy o F. V. Karzhavine (from the collection of P. Ya. Dashkov), f. 98, op. 2, d. 100-103.

Manuscript Division of the V.I. Lenin State Library of the USSR,
cited GBL OR (Otdel rukopisyey Gosudarstvennoy Biblioteki
SSSR i. V.I. Lenina), Moscow. f. 222 (Panins), karton IV, yed. khr. 1
(orders and letters).

Manuscript Division of the M. Ye. Saltykov-Shchedrin Public Library,
cited as GPB (Otdel rukopisyey Gosudarstvennoy publichnoy
biblioteki im. M. Ye. Saltykova-Shchedrina), Leningrad. f. Sukh-
telina, kn. 102, Collection of Autographs of Washington, Franklin,
John Adams, Madison, Jefferson, and others.

II. PUBLISHED SOURCES
1. PUBLICATIONS OF OFFICIAL DOCUMENTS, DIPLOMATIC CORRESPONDENCE, AND PROTOCOLS.

A. I. Andreyev, ed., *Russkiye otkrytiya v Tikhom okeanye i Severnoy Amerikye.* Moscow, 1948.

Collection of the Imperial Russian Historical Society, cited as Sb. RIO (Sbornik imperatorskogo russkogo istoricheskogo obshchestva). Among the materials published in these collections we note: *Bumagi imp. Yekateriny II, khranyashchiyesya v gosudarstvennom arkhivye ministerstva inostrannykh del,* pts. I-V, vols. 7, 10, 13, 27, 42; *Diplomaticheskaya perepiska angliyskikh poslov i poslannikov pri russkom dvorye (1762-1776),* vols. 12, 19; *Diplomaticheskaya perepiska imp. Yekateriny II, pts. I-IX (1762-1777),* vols. 48, 51, 57, 67, 87, 97, 118, 135, 145; *Pisma imp. Yekateriny II baronu Melkhioru Grimmu,* vols. 23; *Pisma barona Melkhiora Grimma k imp. Yekaterinye II,* vols. 33, 44.

F. Martens, ed., *Sobraniye traktatov i konventsiy, zaklyuchennykh Rossiyeyu s inostrannymi derzhavami.* 15 vols. St. Petersburg, 1874-1909.

"Iz istorii russko-amerikanskikh otnosheniy." *Mezhdunarodnaya zhizn,* 1974, No. 7.

"Novyye dokumenty o mirnom posrednichestvye Rossii v voynye SShA za nezavisimost (1780-1781)." Sost. i avt. vstup. stati N. N. Bokhovitinov. *Amerikansky yezhyegodnik. 1975.* Moscow, 1975.

"O vooruzhennom morskom neytralitetye. Sostavleno . . . po dokumentam Moskovskogo glavnogo arkhiva ministerstva inostrannykh del." *Morskoy sbornik,* vol. 11(3)-11(4), Nos. 9-12. September-December, 1859. St. Petersburg, 1859.

Polnoye sobraniye zakonov Rossiyskoy imperii s 1649 g. First Edition. St. Petersburg, 1830.

Protokoly zasedaniy konferentsii imperatorskoy Akademii nauk s 1725 po 1803 g. (1771-1785). St. Petersburg, 1900, vol. IV (1786-1803). St. Petersburg, 1911.

"Zapiska o buntye, proizvedennom Beniovskim v Bolsheretskom ostrogye i o posledstviyakh onogo." *Russky arkhiv,* No. 4, 1865.

2. PAPERS FROM PRIVATE ARCHIVES. CORRESPONDENCE, COLLECTIONS, MEMOIRS, AND DIARIES OF POLITICAL AND SOCIAL LEADERS, SCHOLARS, AND LITERARY PEOPLE.

Franz U. T. Aepinus, *Teoriya elektrichestva i magnetizma.* Leningrad, 1951.

Arkhiv knyazya Vorontsova. kn. 1-40. Moscow, 1870-1895: *Rospis soroka knigam knyazya Vorontsova s azbuchnym ukazatelyem lichnykh imen.* Moscow, 1897.

Ye. R. Dashkova, (N. D. Chichulin, ed.), *Zapiski knyagini Dashkovoy.* St. Petersburg, 1907.

D. I. Fonvizin, *Sochineniya, pisma i izbrannyye perevody.* St. Petersburg, 1866.

D. I. Fonvizin, *Pervoye polnoye sobraniye sochinenii.* Moscow, 1883.

Benjamin Franklin, *Izbrannyye proizvedeniya.* Moscow, 1956.

——————— , *Kak blagopoluchno vek prozhit, nauka dobrogo cheloveka Rikharda.* Moscow, 1791.

——————— , *Opyty i nablyudeniya nad elektrichestvom.* Moscow, 1956.

——————— , *Otryvok iz zapisok Franklinovykh s prisovokupleniyem kratkogo opisaniya ego zhizni i nekotorykh ego sochinenii.* Translation of A. T. from the French. Moscow, 1799.

——————— , *Sobraniye raznykh sochineniy Venyamina Franklina.* Moscow, 1803.

——————— , *Ucheniye dobrodushnogo Rikharda.* St. Petersburg, 1784.

Alexander Hamilton, *Otchyot general-kasnachyeya A. Gamilton, uchinenny Amerikanskim Shtatam 1791 g. o polzye manufaktur v otnoshenii onykh k torgovlye i zemlyedeliyu.* St. Petersburg, 1807.

N. M. Karamzin, *Sochineniya* (in various editions, in particular, vol. 1, Petrograd, 1917; vol. 3, St. Petersburg, 1848; Translations, vol. VIII, St. Petersburg, 1833.)

A. V. Khrapovitsky, *Dnevnik.* Moscow, 1901.

M. V. Lomonosov, *Polnoye sobraniye sochinenii.* 10 vols. Moscow-Leningrad, 1950-1957.

N. M. Maykov, ed., *Pisma A. A. Bezborodko k grafu P. A. Rumyantsovu, 1775-1793 gg.* St. Petersburg, 1900.

N. I. Novikov, *Izbrannyye proizvedeniya.* Moscow-Leningrad, 1951.

N. I. Novikov i ego sovremenniki. Izbrannyye sochineniya. Moscow, 1961.

N. P. Panin, *Materialy dlya zhiznyeopisaniya grafa Nikity Petrovicha*

Panina (1770-1837), especially vol. VI. 7 vols. St. Petersburg, 1888-1892.

Pisma i bumagi imp. Yekateriny II, khranyashchiyesya v Publichnoy bibliotekye. St. Petersburg,1873.

A. N. Radishchev, *Polnoye sobraniye sochinenii.* 3 vols. Moscow-Leningrad, 1938-1952.

G V. Rikhman, *Trudy po fizikye.* Moscow, 1956.

L. F. Segur, *Zapiski grafa Segyura o prebyvanii ego v Rossii (1785-1789).* Translated from the French. St. Petersburg, 1865.

A. V. Suvorov, *Dokumenty*, vol. II. Moscow, 1951.

M. F. Ushakov, *Dokumenty*, vol. I. Moscow, 1951.

3. WORKS OF TRAVELLERS AND OTHER WORKS OF CON-TEMPORARIES OF EVENTS STUDIED.

V. Baranshchikov, *Neschastnyye priklyucheniya Vasiliya Baran-shchikova meshchanina Nizhnego* Novgoroda v *3-kh chastyakh sveta, v Amerikye, Azii i Yevropye s 1780 po 1787 g.* St. Petersburg, 1787, 1788, 1793.

J. B. Bossiev, *Novyye putechestviya v Zapadnuyu Indiyu, soder-zhashchiya v sebe opisaniye raznykh narodov, zhivushchikh v okruzh-nostyakh bolshoy reki Sent Lui, obyknovyenno nazyvayemoy Missisipi, ikh zakony, pravleniye, nravy voyny i otpravleniye torgovli, pisannyye g. Bossyu.* Translated from the French language. Publishers, N. Novikov and Company. Pts. 1-2. University Press of N. Novikov. Moscow, 1783.

G. Cooper, *Sokrashchennaya aglinskaya istoriya s drevneyshikh do nyneshnikh vremen, sochinennaya G. Kuperom, po rasporya-zheniyu grafa Chesterfilda, s prisovokupleniyem v dopolneniye iz drugogo avtora opisaniya voyny Anglii s Soyedinyonnymi Ameri-kanskimi oblastyami.* Translated from the English. St. Petersburg, 1790.

Ye. N. Karzhavin (and F. V. Karzhavin), *Remarques sur la langue russiènne et sur son alphabet.* Publ., corr. et augm. par Phéodore Karjavine. . . . St. Petersburg, 1789, 1791.

F. V. Karzhavin, *Sokrashchennyy Vitruviy, ili Sovershennyy ar-khitektor.* Translation of the Architect-Deputy Fyodor Karzhavin. Moscow, 1789.

_____, *Opisaniye khoda kupecheskikh karavanov v step-noy Aravii* . . . St. Petersburg, 1790.

——————————, *Slovar, v kotorom, po vozmozhnosti moyey, izyasneny, inoyazychnyye, obretayushchiyesya v arkhitektonicheskikh sochineniyakh rechi, iz kotorykh mnogiye prinyaty nashimi zodchimi bez nuzhdy ot inozemelnykh masterov* . . . Moscow, 1791.

——————————, *Kratkoye izvestiye o dostopamyatnykh priklyucheniyakh kapitana d'Sivilya, trizhdy umershego, i proch* . . . Translation of Fyodor Karzhavin. Moscow, 1791.

——————————, *Frantsuzskiye, rossiyskiye i nemetskiye razgovory v polzu nachinatelyey.* St. Petersburg, 1791, 1803 (the book was republished many times both during the lifetime and after the death of F. V. Karzhavin).

—————— ., ——————, *Vozhak, pokazyvayushchiy put k luchshemu vygovoru buku i recheniy frantsuzskikh. Le guide francais par Théodore Karjavine.* St. Petersburg, 1794.

——————————, *Fokus-pokus, ili Sobraniye lyubopytnoye redkikh udivitelnykh i zabavnykh ruchnykh iskusstv.* St. Petersburg, 1795.

——————————, *Novoyavlennyy vedun, povedayushchiy gadaniya dukhov* . . . St. Petersburg, 1795.

——————————, *Modèle des jeunes gens. Lecture pour l'étude de la langue francaise.* (Ed. rev. et corr. par Théodore Karjavine). St. Petersburg, 1796.

D. M. Ladygin, *Izvestiye v Amerikye o seleniyakh aglitskikh v tom chisle nyne pod nazvaniyem Soyedinyonnykh Provintsiy, vybrano perechnem iz noveyshikh o tom prostrannykh sochinitelyey.* St. Petersburg, 1783.

Opisaniye zemel Severnoy Ameriki i tamoshnykh prirodnykh zhitelyey. Translated from the German into the Russian language by A. R. St. Petersburg, 1763.

B. P. Polevoy, *Rossiyskiye kuptsy Grigoriya Shelikhova stranstvovaniya iz Okhotska vo Vostochnomu okeanu k Amerikanskim beregam.* Khabarovsk, 1971.

Guillaume Raynal, *Filosoficheskaya i politicheskaya istoriya o zavedeniyakh i kommertsii yevropeytsyev v obeikh Indiyakh.* Translated from the French, pts. 1-6. St. Petersburg, 1805-1811.

W. Robertson, *Izvestiye o Amerikye, Villiama Robertsona, pervenstvuyushchego professora v Universitetye v Edinburgye i korolevskogo istoriografa po Shotlandii.* Translation from the English (by A. I. Luzhkov), pts. 1-2. St. Petersburg, 1784.

G. A. Sarychev, *Puteshestviye po severo-vostochnoy chasti Sibiri, Ledovitomu moryu i Vostochnomu okeanu.* Moscow, 1952.

K. Ph. M. Snell, *Von den Handlungsvortheilen welche aus der Unabhängigkeit der Vereinigten Staaten von Nord-Amerika für das russische Reich entspringen.* Riga, 1783.

F. V. Taube, *Istoriya o aglinskoy torgovlye, manufakturakh, seleniyakh i moreplavanii onyye v drevniye, sredniye i noveyshiye vremena do 1776 goda, s dostovernym pokazaniyem spravedlivykh prichin nyneshney voyny v Severnoy Amerikye i prochikh tomu podobnykh veshchey do 1776 goda.* Translation from the German. Moscow, 1793.

4. PERIODICALS

Akademicheskiye izvestiya, St. Petersburg, 1779-1781.

Irtysh, prevrashchayushchiysya v Ipokrenu, Tobolsk, 1790.

Moskovskiye vedomosti, 1775-1790.

Moskovsky zhurnal, 1791-1792.

Moskovskoye yezhyemesyachnoye izdaniye, 1781.

Neues St. Peterburgisches Journal vom Jahre 1784.

Nova Acta Academiae Scientiarum Imperialis Petropolitanae, St. Petersburg, 1789 and other years.

Novyye yezhyemesyachnyye sochineniya, 1786-1796.

Politichesky zhurnal, Moscow, 1790-1800.

Pribavleniye k Moskovskim vedomostyam, 1783-1784.

Priyatnoye i poleznoye preprovozhdeniye vremeni, Moscow, 1794-1798.

S. -Petersburgskiye vedomosti, 1775-1790.

S. -Petersburgskiye yezhyenedelnyye sochineniya, 1778.

S. -Peterburgsky vestnik, 1778-1780.

Sobraniye raznykh sochineniy i novostey, St. Petersburg, 1775-1776.

Uyedinyonny poshekhonets, Yaroslavl, 1786.

Zerkalo sveta, St. Petersburg, 1786-1787.

5. STATISTICAL MATERIALS, HANDBOOKS, GUIDEBOOKS

K. Arsenyev, *Nachertaniye statistiki Rossiyskogo gosudarstva,* pts. 1-2, St. Petersburg, 1818-1819.

Bibliothèque Imperiale Publique de St. Petersburg. *Catalogue de la Sec. des Rossica ou Ecrits sur la Russie en Langues Etrangères.* 2 vols. St. Petersburg, 1873.

M. D. Chulkov, *Istoricheskoye opisaniye rossiyskoy kommertsii,* vol. 7. 7 vols. Moscow, 1781-1788.

V. Kamenetsky, "Materialy o russko-amerikanskikh otnosheniyakh XVIII-XIX vv. v russkikh izdaniyakh," *Istorichesky zhurnal,* 1943, Nos. 3-4.

N. Kaydanov, *Sistematichesky katalog delam gosudarstvennoy kommerts-kollegii (1716-1811 gg.).* St. Petersburg, 1884.

Lichnyye arkhivnyye fondy v gosudarstvennykh khranilishchakh SSSR, vols. 1-2, Moscow, 1963.

G. Nebolsin, *Statisticheskiye zapiski o vneshney torgovlye Rossii,* pt. 1-2. St. Petersburg, 1835.

A. N. Neustroyev, *Istoricheskoye rozyskaniye o russkikh povremennykh izdaniyakh i sbornikakh za 1703-1802.* St. Petersburg, 1874.

————————— , *Ukazatel k russkim povremennym izdaniyam i sbornikam za 1703-1802 i k istoricheskomu rozyskaniyu o nikh.* St. Petersburg, 1898.

Rukopisnyye materialy Leonarda Eylera v arkhivyye Akademii nauk SSSR, vol. 1, Moscow-Leningrad, 1962.

Svodny katalog russkoy knigi XVIII veka, 1725-1800, vols. 1-5, Moscow, 1963-1967.

Heinrich Friedrich Storch, *Historisch-statitisches Gemälde des russischen Reichs. . . .* 7 vols. Riga-Leipzig, 1797-1803.

————————— , *Supplementband zum fünften, sechsten und siebenten Teil des historich-statistischen Gemäldes . . .* Leipzig, 1803.

Uchenaya korrespondentsiya Akademii nauk XVIII veka (1766-1782), Moscow-Leningrad, 1937.

6. BIOGRAPHIES

D. S. Babkin, *A. N. Radishchev. Literaturno-obshchestvennaya deyatelnost.* Moscow-Leningrad, 1966.

N. P. Durov, "Fyodor Vasilyevich Karzhavin." *Russkaya starina,* vol. 12. February, 1875.

N. Grigorovich, *Kantsler knyaz Bezborodko.* 2 vols. St. Petersburg, 1879-1881.

R. F. Ivanov, *Franklin.* Moscow, 1972.

P. L. Kapitsa, "Nauchnaya deyatelnost V. Franklina." *Vestnik AN SSSR,* No. 2, p. 72, 1956.

G. P. Makagonenko, *Nikolay Novikov i russkoye prosveshcheniye XVIII veka.* Moscow-Leningrad, 1951.

_____, *Radishchev i yevo vremya*. Moscow, 1956.

V. I. Rabinovich, *Revolyutsionny prosvetitel F. V. Karzhavina*. Moscow, 1966.

_____, *S gishpantsami v Novy York i Gavanu*. Moscow, 1967.

M. I. Radovsky, *Venyamin Franklin*. Moscow-Leningrad, 1965.

B. Polevoy, *Grigory Shelikhov— "Kolumb rossiysky."* Magadan, 1960.

N. N. Yakovlyov, *Vashington*. Moscow, 1973.

III. HISTORICAL ARTICLES AND GENERAL WORKS

V. N. Aleksandrenko, *Russkiye diplomaticheskiye agenty v Londonye v XVIII v.* 2 vols. Warsaw, 1897.

M. P. Alekseyev, "Filologicheskiye nablyudeniya Karzhavina, F. V. Iz istorii russkoy filologii v XVIII v."*Romanskaya filologiya*. Leningrad, 1961.

H. Aptheker, *Istoriya amerikanskogo naroda*. vol. II: *Amerikanskaya revolyutsiya 1763-1783*. Translated from the English. Moscow, 1962.

I. S. Bak, "Dmitry Alekseyevich Golitsyn (filosofskiye, obshchestvenno-politicheskiye i ekonomicheskiye vozzreniya)." Istoricheskiye zapiski, No. 26, 1948.

V. N. Berkh, "Pobeg grafa Beniovskogo iz Kamchatki vo Frantsiyu." *Syn otechestva,* 1821, Nos. 27, 28.

P. N. Berkov, *Istoriya russkoy zhurnalistiki XVIII veka*. Moscow-Leningrad, 1952.

I. A. Belyavskaya, "V. Franklin—deyatel natsionalno-osvoboditelnogo dvizheniya amerikanskogo naroda." *Voprosy istorii,* No. 10, 1956.

V. A. Bilbasov, *Istoriya Yekateriny Vtoroy*. 2 vols. St. Petersburg, 1890-1891.

N. N. Bolkhovitinov, *Stanovleniye russko-amerikanskikh otnosheny, 1775-1815*. Moscow, 1966.

V. Danevsky, *Istorichesky ocherk neytralityeta*. Moscow, 1879.

N. M. Druzhinin, "O periodizatsii istorii kapitalisticheskikh otnosheny v Rossii." *Voprosy istorii,* No. 11, 1949.

_____, "Genezis kapitalizma v Rossii." Desyatyy mezhdunarodnyy kongress istorikov v Rime. Moscow, 1956.

Ye. Dvoychenko-Markova, "Shturman Gerasim Izmaylov." *Morskiye zapiski,* vol. 13, No. 4, New York, 1955.

A. A. Fursenko, *Amerikanskaya burzhuaznaya revolyutsiya XVIII v.* Moscow-Leningrad, 1960.

Yu. Ya. Gerchuk, "Etnograficheskiye nablyudeniya russkogo puteshestvennika F. V. Karzhavina." *Sovetskaya etnografiya,* No. 1, 1972.

Istoriya diplomatii, vol. I. 2nd Edition. Moscow, 1959.

D. Kachenovsky, *O kaperakh i prizovom sudoproizvodstve.* Moscow, 1865.

P. L. Kapitsa. *Zhizn dlya nauki. Lomonosov, Franklin, Rezeford, Lanzheven.* Moscow, 1965.

N. Lazarev, "Pervyye svedeniya russkikh o Novom svetye." *Istorichesky zhurnal,* No. 1, 1943.

L. Lekhtblau, "Iz istorii prosvetitelnoy literatury v Rossii." *Istorik-marksist,* No. 1, 1939.

V. Leshkov, *Istoricheskiye issledovaniye nachal neytraliteta otnositelno morskoy torgovli.* Moscow, 1841.

G. M. Lester, "Znakomstvo uchyonykh Severnoy Ameriki kolonialnogo perioda s rabotami M. V. Lomonosova i Peterburgskoy akademii nauk." *Voprosy istorii yestyestvoznaniya i tekhniki,* vol. 12, Moscow, 1962.

Mezhdunarodnyye svyazi Rossii v XVII-XVIII vv.: Ekonomika, politika, i kultura. Moscow, 1966.

Nauchnyy byuleten LGU, No. 8, 1946.

M. V. Nechkina, "Volter i russkoye obshchestvo," in *Volter. Stati i materialy.* Moscow, 1948.

——————, "K itogam diskussii o 'voskhodyashchyey' i 'niskhodyashchyey' stadiyakh feodalizma." *Voprosy istorii,* No. 12, 1963.

M. N. Nikolskaya, *Russkaya pechat o voynye Severnoy Ameriki za nezavisimost v XVIII vekye.* V. I. Lenin Moscow State Pedagogical Institute. Moscow, 1968. (Doctoral dissertation)

Ocherk istorii SSSR. Period feodalizma. Rossiya vo vtoroy polovinye XVIII v. Moscow, 1956.

V. Orlov, *Russkiye prosvetiteli 1790-1800-kh godov.* Moscow, 1953.

Ot Alyaski do Ognyonnoy Zemli. Istoriya i etnografiya stran Ameriki. Moscow, 1967.

Ye. G. Plimak, "Pravda knigi i lozh kommentariya (k vykhodu v SShA *Puteshestviya iz Peterburga v Moskvu* A. N. Radishcheva), in

Kritika burzhuaznykh kontseptsy istorii Rossii perioda feodalizma. Moscow, 1962.

—————— , "Zloklyucheniya burzhuaznoy komparativistiki." *Istoriya SSSR,* No. 3, 1963.

—————— , *Zapretnaya mysl obretayet svobodu.* Moscow, 1966.

M. I. Radovsky, *Venyamin Franklin i ego svyazi s Rossiyey.* Moscow-Leningrad, 1958.

A. Rochester, *Amerikansky kapitalizm, 1607-1800.* Moscow, 1950.

I. Yu. Rodzinskaya, "Russko-angliyskiye otnosheniya v shestide-syatykh godakh XVIII v.," in *Trudy Moskovskogo gosudarstvennogo istoriko-arkhivnogo instituta,* vol 21, Moscow, 1965.

G. N. Sevostyanov, Chief Ed., I. A. Belyavsky, G. P. Kuropyatnik, and B. Ya. Mikhaylov, eds., *Ocherki novoy i novyeyshyey istorii SShA.* Moscow, 1960.

A. S. Sgibnev, "Bunt Beniovskogo v Kamchatkye v 1771 g." *Russkaya starina,* vol. 15, 1876.

M. N. Shprygova, "Voyna Ameriki za nezavisimost v osveshcheniiy *Moskovskikh vedomostey* N. I. Novikova." *Nauchnyye doklady vysshey shkoly. Istoricheskiye nauki,* No. 3, 1961.

—————— , "Osveshcheniye v *Sankt-Peterburgskikh vedo-mostyakh* voyny Serernoy Ameriki za nezavisimost." *Uchyonyye zapiski MGPI im. V. I. Lenina,* No. 286, Moscow, 1967.

G. Shtorm, "Potayennyy Radishchev." *Novyy mir,* No. 11, 1964.

M. M. Shtrange, *Russkoye obshchestvo i frantsuzskaya revolyutsiya 1789-1794.* Moscow, 1956.

L. A. Shur, "Ispanskaya i Portugalskaya Amerika v russkoy pechati pervoy chetverti XIX v." *Latinskaya Amerika v proshlom i nastoyashchem.* Moscow, 1960.

A.M. Stanislavskaya, "Rossiya i Angliya v gody vtoroy turetskoy voyny 1787-1791." *Voprosy istorii,* No. 11, 1948.

—————— , "Anglo-russkiye otnosheniya v kontsye XVIII veka." *Doklady i soobshcheniya Instituta istorii AN SSR,* No. 12, 1956.

A. Startsev, "Venyamin Franklin i russkoye obshchestvo XVIII veka." *Internatsionalnaya literatura,* Nos. 3-4, 1940.

—————— , "O zapadnykh svyazyakh Radishcheva." *Internatsionalnaya literatura.* Nos. 708, 1940.

—————— , "Amerikanskaya voyna za nezavisimost v russkoy

pechati kontsa XVIII v. Obzor redkikh izdaniy." *Istoricheskaya litera-tura,* vol. 5-6, 1940.

—————————, *Amerika i russkoye obshchestvo.* Moscow, 1942.

—————————, "F. V. Karzhavin i ego amerikanskoye puteshest-viye." *Istoriya SSSR,* No. 3, 1960.

A I. Startsev-Kunin, *Amerikanskaya revolyutsiya, Radishchev i russkoye obshchestvo XVIII veka.* Dissertation. Moscow, 1946.

Dzh. Stroykh, *Stanovleniye nauki v SShA.* Translated from the English. Moscow, 1966.

Ye. V. Tarle, "Byla li Yekaterininskaya Rossiya ekonomicheski otstaloyu stranoyu?" *Sochineniya,* vol. IV. Moscow, 1958.

V. K. Yatsunsky, "Osnovnyye etapi genezisa kapitalizma v Rossii." *Istoriya SSSR,* No. 5, 1958.

A. V. Yefimov, *SShA. Puti razvitiya kapitalizma.* Moscow, 1969.

————————— "Obshchestvennaya deyatelnost Venya-mina Franklina." *Vestnik AN SSSR,* No. 3, 1956.

A. V. Yefimov and S. A. Tokarev, eds., *Narody Ameriki,* vol. 1. Mos-cow, 1959.

M. N. Zakharov, "O genezise idey T. Dzheffersona." *Voprosy istorii,* No. 3, 1948.

B. AMERICAN-WEST EUROPEAN BIBLIOGRAPHY

I. UNPUBLISHED MATERIAL

National Archives, Washington, D. C.
Papers of the Continental Congress, 1774-1789. 204 rolls (M247). Individual rolls, in particular No. 117 (Mission of Francis Dana to St. Petersburg.).
Library of Congress, Manuscript Division, Washington, D. C.
Russian Collections. G. V. Yudin. Russian-American Company Papers, 1786-1830. 3 boxes.
Massachusetts Historical Society, Boston, Mass.
The Adams Papers.
Boston Athenaeum, Boston, Mass.
American Academy of Arts and Sciences Records.
The Historical Society of Pennsylvania, Philadelphia, Pa.

Lewis-Neilson Papers. W. D. Lewis. Miscellaneous Letters and Documents.

The American Philosophical Society, Philadelphia, Pa.
Papers of Dr. Franklin. Materials on the Election of the first Russian Members and Correspondence with the Petersburg Academy of Sciences.

Stanford University, Stanford, Calif. Hoover Institution on War, Revolution; and Peace.
Frank Golder Collection. Boxes XIV, XX.

II. OFFICIAL DOCUMENTS, PAPERS, MEMOIRS, LITERARY WORKS, AND OTHER WORKS OF THE REVOLUTIONARY WAR GENERATION

Charles Francis Adams, ed., *The Works of John Adams, Second President of the United States*, vols. IV-V. 10 vols. Little, Brown. Boston: 1850-1856.

Alfred, Ritter von Arneth, ed., *Maria Theresa und Joseph II: Ihre Correspondenz sammt briefen Joseph's an seinen Bruder Leopold*, vol. III. 3 vols. C. Gerold's Sohn. Vienna: 1867-1868.

——————, ed., *Joseph II und Katharina von Russland: Ihr Briefwechsel.* W. Braumüller. Vienna, 1869.

Max Beloff, ed., *The Debate on the American Revolution, 1761-1783.* N. Kaye. London: 1949.

T. Bond, "Anniversary Oration, Delivered May 21st, before the American Philosophical Society, Held in Philadelphia for the Promotion of Useful Knowledge, for the Year 1782," 31-32. Printed by John Dunlop. Philadelphia, 1782.

Julian P. Boyd, ed., *The Papers of Thomas Jefferson.* 18 vols. Princeton University Press. Princeton: 1950-1971.

Marvin L. Brown, ed. & trans., *American Independence through Prussian Eyes. A Neutral View of the Peace Negotiations of 1782-1783: Selections from Prussian Diplomatic Correspondence.* Duke University Press. Durham: 1959.

Edmund C. Burnett, ed., *Letters of Members of the Continental Congress.* 8 vols. The Carnegie Institution of Washington. Washington: 1921-1936.

Lyman H. Butterfield, ed., *Diary and Autobiography of John Adams.* 4 vols. Belknap Press of Harvard University Press. Cambridge: 1961.

Lester J. Cappon, ed., *The Adams-Jefferson Letters.* 2 vols. University of North Carolina Press. Chapel Hill: 1959.

"Circular Letter Issued by the British Foreign Office, 1777. The London *Chronicle,* June 17-19, 1777." *Pennsylvania Magazine of History and Biography,* vol. XVI, 1892.

Henry S. Commager, ed., *Documents of American History.* 8th Edition. Appleton-Century-Crofts. New York: 1968.

Marie Daniel Bourée, Baron de Corberon, *Un diplomat francais à la cour de Catherine II, 1775-1780: Journal intime du Chevalier de Corberon, Chargé d'Affaires de France en Russie,* vol. I. 2 vols. Plon, Nourrit et Cie. Paris: 1901.

Tench Coxe, *View of the United States of America in a Series of Papers Written at Various Times between the Years 1787 and 1794.* Philadelphia, Printed 1794; London, Reprinted for J. Johnson, 1795.

Henri Doniol, *Histoire de la participation de la France à l'établissement des Etats-Unis d'Amerique. Correspondence diplomatique et documents.* 5 vols. Imprimerie nationale. Paris: 1886-1892.

John C. Fitzpatrick, ed., *The Writings of George Washington. From the Original Manuscript Sources, 1745-1799.* 40 vols. U. S. Government Printing Office. Washington: 1931-1944.

Worthington C. Ford, ed., *Writings of John Quincy Adams.* 7 vols. The Macmillan Company. New York: 1913-1917.

Guillaume de Garden, *Histoire générale des traités de paix et autres transactions principales entre toutes les puissances de l'Europe depuis la paix de Westphalie.* 15 vols. Amyot. Paris: 1848-1887.

James Howard Harris, 3rd Earl of Malmesbury, ed., *Diaries and correspondence of the First Earl of Malmesbury,* vols. I-II. 4 vols. R. Bentley. London: 1844.

Gaillard Hunt, ed., *The Writings of James Madison.* 9 vols. G. P. Putnam's Sons. New York and London: 1900-1910.

William T. Hutchison and William M. E. Rachal, eds., *The Papers of James Madison.* Chicago: 1962-

John Paul Jones, *Memoirs of Paul Jones, Late Rear-Admiral in the Russian Service . . . Now First Compiled from His Original Journals and Correspondence, Including an Account of His Services under Prince Potemkin. Prepared for Publication by himself.* 2 vols. Washbourne. London: 1843.

Leonard W. Labaree, ed., *The Papers of Benjamin Franklin.* 17 vols. Yale University Press. New Haven: 1959-1973.

Andrew A. Lipscomb and Albert E. Bergh, eds., *The Writings of*

Thomas Jefferson. 20 vols. U.S. Government Printing Office. Washington: 1905.

Georg Friedrich von Martens, *Recueil des principaux traités d'alliance, de paix, de treve, de neutralité, de commerce, de limites, d'echanges, etc. conclus par les puissances et Etats dans d'autres parties du monde depuis 1761 jusqu'à present.* 7 vols. J. C. Dieterich. Göttingen: 1791-1801.

Hunter Miller, ed., *Treaties and Other International Acts of the United States of America, 1776-1863,* vol. I. 8 vols. U. S. Government Printing Office. Washington: 1931-1948.

Gouverneur Morris (Beatrix Cary Davenport, ed.), *A diary of the French Revolution.* 2 vols. Houghton Mifflin Co. Boston: 1939.

Guillaume-Thomas-Francois Raynal, *Histoire philosophique et politique des établissements et du commerce des Européens dans les deux Indes.* 10 vols. Chez J.-L. Pellet. Geneva: 1780-1781.

_____ ., *Revolution de l'Amerique.* London, L. Davis, and sold at the Hague at P. F. Gosse, 1781.

James B. Scott, *The Armed Neutralities of 1780 and 1800: A collection of Official Documents.* New York: 1918.

Albert H. Smyth, ed., *The Writings of Benjamin Franklin.* 10 vols. The Macmillan Company. New York: 1907.

Jared Sparks, ed., *The Life of John Ledyard, the American Traveller, Comprising Selections from his Journals and Correspondence.* Cambridge, Hilliard and Brown; New York, C. & C. Carvill, 1828. Subsequent editions, of which the author used one published in 1864.

_____ , ed., *The Works of Benjamin Franklin.* 10 vols. Hilliard, Gray, & Co. Boston: 1836-1840.

Transactions of the American Philosophical Society held at Philadelphia for promotion of Useful Knowledge, vol. I, Philadelphia, 1771 and other years.

United States. Library of Congress. *Journals of the Continental Congress, 1774-1789.* 34 vols. Government Printing Office. Washington: 1904-1937.

United States. The President of the United States. *Secret Journals of the Acts and Proceedings of Congress From the First Meeting Thereof to the Dissolution of the Confederation, By the Adoption of the Constitution of the United States.* 4 vols. Thomas B. Wait. Boston: 1820-1821.

United States. Secretary of State. *Diplomatic Correspondence of the United States of America from the Signing of the Definitive Treaty of Peace, 10th September, 1783 to the Adoption of the Constitution, March 4, 1789.* 7 vols. Printed by Francis Preston Blair. Washington: 1833-1834.

Stephen D. Watrous, ed., *John Ledyard's Journey Through Russia and Siberia, 1787-1788. The Journal and Selected Letters.* University of Wisconsin Press. Madison: 1966.

F. Wharton, ed., *The Revolutionary Diplomatic Correspondence of the United States.* 6 vols. 50th Congress. 1st Session. House of Representatives Misc. Doc. 603. Government Printing Office. Washington: 1889.

III. SECONDARY SOURCES

A. Pre-1940 Works

Anna Mary Babey, *Americans in Russia, 1776-1917. A Study of the American Travellers in Russia from the American Revolution to the Russian Revolution.* The Comet Press. New York: 1938.

Hubert H. Bancroft, *History of Alaska, 1730-1885,* vol. 33 of *The Works of Hubert Howe Bancroft.* A. L. Bancroft & Co. San Francisco: 1886.

Samuel F. Bemis, *The Diplomacy of the American Revolution: The Foundations of American Diplomacy, 1775-1823.* D. Appleton Century Co. New York and London: 1935. Revised Edition: Indiana University Press. Bloomington: 1957.

_____ , *Pickney's Treaty. A Study of America's Advantage from Europe's Distress, 1783-1800.* Johns Hopkins University Press. Baltimore: 1926. Revised Edition: Yale University Press. New Haven: 1960.

Carl Bergbohm, *Die bewaffnete Neutralität, 1780-1783.* Puttkamer & Mühlbrecht. Berlin: 1884.

A. Bernstorff, Denkwürdigkeiten aus dem Leben des K. dänischen *staatsministers Andreas Peter Graven v. Bernstorff.* Copenhagen: 1800.

Sarah M. Brownson, *Life of Demetrius Augustine Gallitzin, Prince and Priest.* New York and Cincinnati, F. Pustet & Co., 1873. Paris, Didier, 1880.

William P. Cresson, *Francis Dana, A Puritan Diplomat at the Court of Catherine the Great.* L. McVeagh, The Dial Press. New York: 1930.

Christian Wilhelm von Dohm, *Denkwürdigkeiten meiner Zeit.* 5 vols. Helwing. Hannover: 1814-1819.

Paul Fauchille, *La diplomatie francaise et la ligue des neutres de 1780 (1776-1783).* G. Pedone-Lauriel. Paris: 1893.

Comte de Goertz, *Mémoire ou précis historique sur la neutralité armée et son origine suivi de pièces justificatives.* Basel: 1801.

Thomas Heyden, *A Memoir of the Life and Character of the Rev. Prince Demetrius A. de Gallitzin, Founder of Loretto and Catholicity in Cambria County, Pa., Apostle of the Alleghanies.* Baltimore, J. Murphy & Co., New York, Catholic Publication Society, 1869. German Translation used by Author: *Der Missioner Fürst Augustin Gallitzin.* Hamburg: 1859.

John C. Hildt, *Early Diplomatic Negotiations of the United States with Russia.* The Johns Hopkins Press. Baltimore: 1906.

Charles S. Hyneman, *The First American Neutrality. A Study of the American Understanding of Neutral Obligations During the Years 1792 to 1815.* Illinois Studies in the Social Sciences, vol. XX, Nos. 1-2. University of Illinois Press. Urbana: 1935.

E. R. Johnson, T. W. Van Metre, G. G. Hebner, and D. S. Hanchett, *History of Domestic and Foreign Commerce of the United States.* vols. I-II in one vol. Washington: 1915. Reprint: 1922.

Francis P. Renaut, *Les rélations diplomatiques entre la Russie et les États-Unis (1776-1825).* Éditions du Graouli. Paris: 1923.

—————— , *Les Provinces-Unies et la Guerre d'Amerique (1775-1784).* 3 vols. Éditions du Graouli. Paris: 1924.

Philip S. Russell, *John Paul Jones: Man of Action.* Brentano's. New York: 1927.

B. Post-1940 Works

Victor Alexandrov. *L'Ours et la baleine, L'histoire des relations extraordinaires russo-americaines.* Librairie Stock. Paris: 1958.

Thomas A. Bailey, *America Faces Russia: Russian-American Relations from Early Times to Our Day.* Cornell University Press. Ithaca: 1950.

Samuel F. Bemis, *John Quincy Adams and the Foundations of American Foreign Policy.* A. A. Knopf. New York: 1949.

Ulane Bonnel, *La France, les États-Unis et la guerre de course (1797-1815).* Nouvelles Éditions latines. Paris: 1961.

Irving Brant, *James Madison*. 6 vols. Bobbs-Merrill. Indianapolis: 1941-1961.

Edward S. Corwin, *French Policy and the American Alliance of 1778*. Archon Books. Hamden: 1962.

Alfred W. Crosby, *America, Russia, Hemp, and Napoleon: American Trade with Russia and the Baltic, 1783-1812*. Ohio State University Press. Columbus: 1965.

Paul Dukes, *The Emergence of the Super-Powers. A Short Comparative History of the U.S.A. and the U.S.S.R.* Macmillan. London: 1970.

Foster Rhea Dulles, *The Road to Teheran: The Story of Russia and America, 1781-1943.* Princeton University Press. Princeton: 1944.

Francis Franklin, *The Rise of the American Nation, 1789-1824.* International Publishers. New York: 1943.

Erwin Hölzle, *Russland und Amerika. Aufbruch und Begegnung zweier Weltmächte.* R. Oldenbourg. Munich: 1953.

Merrill Jensen, *The Founding of a Nation: A History of the American Revolution, 1763-1776.* Oxford University Press. New York: 1968.

Gerald W. Johnson, *The First Captain: The Story of John Paul Jones.* Coward-McCann. New York: 1947. Reprint: University of Michigan Press. Ann Arbor: 1967.

Walter Kirchner, *Eine Reise durch Sibirien in achtzehnten Jahrhundert.* Munich: 1955.

Max M. Laserson, *The American Impact on Russia, Diplomatic and Ideological, 1784-1917.* New York: 1950. Second Edition: Collier Books. New York: 1962.

Isabel de Madariaga, *Britain, Russia, and the Armed Neutrality of 1780. Sir James Harris's Mission to St. Petersburg during the American Revolution.* Yale University Press. New Haven: 1962.

Samuel E. Morison, *The Maritime History of Massachusetts, 1783-1860.* Houghton, Mifflin Co. Boston: 1941.

——————— , *John Paul Jones: A Sailor's Biography.* Little, Brown. Boston: 1959.

Richard B. Morris, *The Peacemakers. The Great Powers and American Independence.* Harper & Row. New York: 1965.

Jacob M. Price, *The Tobacco Adventure to Russia; Enterprise, Politics, and Diplomacy in the Quest for a Northern Market for*

English Colonial Tobacco. American Philosophical Society. Philadelphia: 1961.

C. Stourzh, *Benjamin Franklin and American Foreign Policy.* Chicago: 1954.

A. Tarsaidze, *Czars and Presidents. The Story of a Forgotten Friendship.* McDowell, Obolensky. New York: 1958.

William A. Williams, *American-Russian Relations (1781-1947).* Rinehart. New York: 1952.

Avrahm Yarmolinsky, *Russian Americana. Sixteenth to Eighteenth Centuries. A Bibliographical and Historical Study.* New York Public Library. New York: 1943.

IV. ARTICLES

E. Albrecht, "Die Stellung der Vereinigten Staaten von Amerika zur bewaffneten Neutralität von 1780." *Zeitschrift für Völkerrecht,* VI, 1913.

Lyman H. Butterfield, "The Papers of the Adams Family: Some Account of Their History." *Proceedings* of the Massachusetts Historical Society, vol. LXXI, 1953-1957.

W. S. Carpenter, "The United States and the League of Neutrals of 1780." *American Journal of International Law,* vol. XV, 1921.

C. F. Carusi and C. Kojouharoff, "The First Armed Neutrality." *National University Law Review,* No. 9, 1929.

A. Chaboseau, "Les premières rélations diplomatiques entre les États-Unis et la Russie (1776-1809)." *Revue Bleu,* No. 16, Paris, 1926.

Paul Dukes, "Russia and the Eighteenth Century Revolution." *History,* vol. LVI, No. 188, 1971.

Eufrosina Dvoichenko-Markoff, "Benjamin Franklin, the American Philosophical Society and the Russian Academy of Sciences." *Proceedings* of the American Philosophical Society, vol. 94, No. 6, Dec., 1950.

————— , "A Russian Traveller to Eighteenth-Century America." *Proceedings* of the American Philosophical Society, vol. 97, No. 4, Sept., 1953.

————— , "The Russian Members of the American Academy of Arts and Sciences," *Proceedings* of the American Philosophical Society, vol. 109, No. 1, Feb., 1965.

_____ , "John Ledyard and the Russians." *Russian Review,* No. 4, 1952.

J. M. Frederickson, "American Shipping in the Trade with Northern Europe, 1783-1850." *Scandinavian Economic History Review.* vol. 4, No. 2, 1956.

F. A. Golder, "Catherine and the American Revolution." *American Historical Review,* vol. 21, No. 1, Oct., 1915.

D. M. Griffiths, "Nikita Panin, Russian Diplomacy, and the American Revolution." *Slavic Review,* vol. 28, No. 1, March, 1969.

_____ , "American Commercial Diplomacy in Russia, 1780 to 1783." *William and Mary Quarterly,* vol. XXVII, No. 3, July, 1970.

_____ , "An American Contribution to the Armed Neutrality of 1780." *Russian Review,* vol. 30, No. 2, April, 1971.

_____ , "The Rise and Fall of the Northern System." *Canadian Slavic Studies,* vol. IV, No. 3, Fall, 1970.

_____ , "Soviet Views of Early Russian-American Relations." *Proceedings* of the American Philosophical Society, vol. 116, No. 2, April, 1972.

R. W. Home, "Science as a Career in Eighteenth Century Russia: The Case of F.U.T. Aepinus." *The Slavonic and East European Review,* vol. 41, pp. 75-94, 1973.

Merrill Jensen, "The American People and the American Revolution." *The Journal of American History,* vol. LVII, June, 1970.

Walter Kirchner, "Ukrainian Tobacco for France." *Jahrbücher für Geschichte Osteuropas.* Band X, Heft 4, Dec., 1962.

J. D. Phillips, "Salem Opens American Trade with Russia." *The New England Quarterly,* vol. XIV, No. 4, Dec., 1941.

A. Rasch, "American Trade in the Baltic, 1783-1807." *Scandinavian Economic History Review,* vol. XIII, No. 1, 1965.

N. S. Saul, "The Beginnings of American-Russian Trade, 1763-1766." *William and Mary Quarterly,* vol. XXVI, No. 4, Oct., 1969.

O. Straus, "The United States and Russia: Their Historical Relations." *The North American Review,* vol. 181, No. 2, Aug., 1908.

V. MISCELLANEOUS

Samuel F. Bemis and Grace G. Griffin, *Guide to the Diplomatic History of the United States, 1775-1921.* U.S. Government Printing

Office. Washington: 1935. Reprint: P. Smith. New York: 1951.

Clarence S. Brigham, *History and Bibliography of American Newspapers, 1690-1820.* 2 vols. American Antiquarian Society. Worcester, Mass.: 1947.

Allen Johnson and Dumas Malone, eds., *Dictionary of American Biography.* 20 vols. New York: 1928-1936.

Charles H. Evans, ed., "Exports, Domestic, From the United States to All Countries from 1789 to 1883, Inclusive." 48th Congress. 1st Session. House of Representatives. Misc. Doc. 49, Pt. 2. U.S. Government Printing Office. Washington: 1884.

Wilhelm Christian Friebe, *Ueber Russlands Handel, landwirthschaftliche Kultur, Industrie und Produkte.* Gerstenberg und Dittmar. Gotha: 1796-1798.

Frank A. Golder, *Guide to Materials for American History in Russian Archives.* 2 vols. Carnegie Institution of Washington. Washington: 1917-1937.

Philip M. Hamer, ed., *Guide to Archives and Manuscripts in the United States. Compiled for the National Historical Publications Commission.* Yale University Press. New Haven: 1961.

Oscar Handlin, A. M. Schlesinger, Sr., and S. E. Morison, et al., *Harvard Guide to American History.* Belknap Press. Cambridge, 1954.

John Quincy Adams and Russia. A Sketch of Early Russian-American Relations as Recorded in the Papers of the Adams Family and Some of Their Contemporaries. Quincy, Mass.: 1965.

John J. Oddy, *European Commerce . . .* London, W. J. & J. Richardson, 1805.

Timothy A. Pitkin, *Statistical View of the Commerce of the United States of America.* New Haven, Durrie & Peck, 1835.

Adam Seybert, *Annales statistiques des Etats-Unis.* Paris, 1820.

U.S. Bureau of he Census, *Historical Statistics of the United States: Colonial Times to 1957.* U.S. Government Printing Office. Washington: 1960.

United States Congress. *Biographical Directory of the American Congress, 1774-1949.* U.S. Government Printing Office. Washington: 1950.

Index

Academy of Sciences, Imperial Russian (St. Petersburg), 96-116.

Adams, John, second President of the United States, 36, 39-43, 55-58, 64, 72-74, 84, 87, 144, 180, 184.

Adams, John Quincy, sixth President of the United States, 64.

Aepinus, Franz Ulrich Theodor, Russian scientist, 37, 92, 98-106.

Aleutian Islands: visit of Cook Expedition, 22-23.

American Academy of Arts and Sciences (Boston), 99-101, 114-115.

American Philosophical Society (Philadelphia), 100-3, 106, 110-13.

American Revolution: perceptions of Russian Government, 10-12, 19-29, 45-61, 120-24, 129; perceptions of Russian diplomats in London and Paris, 7-10, 13-16, 25-26, 191-215; perceptions of Russian society, 125-51; perceptions of A. N. Radishchev, 152-63; perceptions of F. V. Karzhavin, 164-77.

Austria: alliance with Russia and role in Russian mediation efforts, 46, 50-61.

Bakunin, Pyotr Vasilyevich, Sr., and Pyotr Vasilyevich, Jr., officials of Russian College of Foreign Affairs, 27, 37, 60, 66.

Baranshchikov, Vasily, Russian visitor to West Indies, 178.

Baryatinsky, Ivan Sergeyevich, Russian Minister in Paris, 5, 7, 13-19, 21, 69-71, 75, 87, 200-1, 208-9, 213-15.

Bellini, Carlo, professor at College of William and Mary, and friend of F. V. Karzhavin, 172-74.

Bernstorff, Count Andreas Peter Graven von, Danish Foreign Minister, 35-36.

Benyowski, Mauritius August, Hungaro-Polish adventurer, 19, 23.

Bezborodko, Aleksandr Alekseyevich, favorite of Empress Catherine II, 13, 65, 69, 72.

Bjelke, Madame, correspondent of Empress Catherine II, 10.

Bogdanovich, Ippolit Fyodorovich, Russian writer and journalist, 133-35.

Bogdanovich, Pyotr Ivanovich, Russian writer and journalist, 130, 133.

Bond, Thomas, Vice President of American Philosophical Society, 92, 111.

Boston: siege of, 1, 10, 13, 191-92, 194-96, 200; role in Russo-American trade, 76, 86; role in Russo-American cultural relations, 99-101, 113-15.

Bowdoin, James, Massachusetts merchant, politician, and patron of learning, 99, 115.

Branko, G. L., Russian journalist, 133.

Braun, Josef Adam, Russian scientist, 101-4.

Breteuil, Baron de (Louis-August le Tonnelier), French diplomatist, 55.

Buchanan, James, fifteenth President of the United States, 187.

Buckinghamshire, Earl of (James Hobart), British Minister in St. Petersburg, 4.

Burgoyne, General John, 16, 140, 211, 214.

Canada: role in War of American Revolution, 20-22, 197-200.

Catherine II (Yekaterina Alekseyevna), Empress of Russia, 1762-1796, 3-87 passim, 109-11, 121-24, 126, 129-30, 133-35, 148, 153, 162-63.

Chernyshev, Ivan Grigoryevich, Russian Minister in London, 4, 12, 17.

Cist, Charles (Thiel, Charles Jacob Sigismund), Russian migrant to United States, 177-78.

Clinton, General Sir Henry, 203, 211.

Cornwallis, General Charles, 47, 59, 63, 212.

Cook, Captain James, British explorer, 22-24, 119.

273

BOOKS FROM THE DIPLOMATIC PRESS, INC.

1001 Lasswade Drive, Tallahassee, Florida 32303, U.S.A.

Satow, Sir Ernest. *Korea and Manchuria between Russia and Japan 1895–1904. The Observations of Sir Ernest Satow, British Minister and Plenipotentiary to Japan and China.* Selected and edited with a historical introduction by George Alexander Lensen. First published 1966; second printing 1968. 300 pp., collotype frontispiece. cloth. ISBN 0-910512-01-9. $12.50.
". . . a welcome addition to primary source material for the study of Far Eastern diplomatic history." — *The Journal of Asian Studies*
". . . full of interesting and illuminating views from a diplomat of experience and wisdom. . ." — *The American Historical Review*

D'Anethan, Baron Albert. *The d'Anethan Dispatches from Japan 1894–1910. The Observations of Baron Albert d'Anethan, Belgian Minister Plenipotentiary and Dean of the Diplomatic Corps.* Translated and edited with a historical introduction by George Alexander Lensen. 1967. 272 pp., collotype frontispiece. cloth. ISBN 0-910512-02-7. $15.00.
"A companion volume to . . . Sir Ernest Satow . . . Masterfully selected excerpts of heretofore unpublished official dispatches . . ." — *Historische Zeitschrift*
"Valuable to students in East Asian international relations." — *Choice*

Lensen, George Alexander. *The Russo-Chinese War.* 1967. 315 pp., collotype frontispiece, maps, extensive bibliography. cloth. ISBN O-910512-03-05. $15.00.
"The first full-length treatment of Sino-Russian hostilities in Manchuria during the Boxer Rebellion of 1900 . . . Lensen writes clearly, vividly, and with full mastery of his subject." — *Choice*

Will, John Baxter. *Trading Under Sail off Japan 1860–1899.* The Recollections of Captain John Baxter Will, Sailing-Master and Pilot. Edited with a historical introduction by George Alexander Lensen. 1968. 190 pp., lavishly printed and illustrated, cloth. ISBN 0-910512-04-3./$12.50.
". . . this extremely interesting story . . . ranks with the few which, while not perhaps of the type to keep young children from play, should keep most men 'in the chimney corner.' " — *The Japan Times*

Lensen, George Alexander (comp.). *Japanese Diplomatic and Consular Officials in Russia. A Handbook of Japanese Representatives in Russia from 1874 to 1968.* 1968. 230 pp., hardcover. ISBN 0-910512-05-1. $15.00.
"A useful handbook for every serious student of the relations between Japan and the U.S.S.R." — *Narody Azii i Afriki*

Lensen, George Alexander (comp.). *Russian Diplomatic and Consular Officials in East Asia. A Handbook of the Representatives of Tsarist Russia and the Provisional Government in China, Japan and Korea from 1858 to 1924 and of Soviet Representatives in Japan from 1925 to 1968.* 1968. 294 pp., hardcover. ISBN 0-910512-06-X. $15.00

"The two handbooks are essential reference works for every library of East Asian or Russian history: for specialists in the field of Russian-East Asian relations where the author is known as a distinguished pioneering scholar, they will be indispensable companions." — *Pacific Affairs*

Lensen, George Alexander. *Faces of Japan: A Photographic Study.* 154 large collotype reproductions, beautifully printed in a limited edition. 1968. 312 pp., cloth. ISBN 0-910512-07-8. $25.00 (originally $30.00).

Japanese of all walks of life at work and at play, as seen through they eyes of a historian.

"A terrifically beautiful book." — *Wilson Hicks*

Westwood, J. N. *Witnesses of Tsushima.* 1970. xiv, 321 pp. plus 38 illustrations, cloth. ISBN 0-910512-08-06. $15.00.

·"Dr. Westwood by interweaving his own narrative with eyewitness accounts and the official reports both Russian and Japanese gives us a far more accurate version of the famous Russian voyage out of Kronstadt to the Straits of Tsushima and the subsequent battle than has been available heretofore." — *Journal of Asian Studies*

Lensen, George Alexander. *Japanese Recognition of the U.S.S.R.: Soviet-Japanese Relations 1921 – 1930.* 1970. viii, 425 pp. illustrated. cloth. ISBN 0-910512-09-4. $15.00.

"This book is a careful detailed treatment of an important period in Russo-Japanese relations. It will be of special interest to diplomatic and economic historians and of more general interest to those concerned with Japan's position in East Asia or the Soviet Union's relations there." — *Choice*

Lensen, George Alexander. *April in Russia: A Photographic Study.* 100 large collotype reproductions, beautifully printed in a limited edition. 1970. 208 pp., cloth. ISBN 0-910512-10-8. $30.00 (originally $40.00).

A historian's view of daily life in the U.S.S.R.

"An enlightening education tool as well as an artistic, almost poetic, addition to personal libraries." — *Tallahassee Democrat*

". . . this historian has the soul of a poet and the eye of an artist." — *Novoye Russkoye Slovo*

McNally, Raymond T. *Chaadayev and his Friends. An Intellectual History of Peter Chaadayev and his Russian Contemporaries.* 1971. vi, 315 pp., frontispiece, imitation leather. ISBN 0-910512-11-6. $15.00.

A new and highly readable interpretation of the place of Peter Chaadayev (1794 – 1856), the first Russian Westernizer and a unique thinker, in intellectual history, based on research in Soviet archives.

Poutiatine, Countess Olga. *War and Revolution. Excerpts from the Letters and Diaries of the Countess Olga Pontiatine.* Translated and edited by George Alexander Lensen. 1971. vi, 111 pp., illustrated, cloth. ISBN 0-910512-12-4. $12.50.

A moving eyewitness account of the Russian Revolution and of conditions in Russian and Anglo-Russian military hospitals during the First Wold War by the granddaughter of the Russian admiral who competed with Commodore Perry in the opening of Japan.

Sansom, Lady Katherine. *Sir George Sansom and Japan.* A memoir of Sir George Sansom, G. B. E., K. C. M. G., Diplomat Historian, by his wife. 1972. 183 pp., illustrated, cloth. ISBN 0-910512-13-2. $15.00.

The diplomatic and scholarly life of Sir George Sansom, the foremost Western authority on Japan, mirrored in the letters and diary entries of his wife and himself, with unforgettable thumbnail sketches of leading diplomatic, political, military and literary figures in Japan from 1928—1950.

Kutakov, Leonid N. *Japanese Foreign Policy on the Eve of the Pacific War. A Soviet View.* 1972. xiii, 241 pp., frontispiece, cloth. ISBN 9105012-15-0. $15.00.

". . . a tightly knit interpretation of an epochal aspect of modern history (particularly the long essay on Japanese-Russian relations) which will intrigue students of the background of World War II." — *Library Journal*

"Of special interest to students of East Asian international relations and to diplomatic historians generally." — *Choice*

Lensen, George Alexander. *The Strange Neutrality: Soviet-Japanese Relations During the Second World War, 1941—1945.* 1972. xii, 335 pp., illustrated, cloth. ISBN 910512-14-0. $15.00.

"A dispassionate and authoritative account which has a place in every collection on the history of World War II in Asia and the Pacific." — *Library Journal*

". . . written with cogency, balance, and depth." — *History*

"A first rate historical work." — *Choice*

Vishwanathan, Savitri. *Normalization of Japanese-Soviet Relations 1945—1970.* 1973. xii, 190 pp. illustrated, cloth. ISBN 910512-14-0. $15.00.

An examination of the political, economic and diplomatic relations between Japan and the U.S.S.R. since the Pacific War, with chapters on trade, fisheries, and the territorial dispute. Written by an Indian scholar on the basis primarily of Japanese sources.

Lensen, George Alexander. *The Damned Inheritance: The Soviet Union and the Manchurian Crises, 1924—1935.* 1974. xiv, 533 pp., illustrated, cloth. ISBN 910512-17-5. $19.80.

An account of the triangular Russo-Chinese-Japanese struggle over Manchuria and the Chinese Eastern Railway and of American and British reaction thereto, written on the basis of Soviet, Japanese, and British documents.

Mazour, Anatole G. *Women in Exile: Wives of the Decembrists.* 1975. 134 pp., illustrated, cloth, ISBN 910512-19-1. $15.00.

The dramatic story of the wives and fiancees of Russia's first revolutionaries, who following the abortive Decembrist revolt of 1825 chose to follow their men into exile in Siberia.

Bolkhovitinov, Nikolai N. *Russia and the American Revolution.* Translated and edited by C. Jay Smith. June 1976. About 425 pp., illustrated, cloth. ISBN 0-910512-20-5. $29.70.

A detailed account by a distinguished Soviet historian on the basis of unpublished archival material of Russian policy toward the American Revolution. Traces the refusal of Catherine the Great to assist George III in suppressing the rebellion, Russia's declaration of armed neutrality, her offer of peaceful mediation, and the origins of commercial and cultural ties between Russia and the United States. Throws much new light on the international impact of the American Revolution and on the roots of present-day Soviet-American relations. Belongs in every college and public library.